University Success

WRITING

Success

TRANSITION LEVEL

Charl Norloff and Amy Renehan

Series Editor: Maggie Sokolik

Authentic Content Contributors: Ronnie Alan Hess II and Victoria Solomon

University Success Writing, Transition Level

Copyright © 2017 by Pearson Education, Inc.

Pearson Education, 221 River Street, Hoboken, NJ 07030

Staff credits: The people who made up the *University Success Writing, Transition Level* team, representing content creation, design, manufacturing, marketing, multimedia, project management, publishing, rights management, and testing, are Pietro Alongi, Rhea Banker, Stephanie Bullard, Tracey Cataldo, Sara Davila, Mindy DePalma, Dave Dickey, Warren Fischbach, Nancy Flaggman, Gosia Jaros-White, Niki Lee, Amy McCormick, Jennifer Raspiller, Paula Van Ells, and Joseph Vella.

Project supervision: Debbie Sistino

Contributing editors: Eleanor Barnes, Andrea Bryant, Nancy Matsunaga, and Leigh Stolle

Cover image: © Wiliam Perry / Alamy Stock Photo

Text and cover design: Yin Ling Wong

Video research: Constance Rylance

Video production: Kristine Stolakis

Text composition: MPS Limited

Library of Congress Cataloging-in-Publication Data

A catalog record for the print edition is available from the Library of Congress.

ISBN-10: 0-13-440028-3

ISBN-13: 978-0-13-440028-0

Printed in the United States of America

1 16

Contents

PART 1: FUNDAMENTAL WRITING SKILLS

PART 2: CRITICAL THINKING SKILLS

PART 3: EXTENDED WRITING

Welcome to *University Success*

INTRODUCTION

University Success is a new academic skills series designed to equip transitioning English learners with the reading, writing, and oral communication skills necessary to succeed in courses in an English-speaking university setting. The blended instructional model provides students with an inspiring collection of extensive authentic content, expertly developed in cooperation with five subject matter experts, all "thought leaders" in their fields. By utilizing both online and in-class instructional materials, *University Success* models the type of "real life" learning expected of students studying for a degree. Unlike a developmental textbook, *University Success* recognizes the unique linguistic needs of English language learners. The course carefully scaffolds skill development to help students successfully work with challenging and engaging authentic content provided by top professors in their academic fields.

SERIES ORGANIZATION: *THREE STRANDS*

This three-strand series, **Reading**, **Writing**, and **Oral Communication**, includes five distinct content areas: the Human Experience, Money and Commerce, the Science of Nature, Arts and Letters, and Structural Science, all popular fields of study among English language learners. The three strands are fully aligned across content areas and skills, allowing teachers to utilize material from different strands to support learning. Teachers can delve deeply into skill development in a single skill area, or provide additional support materials from other skill areas for richer development across the four skills.

THE *UNIVERSITY SUCCESS* APPROACH: *AN AUTHENTIC EXPERIENCE*

This blended program combines the utility of an interactive student book, online learner lab, and print course to create a flexible approach that adjusts to the needs of teachers and learners. The skill-based and step-by-step instruction helps students master essential skills and become confident and successful in their ability to perform in academic-degree-bearing courses taught in English. Students at this level need to engage with content that provides the same challenges faced by native speakers in a university setting. Many English language learners are not prepared for the quantity of reading and writing required in college-level courses, nor are they properly prepared to listen to full-length lectures that have not been scaffolded for them. These learners, away from the safety of an ESL classroom, must keep up with the rigors of a class led by a professor who may be unaware of the challenges a second-language learner faces. *University Success* steps up to the podium to represent academic content realistically with the appropriate skill development and scaffolding essential for English language learners to be successful.

The program features the following:

- **Rigorous academic preparation** that allows students to build on their strengths and prior knowledge, develop language and study skills, and increase their knowledge of academic content related to the STEAM areas of study
- **Systematic skill development,** from strategies to critical thinking to application and assessment, that explicitly teaches students to notice, understand, and employ English language features in the comprehension and synthesis of new information
- **A fluency driven approach** designed to help learners with fluency, accuracy, and automaticity allowing them to process linguistically complex texts of significant length
- **Flexible three-part developmental English approach** that includes intensive skill development and extensive practice
- **Extensive work with authentic texts** and videotaped **lectures** created by dynamic Stanford University professors providing a challenging experience that replicates the authentic experience of studying in a mainstream university classroom
- **Flexible format** and sophisticated design for students who are looking for authentic academic content, comprehensive practice, and a true college experience
- **Global Scale of English for Academic Learners** alignment with content tied to outcomes designed to challenge students who have achieved a B2+ level of proficiency or higher
- **Content and fluency vocabulary approach** that develops learner ability to read words as multiword units and to process text more quickly and with greater ease
- **Strategies for academic success,** delivered via online videos, including how to talk to professors during office hours and time management techniques, that help increase students' confidence and ability to cope with the challenges of academic study and college culture
- **Continuous formative assessment** and extensive formative assessment built into the series, offering multiple points of feedback, in class or online, assessing the ability of students to transfer and apply skills with rigorous academic challenges

TEACHER SUPPORT

Each of the three strands is supported with:

- **Comprehensive downloadable teaching notes** in MyEnglishLab that detail key points for all of the specialized academic content in addition to tips and suggestions for teaching skills and strategies
- **An easy-to-use online learning management system** offering a flexible gradebook and tools for monitoring student progress
- **Audioscripts, videoscripts, answer keys, and word lists** to help in lesson planning and follow-up

BOOK ORGANIZATION: *THREE PARTS*

University Success is designed with a part structure that allows for maximum flexibility for teachers. The series is "horizontally" aligned allowing teachers to teach across a specific content area and "vertically" aligned allowing a teacher to gradually build skills. Each part is a self-contained module, offering teachers the ability to customize a nonlinear program that will best address the needs of students. The skills, like the content areas, are aligned, giving teachers and students the opportunity to explore the differences in application based on the type of study experience the students need.

In Part 1 and Part 2 students work with comprehensive skills that include:

- Working with and developing complex ideas reflecting areas of academic interest
- Using, creating, and interpreting visuals from data, experiments, and research
- Distinguishing facts and opinions and hedging when presenting, reviewing, or writing academic research
- Recognizing and using inference and implications in academic fields
- Identifying, outlining, and describing complex processes in research, lab work, and experiments

Part 3 provides a truly authentic experience for students with an extended essay (Reading strand), lecture (Oral Communication strand), and interview about the writing process (Writing strand) provided by the thought leader. Part 3 functions as a final formative assessment of a student's ability to apply skills with mainstream academic content. Part 3 content includes:

- Subject matter to which students can find personal connections
- Topics with interdisciplinary appeal
- Material that draws students into the most current debates in academia
- Topics that strengthen the cultural and historical literacy of students

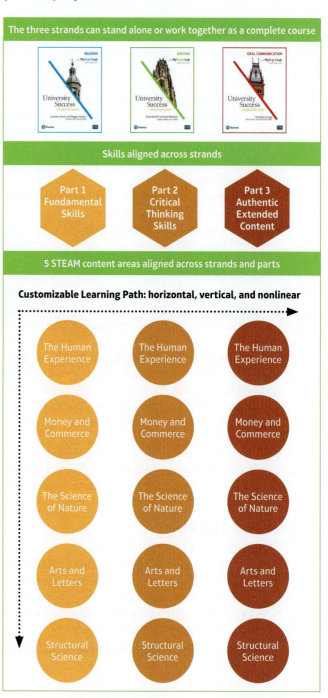

The three strands can stand alone or work together as a complete course

Skills aligned across strands

Part 1 Fundamental Skills

Part 2 Critical Thinking Skills

Part 3 Authentic Extended Content

5 STEAM content areas aligned across strands and parts

Customizable Learning Path: horizontal, vertical, and nonlinear

The Human Experience · Money and Commerce · The Science of Nature · Arts and Letters · Structural Science

SUBJECT MATTER EXPERTS

Marcelo Clerici-Arias teaches undergraduate courses at Stanford University's Department of Economics, from principles of micro- and macroeconomics to upper-level courses in computational economics, behavioral economics, and economic policy. He has researched innovative pedagogies used in economics and other social and natural sciences. His main research areas are game theory, computational economics, and teaching and learning. Professor Clerici-Arias is a popular speaker and presenter, has participated in NSF-sponsored projects, and has co-edited an economics textbook.

Jonathan D. Greenberg is a lecturer in law at Stanford Law School; teaching fellow for the school's advanced degree program in International Economic Law, Business and Policy; and scholar-in-residence at the school's Gould Center for Conflict Resolution. He has published scholarly articles and chapters in a broad range of interdisciplinary journals and books.

Robert Pogue Harrison is a professor of French and Italian literature at Stanford University and author of six books, the most recent of which is *Juvenescence: A Cultural History of Our Age* (2014). He writes regularly for the *New York Review of Books* and hosts the radio podcast *Entitled Opinions*. He is a member of the American Academy of Arts and Sciences, and in 2014 he was knighted Chevalier of the French Republic.

Lynn Hildemann is a professor of civil and environmental engineering at Stanford University and currently is serving as department chair. She is an author on over 80 peer-reviewed publications. Her research areas include the sources and dispersion of airborne particulate matter in indoor environments and assessment of human exposure to air pollutants. She has served on advisory committees for the Bay Area Air Quality Management District and the California Air Resources Board and as an associate editor for *Environmental Science & Technology*.

Robert Siegel is a professor in the Department of Microbiology and Immunology at Stanford University. He holds secondary appointments in the Program in Human Biology, the Center for African Studies, and the Woods Institute for the Environment. He is the recipient of numerous teaching awards including Stanford's highest teaching accolade, the Walter Gores Award. Dr. Siegel's courses cover a wide range of topics including virology, infectious disease, and global health, as well as molecular biology, Darwin and evolution and island biogeography, and photography. He is an avid hiker, photographer, and dromomaniac.

SERIES EDITORS

Robyn Brinks Lockwood teaches courses in spoken and written English at Stanford University in the English for Foreign Students graduate program and is the program education coordinator of the American Language and Culture undergraduate summer program. She is an active member of the international TESOL organization, serves as chairperson of the Publishing Professional Council, and is a past chair of the Materials Writers Interest Section. She is a frequent presenter at TESOL regional and international conferences. She has edited and written numerous textbooks, online courses, and ancillary components for ESL courses and TOEFL preparation.

Maggie Sokolik holds a BA in anthropology from Reed College, and an MA in romance linguistics and a PhD in applied linguistics from UCLA. She is the author of over 20 ESL and composition textbooks. She has taught at MIT, Harvard, Texas A&M, and currently UC Berkeley, where she is director of College Writing Programs. She has developed and taught several popular MOOC courses in English language writing and literature. She is the founding editor of *TESL-EJ*, a peer-reviewed journal for ESL/EFL professionals, one of the first online journals. She travels frequently to speak about grammar, writing, and instructor education. She lives in the San Francisco Bay area, where she and her husband play bluegrass music.

Lawrence J. Zwier is an associate director of the English Language Center, Michigan State University. He holds a bachelor's degree in English literature from Aquinas College, Grand Rapids, MI, and an MA in TESL from the University of Minnesota. He has taught ESL/EFL at universities in Saudi Arabia, Malaysia, Japan, Singapore, and the United States. He is the author of numerous ELT textbooks, mostly about reading and vocabulary, and also writes nonfiction books about history and geography for middle school and high school students. He is married with two children and lives in Okemos, Michigan.

Key Features of *University Success Writing*

UNIQUE PART STRUCTURE

University Success employs a unique three-part structure, providing maximum flexibility and mulitple opportunities to customize the flow of content.

Each part is a self-contained module allowing teachers to focus on the highest value skills and content. Parts are aligned around science, technology, engineering, arts, and mathmatic (STEAM) content relevant to mainstream academic areas of study.

Part 1 and Part 2 focus on the fundamental and critcal thinking skills most relevant for students preparing for university degrees. **Part 3** introduces students to extended practice with the skills. Students work directly with the authentic content created by top professors in their academic fields.

PART 1 AND PART 2

A **Unit Profile** outlines the content.

Outcomes aligned with the Global Scale of English (GSE) are clearly stated to ensure student awareness of skills.

Getting Started questions explore the content, develop context, and engage students' prior knowledge.

An **online self-assessement** identifies students' confidence with skills and helps them create personal learning objectives.

Professors greet students at the beginning and end of each part providing a preview and a wrap of the content.

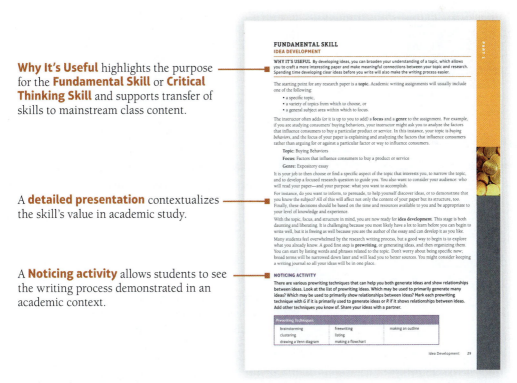

Why It's Useful highlights the purpose for the **Fundamental Skill** or **Critical Thinking Skill** and supports transfer of skills to mainstream class content.

A **detailed presentation** contextualizes the skill's value in academic study.

A **Noticing activity** allows students to see the writing process demonstrated in an academic context.

Each skill is divided into discreet **Supporting Skills**.

Multiple **excercises**, including authentic university writing assignments, encourage application of the skills and build fundamental and critical thinking skills.

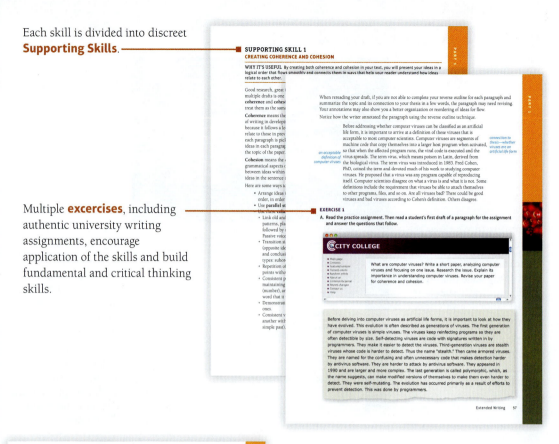

SUPPORTING SKILL 1
CREATING COHERENCE AND COHESION

WHY IT'S USEFUL By creating both coherence and cohesion in your text, you will present your ideas in a logical order that flows smoothly and connects them in ways that help your reader understand how ideas relate to each other.

Good research, great [...] multiple drafts is one [...] **coherence** and **cohes** [...] treat them as the same [...]

Coherence means the [...] of writing in developing [...] because it follows a lo [...] relate to those in prev [...] each paragraph is pick [...] ideas in each paragrap [...] the topic of the paper. [...]

Cohesion means the [...] grammatical aspects c [...] between ideas within [...] ideas in the sentence [...]

Here are some ways t [...]
• Arrange ideas [...] order, in order [...]
• Use **parallel st** [...]
• Use these code [...]
• Link old and [...] patterns, pla [...] followed by [...] Passive voice [...]
• Transition s [...] (opposite ide [...] and conclusi [...] types: subor [...]
• Repetition o [...] points witho [...]
• Consistent p [...] maintaining [...] (number), a [...] word that it [...]
• Demonstrati [...] ones.
• Consistent v [...] another with [...] simple past), [...]

When rereading your draft, if you are not able to complete your reverse outline for each paragraph and summarize the topic and its connection to your thesis in a few words, the paragraph may need revising. Your annotations may also show you a better organization or reordering of ideas for flow.

Notice how the writer annotated the paragraph using the reverse outline technique.

an acceptable definition of computer viruses

Before addressing whether computer viruses can be classified as an artificial life form, it is important to arrive at a definition of these viruses that is acceptable to most computer scientists. Computer viruses are segments of machine code that copy themselves into a larger host program when activated, so that when the affected program runs, the viral code is executed and the virus spreads. The term *virus*, which means poison in Latin, derived from the biological virus. The term virus was introduced in 1983. Fred Cohen, PhD, coined the term and devoted much of his work to studying computer viruses. He proposed that a virus was any program capable of reproducing itself. Computer scientists disagree on what a virus is and what it is not. Some definitions include the requirement that viruses be able to attach themselves to other programs, files, and so on. Are all viruses bad? There could be good viruses and bad viruses according to Cohen's definition. Others disagree.

connection to thesis—whether viruses are an artificial life form

EXERCISE 1

A. Read the practice assignment. Then read a student's first draft of a paragraph for the assignment and answer the questions that follow.

CITY COLLEGE

• Main page
• Contents
• Featured content
• Current events
• Random article
• About us
• Community portal
• Recent changes
• Contact us
• Help

What are computer viruses? Write a short paper, analyzing computer viruses and focusing on one issue. Research the issue. Explain its importance in understanding computer viruses. Revise your paper for coherence and cohesion.

Before delving into computer viruses as artificial life forms, it is important to look at how they have evolved. This evolution is often described as generations of viruses. The first generation of computer viruses is simple viruses. The viruses keep reinfecting programs so they are often detectible by size. Self-detecting viruses are code with signatures written in by programmers. They make it easier to detect the viruses. Third-generation viruses are stealth viruses whose code is harder to detect. Thus the name "stealth." Then came armored viruses. They are named for the confusing and often unnecessary code that makes detection harder by antivirus software. They are harder to attack by antivirus software. They appeared in 1990 and are larger and more complex. The last generation is called polymorphic, which, as the name suggests, can make modified versions of themselves to make them even harder to detect. They were self-mutating. The evolution has occurred primarily as a result of efforts to prevent detection. This was done by programmers.

Extended Writing   57

B. Complete the graphic organizer with the information you highlighted in the article. Compare with a partner and practice summarizing the text orally with each other.

Article title	
Author name	
Publication information	
Main idea of article	
Essential detail(s) that support main idea	
Keywords you will use in summary	

C. Write a 4–5 sentence summary of this article, using your notes.

_____
_____
_____
_____
_____

D. <u>PEER REVIEW</u>. Exchange your summary with a partner. Respond to the questions to evaluate each other's work. For responses marked No, give feedback in the Notes column to help your partner revise.

	Yes	No	Notes
Does the summary include the title, author, date, and publisher of the original text?	☐	☐	
Does the writer clearly state the topic and main idea of the text?	☐	☐	
Does the summary include support for the main idea?	☐	☐	
Does the summary include only essential information?	☐	☐	
Does the writer repeat information?	☐	☐	
Is the summary well organized?	☐	☐	
Does the writer use transition cues well?	☐	☐	
Does the writer remind the reader of the source several times?	☐	☐	
Does the writer use keywords from the reading correctly?	☐	☐	
Is the length appropriate?	☐	☐	

Go to **MyEnglishLab** to complete vocabulary exercises and skill practices and join in collaborative activities.
For more about SUMMARIZING, see | R | ECONOMICS 🔷.

Idea Development   43

Peer reviews allow students to evaluate each others' writing, provide objective feedback, and work collaboratively.

Online activities encourage students to personalize content with collaborative research activities.

x   KEY FEATURES

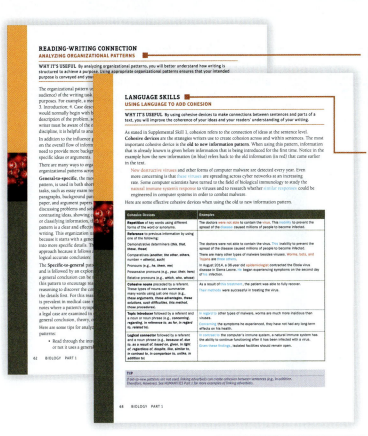

Reading-Writing Connection aligns the Reading and Writing strands establishing how strategies apply across language skills and using authentic academic content relevant to mainstream study.

The **Language Skill** study provides support for complex lexical and grammatical skills.

An **Apply Your Skills** section at the end of Part 1 and 2 functions as a formative assessment.

A **Before You Write** activity gives students the opportunity to discuss questions related to the topic of their final assignment and begin planning their writing.

Thinking about Language and additional critical thinking activities allow students to practice critical writing skills in preparation for their final assignment.

In **Write**, students complete a final writing assignment which allows them to integrate content and use all aspects of the writing process.

In addition, students are given the opportunity to go **Beyond the Assignment** to write a research paper that extends beyond what they have just completed.

PART 3

Students view **authentic interviews** with professors discussing their own writing processes.

Thinking Critically activities ask learners to engage at a deep level with the content, using information from the interview to address specific real-world applications.

Thinking About Language reviews language skills developed in Part 1 and Part 2, using authentic content.

A final **Assignment** includes **Research** and encourages in-class and online project collaboration.

TEACHER SUPPORT

Each of the three strands is supported with comprehensive **downloadable teaching notes** in MyEnglishLab that detail key points for all of the specialized, academic content in addition to tips and suggestions for how to teach skills and strategies.

Assessments on selected topics provide extra opportunities for students to demonstrate learning. Flexible design allows assessments to be used as unit reviews, mid-terms, or finals. Test bank presents multiple test versions for easy test proctoring.

An easy to use online learning management system offering a **Flexible Gradebook** and tools for monitoring student progress, such as audioscripts, videoscripts, answer keys, and word lists to help in lesson planning and follow up.

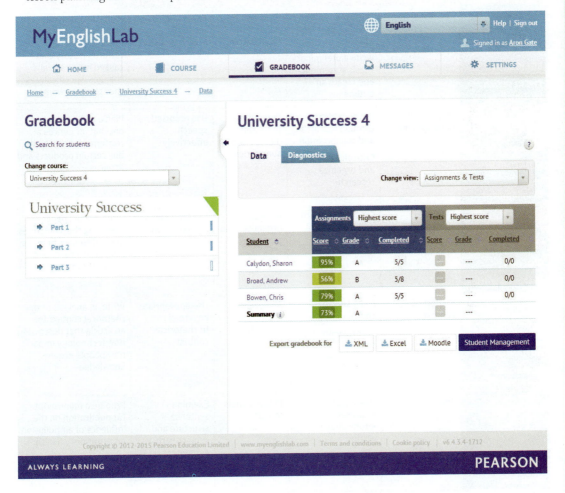

Continued

Scope and Sequence

PART 1

Fundamental Writing Skills is designed to build fundamental skills step by step through exploration of rigorous academic content.

	FUNDAMENTAL WRITING SKILLS	SUPPORTING SKILLS	READING-WRITING CONNECTION	LANGUAGE SKILLS	APPLY YOUR SKILLS
SOCIOLOGY **The Research Writing Process**	The research writing process	Narrow a topic and develop a research question Write a preliminary thesis statement and create an outline	Assemble an annotated bibliography	Explore verb tenses in academic writing	Plan a research paper on an important event in your country's or culture's history that caused major social changes, specifically as they relate to women.
ECONOMICS **Idea Development**	Idea development	Develop ideas through research and collaboration Critically evaluate and organize research	Summarize texts and incorporate summaries	Use reported speech effectively	Plan a research paper on what influences a consumer's decision to buy certain products and services
BIOLOGY **Extended Writing**	Extended writing	Create coherence and cohesion Revise writing	Analyze organizational patterns	Use language to add cohesion	Write a short paper analyzing the similarities and differences between biological viruses and computer viruses
HUMANITIES **Rhetorical Context**	Rhetorical context	Make stylistic choices Control voice and tone	Analyze the rhetorical context	Use appropriate adverbials to fit rhetorical context	Write an analysis of the rhetorical context for an article that describes how technology impacts how people acquire knowledge
ENVIRONMENTAL ENGINEERING **Publishing**	Publishing	Use visuals to present information in writing Edit text and visuals	Relate visuals to text	Examine sentence structure and subject-verb agreement	Prepare a manuscript for publication on the influence of air pollution on respiratory health.

PART 2
Critical Thinking Skills moves from skill building to application of the skills that require critical thinking.

	CRITICAL THINKING SKILLS	SUPPORTING SKILLS	READING-WRITING CONNECTION	LANGUAGE SKILLS	APPLY YOUR SKILLS
SOCIOLOGY Fact and Opinion	Fact and opinion	Support claims with facts and opinions Evaluate others' opinions	Distinguish facts and opinions and make claims	Signpost facts and opinions	Use facts and opinions to construct an analysis in a research paper about an event or moment in a civil rights movement. Write a thesis statement and an outline of your claims and support
ECONOMICS Reading Critically for Effective Writing	Reading critically for effective writing	Select sources Integrate sources to provide evidence Respond to inference	Write a critical response	Use direct quotations and reported speech	Write a critical response to ideas in an article that discusses how positive and/or negative externalities of a particular good or service impact society
BIOLOGY Process Writing	Process writing	Structure a process Explain a procedure	Formulate a hypothesis	Form conditional clauses	Write an analytical process paper explaining the characteristics of and latest treatment methods for a virus you have researched.
HUMANITIES Descriptive Writing	Descriptive writing	Explore figurative language Appeal to the senses	Analyze descriptive writing	Use grammar to vary description	Write a descriptive essay about an interaction with something you read, heard, or saw that changed your understanding or knowledge about a concept or idea.
ENVIRONMENTAL ENGINEERING Research Writing	Research writing	Write research proposals Develop an abstract	Analyze research posters	Relate form to function	Create text for a research poster that presents the aim and results of a study about the effects of temperature inversions on air quality

PART 3

Extended Writing presents authentic content written by university professors. Academically rigorous application and assessment activities allow for a synthesis of the skills developed in Parts 1 and 2.

	INTERVIEWS AND READINGS	RESEARCH
SOCIOLOGY Writing as a Sociologist	Writing as a Sociologist *The 1963 Birmingham Campaign: The Turning Point in the American Civil Rights Movement*	Write a research paper on a particular act of nonviolent civil disobedience in the US Civil rights movement and its impact on the movement.
ECONOMICS Writing as an Economist	Writing as an Economist *Minimum Wages*	Write a research paper analyzing the development of a new product or service and its likelihood of succeeding.
BIOLOGY Writing as a Biologist	Writing as a Biologist *Vaccines That Prevent Virally-Induced Cancer*	Write a research paper on the causes of a cancer known to be associated with a particular virus.
HUMANITIES Writing as a Literary Expert	Writing as a Literary Expert *The Golden Bough*	Write a literary analysis of the poem, "Do Not Go Gentle into That Good Night" by Dylan Thomas, including a summary of the poem and a response to one or more ideas or images in it.
ENVIRONMENTAL ENGINEERING Writing as an Environmental Engineer	Writing as an Environmental Engineer *Increasing Energy Efficiency vs. Maintaining Indoor Air Quality*	Write a research paper comparing and contrasting the methods, findings, and conclusions of three to five case studies of 'sick building syndrome' caused by indoor air quality problems.

A Note from Maggie Sokolik

Series Editor for *University Success Writing*

Transition-level EAP students, whether just crossing the bridge from ESL to academic study in a university or already into their graduate or undergraduate studies are often still lacking in both the skills and confidence to tackle writing at the university level. Despite having proficiency in speaking and having developed basic reading and writing skills in their own country or in an IEP, they may still struggle with academic discourse practices, especially in writing beyond the five-paragraph essay and in incorporating the ideas of others into their writing.

To help students make the transition to academic study, *University Success Writing* approaches writing in a manner more aligned with how it is taught at the university level and across disciplines, rather than from an ESL stance. The focus is on inquiry-based and research writing, on writing in the subject areas, and on critical and creative thinking that results in strong content development. What *University Success Writing* does is to break down, explain, and carefully scaffold the processes involved in various writing tasks to help students see how they can approach writing assignments in different disciplines and achieve papers they can be proud of. The transition level of *University Success* is ideal because it provides content that is appropriate and authentic to get learners on the college track and prepares them to meet their academic goals.

PART 1 – FUNDAMENTAL WRITING SKILLS

In the first five units of *University Success Writing*, each of the five main subject areas (Economics, Sociology, Biology, Humanities, Environmental Engineering) is used to provide content for skill-based learning and practice of inquiry and research-based writing. While students have most likely been taught steps in the writing process, they have not had enough practice with utilizing those skills as they develop their ideas and support them with appropriate source material from authentic content in the subject areas.

PART 2 – CRITICAL THINKING SKILLS

In these units, each main subject area is explored through new topics. Critical thinking is more directly elicited so that transition-level students engage in high-level writing tasks such as critically reading texts to evaluate sources for incorporation into their writing, integrating both fact and opinion to support a thesis, using descriptive writing techniques to more effectively develop content, and analyzing and practicing ways to propose and present authentic research, including visually.

PART 3 – EXTENDED WRITING

Part 3 includes interviews with the Stanford thought leaders on their own writing processes. This provides students with a unique opportunity to hear the professors respond in their own words to questions about how they get their ideas, research, and then develop them, and also what they expect from students writing in their disciplines. These interviews are followed by opportunities for students to engage in critical thinking, analysis and discussion of authentic situations based on assignments in the subject area. Students are also given a research writing assignment designed to bring to bear all the skills they've developed in previous units and provide practice that will help them successfully participate in inquiry-based research and writing in their academic studies.

Acknowledgments

The authors would like to acknowledge all of the people at Pearson who contributed to this project and made this book possible. In particular, we thank Amy McCormick for putting such an amazing team together. We thank the entire team for developing a sound framework: Maggie Sokolik for her work in the development of the writing strand, Debbie Sistino for her patience, guidance, and encouragement, and Sara Davila for her problem solving and invaluable research. We thank Victoria Solomon and Ronnie Hess for their contributions to the Reading-Writing Connection sections. Finally, we'd like to give a special thanks to Andrea Bryant, our Development Editor, whose expertise, insight, and positivity helped shape the manuscript and made the writing process a pleasant one.

The authors thank the many students they have worked with over the years for all they have taught them about language learning. They also thank their colleagues for the support and many collaborations that have resulted in a collective understanding and respect for the challenge of teaching language, and particularly writing, in our profession.

Charl Norloff is grateful for the opportunity to work with her talented co-author, Amy Renehan, and appreciated her unfailing good humor, creative ideas, and hard work. She thanks her husband, Richard, for once again patiently supporting her desire to write, and her sons Jonathan and Joshua, now independent young adults, for their love, continued support, and the time to write!

Amy Renehan would also like to thank Talya Clay for her encouragement and support, and her co-author, Charl Norloff for being a great writing partner. She is also very grateful to her parents, Larry and Donna, and mother-in-law, Annie, for their support during this project. Finally, her deepest appreciation goes to her husband, Evan and daughter, Violet for their patience, love, and support.

Reviewers

We would like to thank the following reviewers for their many helpful comments and suggestions:

Jamila Barton, North Seattle Community College, Seattle, WA; **Joan Chamberlin**, Iowa State University, Ames IA; **Lyam Christopher**, Palm Beach State College, Boynton Beach, FL; **Robin Corcos**, University of California, Santa Barbara, Goleta, CA; **Tanya Davis**, University of California, San Deigo, CA; **Brendan DeCoster**, University of Oregon, Eugene, OR; **Thomas Dougherty**, University of St. Mary of the Lake, Mundelein, IL; **Bina Dugan**, Bergen County Community College, Hackensack, NJ; **Priscilla Faucette**, University of Hawaii at Manoa, Honolulu, HI; **Lisa Fischer**, St. Louis University, St. Louis, MO; **Kathleen Flynn**, Glendale Community College, Glendale, CA; **Mary Gawienowski**, William Rainey Harper College, Palatine, IL; **Sally Gearhart**, Santa Rosa Junior College, Santa Rosa, CA; **Carl Guerriere**, Capital Community College, Hartford, CT; **Vera Guillen**, Eastfield College, Mequite, TX; **Angela Hakim**, St. Louis University, St. Louis, MO; **Pamela Hartmann**, Evans Community Adult School, Los Angeles Unified School District, Los Angeles, CA; **Shelly Hedstrom**, Palm Beach State University, Lake Worth, FL; **Sherie Henderson**, University of Oregon, Eugene, OR; **Lisse Hildebrandt**, English Language Program, Virginia Commonwealth University, Richmond, VA; **Barbara Inerfeld**, Rutgers University, Piscataway, NJ; **Zaimah Khan**, Northern Virginia Community College, Loudon Campus, Sterling, VA; **Tricia Kinman**, St. Louis University, St. Louis, MO; **Kathleen Klaiber**, Genesee Community College, Batavia, NY; **Kevin Lamkins**, Capital Community College, Hartford, CT; **Mayetta Lee**, Palm Beach State College, Lake Worth, FL; **Kirsten Lillegard**, English Language Institute, Divine Word College, Epworth, IA; **Craig Machado**, Norwalk Community College, Norwalk, CT; **Cheryl Madrid**, Spring International Language Center, Denver, CO; **Ann Meechai**, St. Louis University, St. Louis, MO; **Melissa Mendelson**, Department of Linguistics, University of Utah, Salt Lake City, UT; **Tamara Milbourn**, University of Colorado, Boulder, CO; **Debbie Ockey**, Fresno City College, Fresno, CA; **Diana Pascoe-Chavez**, St. Louis University, St. Louis, MO; **Kathleen Reynolds**, William Rainey Harper College, Palatine, IL; **Linda Roth**, Vanderbilt University ELC, Greensboro, NC; **Minati Roychoudhuri**, Capital Community College, Hartford, CT; **Bruce Rubin**, California State University, Fullerton, CA; **Margo Sampson**, Syracuse University, Syracuse, NY; **Sarah Saxer**, Howard Community College, Ellicott City, MD; **Anne-Marie Schlender**, Austin Community College, Austin, TX **Susan Shields**, Santa Barbara Community College, Santa Barbara, CA; **Barbara Smith-Palinkas**, Hillsborough Community College, Dale Mabry Campus, Tampa, FL; **Sara Stapleton**, North Seattle Community College, Seattle, WA; **Lisa Stelle**, Northern Virginia Community College Loudon, Sterling, VA; **Jamie Tanzman**, Northern Kentucky University, Highland Heights, KY; **Jeffrey Welliver**, Soka University of America, Aliso Viejo, CA; **Mark Wolfersberger**, Brigham Young University Hawaii, Laie, HI; **May Youn**, California State University, Fullerton, CA

PART
1

Fundamental Writing Skills

Part 1 is designed to build fundamental skills step by step through the exploration of rigorous, academic content. Practice activities tied to specific learning outcomes in each unit focus on understanding the function and application of the skills.

Struggle influences social change.

SOCIOLOGY

The Research Writing Process

UNIT PROFILE

The world experienced many social changes after World War II. In this unit, you will read and write about the changes specifically related to the entry of women into the workforce. Over the years, there have been both opportunities and barriers to women's fully integrating into many professions, enjoying fulfilling careers, and achieving full equality.

You will plan a research paper on an important event in your country's or culture's history that caused major social changes, specifically as they relate to the role of women.

OUTCOMES

• Narrow a topic and develop a research question

• Write a preliminary thesis statement and create an outline

• Assemble an annotated bibliography

• Explore verb tenses in academic writing

GETTING STARTED

▶ Go to MyEnglishLab to listen to Professor Greenberg and to complete a self-assessment.

Discuss these questions with a partner or group.

1. Do you think women have achieved full equality in the workforce? If so, give examples. If not, why do you think there is still a gap between men and women in the workforce?

2. Many historical events start with individuals making small changes or working to make their voices heard in the government. Talk about an important historical event and how individuals played a role in its evolution. Did the event have a positive or negative outcome?

3. What actions do you think are needed to advance total gender equality in the workplace?

For more about **SOCIOLOGY**, see 2 3. See also R and OC **SOCIOLOGY** 1 2 3.

FUNDAMENTAL SKILL
THE RESEARCH WRITING PROCESS

WHY IT'S USEFUL By treating research writing as a process and breaking down an assignment into steps, you will develop the skills to write a research paper that has a strong thesis statement, is well organized and fully developed, and has ideas that can be easily supported.

Good writers understand that writing is a process; that is, they will not fully get their ideas on paper on their first attempt. They know they will need to work through a series of steps and multiple drafts to arrive at a well-thought-out, organized, and developed research paper.

Look at the four steps in the **research writing process**. Successful research writing begins with exploring a topic, with the goal of **narrowing the topic** to the point where you are able to begin doing comprehensive research. Once you have moved on to researching, **developing a good research question is key.** The critical organizing stage culminates in **writing a preliminary thesis and creating an outline.** Keep in mind that all of this is done before the actual writing begins!

Doing extensive planning and prewriting is one way that writing research papers differs from writing other types of papers.

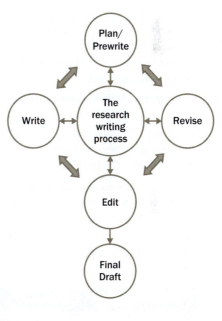

Step 1: Planning and Prewriting
Exploring a topic
Considering purpose and audience
Conducting a preliminary search of sources
Narrowing the topic
Brainstorming and generating ideas
Researching
Developing a research question
Finding and evaluating sources
Critical reading, researching ideas, and taking notes
Assembling an annotated bibliography
Organizing
Writing a preliminary thesis
Creating an outline to organize main and supporting ideas
Step 2: Writing
Writing a first draft
Integrating sources into the text
Step 3: Revising
Getting feedback (from your instructor, peers, and yourself)
Revising additional drafts
Step 4: Editing
Proofreading for vocabulary, grammar, spelling, and punctuation
Editing additional drafts to arrive at a final draft

For most people, the writing process is not linear. A good writer often goes back and forth among the steps, writing one part of the paper, revising another, and doing additional research for yet another part of the paper all at the same time.

When you first receive an academic assignment, the task may seem overwhelming. Break the assignment down into steps and work through a careful process to give yourself a clear starting point to guide you through the successful completion of the task.

STEP 1: PLANNING AND PREWRITING

When you begin to **explore a topic,** it is helpful to draw on your personal experience and collaborate with others when possible as a starting point from which to examine the topic from a more scholarly viewpoint through research. Let's look at how to approach an assignment. The assignment is: **What are the career possibilities in the United States for woman in the 21st century? Choose and analyze an area in which women have achieved equity with men or an area in which they are still lagging behind men in the workforce. Research historical and cultural events that influenced the opportunities or barriers. Include interviews with working women you know. Plan to share your preliminary research findings with your classmates next week.** The assignment includes research on historical and cultural events that have influenced women's job opportunities or barriers, primary research using information from or about working women the writer knows, and an opportunity to share ideas with classmates.

First, **consider the purpose** of the assignment—the reason(s) for writing. Generally, research papers are designed to demonstrate the writer's ability to explore a topic in-depth and develop and explain new ideas. The purpose may or may not be stated directly in the assignment. Learning something new, improving your writing skills, and convincing others of your view on an issue may all be reasons for writing. In this case, the purpose of the assignment—to analyze possible careers for women—is stated directly in the assignment.

Next, **consider your audience**—the people who will read your paper—and what their knowledge about and interest in your topic is. Knowing your audience helps you determine the right style and tone for the paper and how much background information to provide. In this case, while the professor is your primary audience and the person who will most likely assign a grade, your classmates will also be an audience for the paper.

Now, **conduct a preliminary search of sources** using the broad topic given in the assignment. Start by looking online and in university library databases. Here is an example of a source:

> Scott, J, Crompton, R., & Lyonette, C., (Eds.) (2010). *Gender inequalities in the 21st century: New barriers and continuing constraints.* Cheltenham, UK: Edward Elgar Publishing, Inc.

For more on finding appropriate sources, see ECONOMICS, Part 1.

Assignments are often given in broad terms, so you need to **narrow the topic** to make it more specific and manageable. It is helpful to do some preliminary brainstorming, perhaps using a graphic organizer (a list or a diagram) to come to a more specific focus. This chart lists possible career areas for women focusing on opportunities and barriers. We have decided to narrow it down further to the topic of business and why women are lagging behind in achieving high-level management positions in large corporations.

Career Areas for Women	Opportunities	Barriers
Business	• More positions opening up to women	• Still a glass ceiling keeping the number of women in senior positions low • Managing family and work • Attitudes toward women • Gender stereotypes
Medicine	• Rapidly growing field with predictions of many jobs in the future and shortages of doctors and other health professionals	• Still difficult to get into medical school (also very expensive) and even nursing programs
Military	• Women now permitted to hold combat positions in many countries	• Few women able to meet the physical qualifications • Attitudes against women in combat
Science	• Jobs opening to women • More attention being paid to getting women into STEM fields at an earlier age	• Attitude that women don't want these jobs

The final step in exploring the topic involves **brainstorming** and **generating ideas** on the narrowed topic. At this stage, you want to quickly get down on paper what you already know, have learned through your preliminary search, or might think about your topic. Focus on key words that will help guide you through the next phase of the process—research.

For this step, creating a **cluster diagram** helps to generate ideas and key words for an information search—in this case, on the barriers that keep women from getting higher-level positions in large corporations.

CULTURE NOTE
Glass ceiling is a term attributed to Gay Bryant, a magazine editor, and made popular after it was the focus of a Wall Street Journal article in 1986. It is defined as "artificial barriers based on bias that prevent qualified individuals from advancing to management level positions in an organization."

NOTICING ACTIVITY

Look at the cluster diagram. Notice the parts of the diagram. What else could be added to this diagram? Add circles containing any additional information.

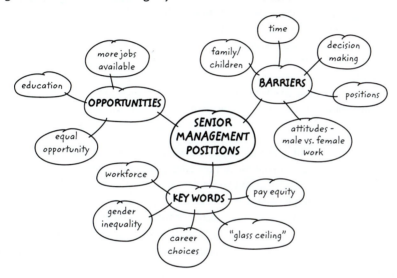

Next, you will do the actual **research** that will support the ideas in your paper. Using your narrowed topic and the ideas you generated by brainstorming, you are ready to **develop a research question, find and evaluate sources, read critically, research ideas, take notes**, and then **assemble them in an annotated bibliography** in order to answer the research question. Here is an example of a **final research question**:

> Although there are increasing numbers of women advancing in the corporate world, why are women still under-represented at the highest levels of management in large corporations, and what are the barriers to their achieving equity with men in both the positions they hold and the salaries they earn?

Resources from the preliminary search can be used to find additional sources. Edited books are often excellent sources because they encompass a collection of articles that focus on one particular topic. The references cited in articles are also good sources. When seeking expert opinions, pay attention to someone who is frequently cited by others; this can help you locate leaders in the field who may lend valuable support to your ideas.

For more on expert opinions, see SOCIOLOGY Part 2.
For more on finding and evaluating sources, see ECONOMICS, Part 2.

Once you have located several sources, read the sources and find information on your topic that will support your ideas. **Critical reading, researching ideas**, and **taking notes** on the sources is essential to identifying ideas for your research paper.

Assembling an annotated bibliography as you find and evaluate sources is an excellent way to keep track of sources and information. Compiling your sources in one place as you read and reread ensures that you do not conduct the same searches over and over again and/or lose important information along the way.

Once you have your narrowed topic, research question, and some useful sources, the next step is to **write a preliminary thesis**. Here is an example:

> Although more women hold senior-level positions in large corporations, they still have not achieved equality because they are still few in number, make less money, and have less real decision-making power than their male counterparts.

The last step in the planning of a research paper is **creating an outline to organize main and supporting ideas.** At this point, you should have notes on the ideas, information from sources, and points you want to include. Organizing those notes into a working outline that lists your main points and the supporting ideas will help you to write a well-organized paper. Writing the outline can highlight areas where there may be gaps in your research so that you can go back and find additional information that will provide adequate support.

STEP 2: WRITING

After completing the planning stage, it is time to **write the first draft**. The more effort you have put into planning, the easier it will be to do the actual writing. Using your preliminary thesis and outline, you are

> For more on developing your ideas, see ECONOMICS, Part 1.
> For more on integrating sources into a research paper, see ECONOMICS. Part 2.

ready to compose the paragraphs of your essay. Introduce your topic in an engaging way and present your thesis. Identify your main ideas by developing and supporting those ideas using the information that you have **integrated from your sources.** Your goal is to convince readers and then conclude your paper in a way that reminds them of the importance of your ideas. You want to leave readers thinking about your topic.

STEP 3: REVISING

Once you have completed your first draft, consider ways to **revise** it to improve it. Focus on how you can develop the content more fully, support your ideas more effectively, and organize your ideas in the clearest way. Do not spend time on grammatical and vocabulary errors at this point unless they have a serious impact on the content. **Getting feedback** is critical to the revision process. You can ask for feedback from an instructor or a peer. You can even get feedback from yourself!

Instructor feedback. In an academic setting, the professor or instructor often provides feedback to students as part of the writing process, prior to submission of the final assignment. If you have this option, take advantage of it.

Peer feedback. This is sometimes done in class, but you can also ask a classmate or another student to read and comment on your draft. Questions from peers or their lack of understanding can be very useful to identify areas in need of additional support or ideas that do not fit your thesis and should be omitted. Here is an example of a peer review form:

	Yes	No	Notes
Does the paper have a purpose?	☐	☐	
Does the paper address the purpose?	☐	☐	
Is there a clear audience?	☐	☐	
Is the paper addressing the needs of the audience?	☐	☐	
Does the organization help the reader?	☐	☐	
Is there a thesis statement?	☐	☐	
Does the thesis statement state exactly what the paper is about?	☐	☐	
Are the main points clear?	☐	☐	
Is there support to develop the main points?	☐	☐	
Do you have questions about the paper's ideas?	☐	☐	

Self-feedback. You can and should go back and read you own paper as you write it. Using a self-feedback form is a good way to make sure you have gone through all of the critical prewriting steps. Here is an example of a self-feedback form:

What is my purpose ? _____

How does my paper address it? _____

_____

Who is my audience? _____

How am I addressing the needs of my audience? _____

_____

How does my organization help my reader? _____

_____

Where is my thesis statement? _____

How does it tell the reader exactly what my paper is about? _____

_____

What are my main points? _____

_____

What support have I offered to develop my main points? _____

_____

What questions might the reader still have about my ideas? _____

_____

At this stage, feedback and revisions should address content and organization only. When you have gotten all the feedback that you can, revise your paper again by writing one or more additional drafts. Some parts of your paper may need little or no revision, and others may require far more work. Remember that most good writers spend quite a bit of time reading, rereading, and revising their papers before they are satisfied with their final work.

Finally, another effective revision strategy is to leave your writing for a while. Time away and some distance can help you look at your work more objectively.

For more on revising, see BIOLOGY, Part 1.

STEP 4: EDITING

The final step in the research writing process is to **proofread and edit** your paper for any vocabulary, grammar, spelling, and punctuation errors. At this stage, it is also important to edit the overall design of your document in order to present a polished-looking paper.

For more on editing, see ENGINEERING, Part 1.

Go to MyEnglishLab to complete a skill practice and join in collaborative activities.

SUPPORTING SKILL 1
NARROWING A TOPIC AND DEVELOPING A RESEARCH QUESTION

WHY IT'S USEFUL By narrowing your topic to one that is appropriate to your assignment, selecting an issue that interests you, and writing a research question to guide you, you will be able to focus your research and later your writing to successfully complete a research paper.

NARROWING THE TOPIC

In all research projects, **narrowing the topic** appropriately is essential. An appropriate topic is one you can analyze, debate, and learn from. As part of planning and prewriting, explore the topic by discussing it with others and finding and reviewing sources. Then examine specific issues in order to further narrow and focus your topic. Choose a topic that interests you and is appropriate for your research paper.

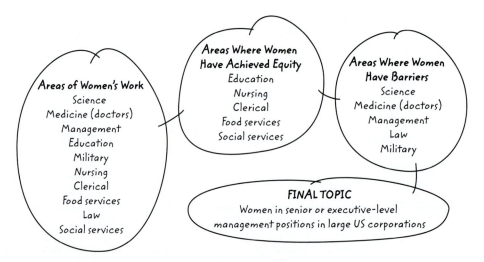

One common problem is choosing a topic that is too broad, which results in a paper that is too general. The sheer amount of information can be overwhelming and make it challenging to decide what to include. For example, *women in management* is too broad. Notice how the final topic in the chart narrowed down women in management further to senior-level management, and the type of business to large US corporations.

Another common problem is having a sufficiently narrowed topic but failing to identify an issue that would focus the project on one specific angle or direction of the topic. Begin to explore your final topic by **identifying the important issues.** Look for patterns in the arguments, ideas, and information in your sources. What are the major themes that the authors discuss? Are there frequently repeated ideas that are referred to by several sources? Are there major disagreements among the sources? Are there authors who are frequently referred to by others or who have a particular perspective on the topic?

As you do a preliminary search of your topic's issues, creating a chart will help you organize your research and identify important issues.

Source	Major Themes	Repeated Ideas	Disagreements	Experts (authors frequently cited or with a particular perspective)

Once you have identified the relevant issues, the next step is to **choose one of the issues** as the focus of your paper. When choosing an issue, think about the following:

- **your personal interest** (This is the most important consideration.)
- purpose and audience
- type of assignment
- requirements and limitations
- available resources
- opportunities (personal experience and knowledge, access to experts)

Narrowing the focus of your research by having an appropriate topic, analyzing the connected issues, and then choosing an important one lays the groundwork for the next step—developing a research question. Here is an example of a final topic and connected issues:

Final topic: Women in senior management positions in large US corporations

Issues: pay equity

    equal representation

    expectations that differ from those placed on men

decision-making power

balancing family with work

attitudes toward women executives

glass ceiling

DEVELOPING A RESEARCH QUESTION

A **research question** is a focused question that helps you to find, critically read, evaluate, and take notes on information and ideas in your sources for use in your research paper. An effective research question focuses on a specific issue, reflects your writing situation, and is narrow enough to meet the parameters of your assignment.

Most research questions begin with a *wh-* question word or a modal such as *would, could,* or *should.* Choosing the type of question is important. Your question can focus on different approaches to the issue, such as current knowledge, history, assumptions, outcomes, or goals and/or policies for carrying out action. Each approach will lead to differences in how you conduct research, organize your information, and draft your paper. Here are some examples:

What barriers still exist that prevent women from achieving upper management corporate positions? (current knowledge about the issue)

When did women first gain entry into senior management positions previously dominated by men? (history)

Could a shift in how society views professions affect the barriers that prevent women from entering the top echelons in corporations? (assumptions and outcomes)

The approach you take will guide your choice of your paper's rhetorical mode, and your research question should fit the mode. You can define or evaluate an issue, compare or contrast two issues, analyze an issue, examine causes or effects of an issue, present a problem and solutions, describe a process, conduct an inquiry, or argue a point of view.

Should there be more government support for working women? (argument)

How can government policies help women achieve salary equity? (process)

Your research question should be flexible because it may change. Writers often find that they need to revise their research questions as their knowledge and understanding of the topic and issue grow. Your answer to the research question is the foundation of your **thesis statement**, which will explain your point of view to your readers.

To **develop a research question,** generate a list of potential questions about your issue that focuses on different approaches and uses different rhetorical modes.

> Why is there still a clear distinction between men's work and women's work, and what is the effect of that on women? (effects)

Choose the research question that best meets your needs, keeping in mind the assignment, your purpose, and your audience.

> What new opportunities are open to women in combat positions in the military? (analysis)

Refine your research question by:

1. replacing words and phrases that may be vague with more specific ones to narrow the scope.

   > ~~Where~~ have women achieved ~~equality~~?

   > **In what professions** have women achieved **equal status with men through equal representation and pay?**

2. asking yourself whether you need to refer to commonly shared assumptions or knowledge about the issue. Use conditional wording such as *although, because, now that, since,* or *while* to introduce these assumptions and frame your question.

   > **Although women's pay has improved relative to men's,** why is there still unequal pay for equal work?

   > **Now that women are graduating from college in greater numbers than men,** when will women achieve greater representation in professions that have been predominantly male?

Use your research question to conduct your preliminary search of sources. If you find vast amounts of information, your research question may be too general and need to be revised to be more focused. If you find little or nothing to answer your question, you may need to expand the scope of your question.

EXERCISE 1

A. Read the practice assignment. Work with a partner to answer the questions that follow.

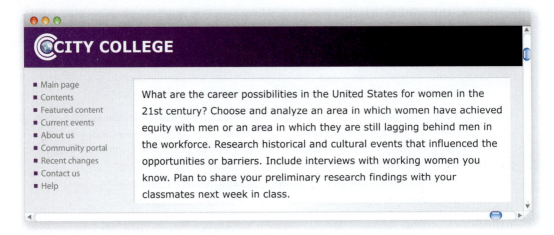

CITY COLLEGE

- Main page
- Contents
- Featured content
- Current events
- About us
- Community portal
- Recent changes
- Contact us
- Help

What are the career possibilities in the United States for women in the 21st century? Choose and analyze an area in which women have achieved equity with men or an area in which they are still lagging behind men in the workforce. Research historical and cultural events that influenced the opportunities or barriers. Include interviews with working women you know. Plan to share your preliminary research findings with your classmates next week in class.

B. Brainstorm possible areas for your research.

   1. List three or more areas in which you believe women have achieved equality with men.

   2. List three or more areas in which you believe women still face barriers to equality with men.

   3. Choose two areas, narrow them, and identify issues associated with them.

      1. Area: ....

        Area narrowed down: ....

        Ideas

      2. Area: ....

        Area narrowed down: ....

        Ideas

C. Choose an area from Part B, and write five possible research questions that consider different issues. Use *what, when, where, who, why, how, would, could,* or *should*. Share your questions with your partner, and discuss the approach and rhetorical mode suggested by each question.

   1. ....

   2. ....

   3. ....

   4. ....

   5. ....

D. Choose the research question from Exercise B on the issue that interests you most. Refine and revise it by changing vague language to be more specific, and rewrite it below. Include an introductory phrase that identifies common assumptions or knowledge about the issue.

Revised research question: ....

....

....

E. Do a preliminary search. Find three or more sources to help you answer your research question.

1. ....

2. ....

3. ....

F. Discuss your research question and preliminary sources with your partner.

Go to MyEnglishLab to complete a skill practice.

SUPPORTING SKILL 2
WRITING A PRELIMINARY THESIS STATEMENT AND CREATING AN OUTLINE

WHY IT'S USEFUL By arriving at a good thesis statement to focus your efforts and creating an outline to organize and manage the ideas you will present, you will be better able to draft an effective research paper.

WRITING A PRELIMINARY THESIS STATEMENT

Your **thesis** is the central idea of your paper. A strong preliminary thesis statement will answer your research question and let the reader know what the answer might be. To arrive at a preliminary thesis, you can brainstorm, freewrite, or list ideas in response to your research question. Review your notes from your preliminary research. Then write a preliminary thesis statement that clearly expresses your opinion about the issue you are addressing. Your thesis statement will continue to guide your critical reading and is a step toward making the shift from learning to adding to existing knowledge on this topic.

A strong thesis statement:

- fits your purpose and is appropriate to the assignment.
- is specific and expresses a particular point of view.
- does not simply announce your topic, state a fact, or make a generalization about the topic.
- is the answer to a question, the solution to a problem, or a position on a debatable issue.
- affects what your reader knows, understands, or believes about the topic.
- is supportable with evidence, facts, and expert opinions.
- frames the structure of your paper by suggesting a rhetorical mode.
- helps you focus and organize your ideas.
- is usually one sentence but can be longer.

Follow these steps to write a preliminary thesis statement:

- Identify key words in your research question and your notes.
- Review your purpose.
- Consider your readers' needs and interests.
- Focus your response to the issue you have chosen.
- Answer your research question.

This chart shows five thesis statements and why they are poor, better, and strong.

Thesis Statement	Analysis	Strength of Thesis Statement
This paper will examine pay inequity for women.	Uses key words, but only announces the topic	Poor thesis statement
Women in executive positions still lack pay equity.	Uses key words and is specific, but only states a fact	Poor thesis statement
Pay inequity is wrong.	Only makes a generalization about the topic	Poor thesis statement
Pay inequities still exist in senior-level management positions, and having lower pay than men negatively affects women.	Uses key words, is specific, expresses a point of view on the topic, and frames the paper by suggesting a rhetorical mode, but doesn't increase the reader's understanding of the issues or focus and organize the paper	Better thesis statement
While women's pay has risen since women entered the workforce in greater numbers in the mid-20th century, pay inequities still exist in senior-level management positions, and having lower pay than men negatively affects women's effectiveness as managers, their ability to manage work and family life, and their opportunities for further advancement.	Addresses assumed knowledge about the topic, frames the structure, helps the reader understand the direction of the paper, and focuses and organizes ideas	Strong thesis statement

CREATING AN OUTLINE

An **outline** provides a framework for your research paper and acts as a guide to its structure and organization. Your outline should include the key points your paper will address, the order in which you will make your points, and the amount of supporting material you have for each point.

An outline can help you see organizational issues or identify places where more support is needed. One way to structure your outlines is to look for common patterns of organization in your sources. A good outline will answer these questions:

- Are you covering all the key points?
- Are you presenting the points in the best order?
- Are you providing enough evidence to support the points?
- Are you balancing the amount of support given to each point?
- Are you relying on enough sources?
- Are you favoring one side of an argument?

Your outline can be **informal**, including simply your preliminary thesis statement and a list of your key points. It can be **topical** (i.e., listing topics and subtopics as words or phrases), or it can comprise **complete sentences that introduce key points** to be used later as the topic sentences of the body paragraphs.

Informal topical outline

Thesis statement

Although more women hold senior-level positions in large corporations, they have not yet achieved equality because they are still few in number, make less money, and have less real decision-making power than their male counterparts.

Topics and subtopics

- Still lack equal representation
  - → Statistics on number of women in upper-management levels
  - → Reasons for low numbers
  - → Negative effects
- Still aren't paid the same as men
  - → Statistics
  - → Negative effects
- Have less decision-making power
  - → Reasons for this
  - → Negative effects

Informal outline focusing on key points

Thesis statement

Although more women hold senior-level positions in large corporations, they have not yet achieved equality because they are still few in number, make less money, and have less real decision-making power than their male counterparts.

Sentences describing key points (written as topic sentences)

- Statistics clearly show that women are still underrepresented in upper management in most US corporations for a number of reasons.

- Women still only make about three-fourths of what men make in most senior management positions in the corporate world, and this negatively affects attitudes about their effectiveness and their ability to do the job.

- While there are more women in top management and executive positions in US corporations, a close examination of their positions and duties reveals that they have significantly less decision-making power than men in comparable situations.

Your outline can also be **formal**, following one of the standard outline styles. A formal outline requires that you limit major sections, keep equal ideas in the same level, use parallel structure, and have at least two items in a section. Using this type of outline clearly classifies and divides your information to show main points and their supporting ideas. A formal outline helps you to visualize if the structure is logical for your thesis and if everything in your outline supports it, either directly or indirectly.

A formal outline, like an informal outline, can be a topical outline or a sentence outline.

Formal topical outline

I. Introduction

    Thesis statement

        Although more women hold senior-level positions in large corporations, they have not yet achieved equality because they are still few in number, make less money, and have less real decision-making power than their male counterparts.

II. Lack of equal representation

    A. Statistics as evidence of claim

    B. Reasons for lack of representation

        1) Glass ceiling

        2) Family responsibilities

III. Pay inequity

    A. Statistics that show inequities

    B. Negative effects of inequities

        1) Attitudes about effectiveness

        2) Ability to do the work

IV. Decision-making power compared to men

    A. Positions

    B. Duties

V. Conclusion

An outline is like a road map. If you create a good one, it is easy to follow it and stay on course to a well-organized first draft of a paper, especially when integrating source material. Like your research question and preliminary thesis, your outline should be flexible and can change as you work through the drafting process.

> For more on developing ideas and evaluating and integrating sources into your writing, see ECONOMICS, Parts 1 and 2.

EXERCISE 2

A. Use your research question from Exercise 1 to write a strong preliminary thesis statement for a research paper.

....

....

....

B. Write a formal topical outline based on your thesis statement. Use the resources you found for Exercise 1 and your own ideas to identify and include at least three main ideas with a minimum of two supporting ideas each.

   I. Introduction

      Thesis statement ....

   II. Main idea ....

      A. Supporting idea ....

      B. Supporting idea ....

   III. Main idea ....

      A. Supporting idea ....

      B. Supporting idea ....

   IV. Main idea ....

      A. Supporting idea ....

      B. Supporting idea ....

   V. Conclusion ....

C. PEER REVIEW. Exchange your thesis statement and outline with a partner. Respond to the questions to evaluate each other's work. For responses marked No, give feedback in the Notes column to help your partner revise.

	Yes	No	Notes
Is the thesis statement specific?	☐	☐	
Does it express a point of view?	☐	☐	
Is it the answer to a question, the solution to a problem, or a position on a debatable issue?	☐	☐	
Does it frame the structure of a paper by suggesting a rhetorical mode?	☐	☐	
Does it suggest how the paper will be focused and organized?	☐	☐	
Does the outline contain at least three key (main) points?	☐	☐	
Are the key points equal and written in parallel structure?	☐	☐	
Does each key point have two supporting ideas?	☐	☐	

Go to MyEnglishLab to complete a skill practice.

READING-WRITING CONNECTION
ASSEMBLING AN ANNOTATED BIBLIOGRAPHY

WHY IT'S USEFUL By assembling an annotated bibliography, you will have another tool to help you prepare to write a research paper. Annotated bibliographies require you to read critically and can help you further develop your thesis. They also help you keep track of the sources you plan to cite in your paper.

A **bibliography** is a list of sources used when writing a scholarly article or paper. This list can include sources you have cited, as well as those that helped to inform your writing but were not actually referenced in it. Each discipline has a preferred citation style, so it is important to check with your instructor to determine which format to use. You may refer to online citation guides to ensure that your bibliography is formatted correctly.

An **annotated bibliography** goes a step further than simply listing sources. The purpose of an annotated bibliography is to demonstrate the relevance of the sources you will use to frame your argument. An **annotation** usually includes a brief summary of the main idea of the text, an assessment of the usefulness or relevance of the source, and an explanation of how the research will inform your thesis. Annotated bibliography entries vary in length, but they usually consist of about 150–200 words.

Process of writing an annotated bibliography

After you have located, reviewed, and assessed your sources, begin your annotated bibliography with a **citation** of the text. In the social sciences, APA style (American Psychological Association) is used to document sources. Look at the example of a book citation using APA style. Note the formatting, punctuation, and type and order of information included.

Honey, M. (1984). *Creating Rosie the Riveter: Class, gender, and propaganda during World War II.* Amherst, MA: University of Massachusetts Press.

The citation is followed by an annotation, which should include a summary, an evaluation, and a reflection on the source.

- The **summary** consists of 2–3 sentences that describe the main points of the work.
- The next part provides an **evaluation** of the ideas or methods presented in the text and may include an assessment of the authority of the author. You may compare and contrast the ideas from this source to others in order to show how reliable the information is. You can also comment on the author's audience for the source if it is significant to your paper.
- Last, include a **reflection** of how you will use the source for your project. You can identify specific ideas, chapters, and pages that will inform your writing. You can also note when a source has influenced you so strongly that it caused you to rethink or even change your original thesis.

A. Read the annotated bibliography entry. Then answer the questions.

Honey, M. (1984). *Creating Rosie the Riveter: Class, gender, and propaganda during World War II.*
Amherst, MA: University of Massachusetts Press.

In *Creating Rosie the Riveter*, Maureen Honey examines how fiction, advertisements, and propaganda published in two magazines widely read by American women during the late 1940s and 1950s were used to encourage women to enter the workforce during World War II. Honey unravels arguments that have been discussed about this subject and moves beyond them by evaluating the factors that hindered the possibility for women to continue working in nontraditional fields after the war.

Honey's systematic research of the strategies used by the government to preserve conventional ideas of women's roles in society while at the same time encouraging them to enter the workforce, is the first of its kind. Unlike historian William Chafe, who believes that the war precipitated women entering the workforce, and Leila Rupp, who posits that the war had no effect on the number of women in the workforce, Maureen Honey believes that images of women in advertising and propaganda had a strong effect on their entry into and exit from the workforce.

Chapter 1 frames the social and political context of the time period. Chapter 4 provides evidence for my claim that working-class women were not driven to work because of a sense of patriotic duty; rather, they worked out of necessity in order to support their families. This book is useful because it makes a distinction between middle-class and working-class women in the workforce during World War II.

B. Answer the questions.

1. Identify the parts of the citation at the beginning of the entry (e.g., title, author, etc.).

   Honey, M. (1984).   _____

   **Creating Rosie the Riveter:
   Class, gender, and propaganda
   during World War II.**   _____

   **Amherst, MA: University of
   Massachusetts Press.**   _____

2. What type of source is this (e.g., journal article, book)? ....

   ....

3. How is the annotation organized? ....

   ....

4. What is the main idea of this source? ....

   ....

   ....

5. How is the source evaluated in the annotation? What information is included?

   ....

   ....

   ....

6. How can you find information about the reliability of the source? What can you find out about Maureen Honey? ....

....

....

7. In your own words, what is the writer of the annotation's thesis?

....

....

....

8. How will the annotation's writer use this source in his or her paper?

....

....

....

EXERCISE 4

A. **Read the article. As you read, note the main idea of each section in the margin. When you are finished, discuss the main ideas with a partner.**

WOMEN IN THE WORKFORCE IN THE UNITED STATES POST-WORLD WAR II *Valerie A. Collier*

1   World War II dramatically changed the landscape of women's participation in the labor force in the United States and gave rise to an eventual shift in gender and social dynamics that led to more women entering the workplace. In the post-war society of the 1950s, despite the fact that women had a limited scope of workplace opportunity, their participation in the labor force steadily increased. Women made up less than a quarter of the workforce in the early decades of the 20th century, but that changed after the war, with women continuing to join the workforce in the decades that followed. The steady addition of women in the workplace had a ripple effect on both industry and society by shaping new jobs and stretching conventional ideas about women's roles. The rise in the number of women in the workforce may be attributed to several major causes and had a number of notable effects on society.

Labor shortages during the war

2   Men entered the armed services, leaving jobs vacant and the wartime manufacturing industry desperate for a labor force. Prior to the war, many professions had insurmountable entry barriers for women, including careers in the sciences, manufacturing, and technology. These fields became open to women during wartime, and in fact, women felt pressure to enter them as a form of patriotic duty. The female labor force grew by 50 percent during the war, and the call to industry at the time can be best illustrated by the US government's iconic stylized character known as Rosie the Riveter. The cartoon was a rallying point to American women to join the war efforts and features a woman wearing the ubiquitous

Rosie the Riveter

Continued

blue-collar manufacturing industry uniform, flexing her bicep, and saying, "We Can Do It!" Women undoubtedly reaped the benefits of being in the workforce by earning their own money and broadening boundaries of what they were thought to be capable of accomplishing.

Financial necessity

3   While the wartime era opened what seemed to be endless workforce possibilities to women, the decade following it just as effectively closed off many opportunities. Men returned home without jobs to a country facing the possibility of another economic depression. The gender-boundary pendulum began to swing in the opposite direction of wartime liberties given to women, and women left their jobs in large numbers, either voluntarily or by being fired or demoted. In addition, schools of law, medicine, and business summarily closed their doors to all but a small percentage of women.

4   However, the decade also bore expanding financial hardships that forced women to earn an income. Women married younger, had more children at a younger age, and the number of people marrying overall rose in society during this time, which came to be known as the baby boom era. There was an intense drive for Americans to be apolitical during the atomic age due to Cold War tension, and many women retreated into the singular focus of providing a secure middle-class lifestyle for their families. However, material possessions found in the idealized middle-class suburban home were expensive, and those, as well as other rising costs of living, slowly pushed women back into the labor force throughout the 1950s.

> **CULTURE NOTE**
> The **baby boom era** is the period between 1946 and 1964 when there was an increased birthrate in the United States.

> **CULTURE NOTE**
> The **atomic age** is the period after the first nuclear "atomic" bomb was used during World War II in 1945.

The women's rights movement and related legislation

5   Author Betty Friedan's influential 1963 book *The Feminine Mystique* launched the feminist movement in America and called into question the happiness of those women who had spent the 1950s at home as "career homemakers." The women's rights movement advocated equal rights and opportunities for women and rose in tandem with other social equality movements, including the civil rights movement. It is arguable that feminism is a cause of, rather than a consequence to, women in the workforce, and perhaps it is a little of both. One of the hallmarks of the movement, preceding the Civil Rights Act by a year, was the Equal Pay Act of 1963. Women made up a third of the work force in the United States, yet earned only 59 cents to the dollar that men earned. The Equal Pay Act was an effort to lay a foundation of fairness for women who, by necessity, joined the workforce but faced gender-based

> **CULTURE NOTE**
> The **Civil Rights Act** is a 1964 US law that prohibited discrimination based on race, color, religion, sex, or national origin.

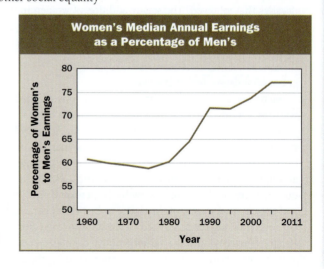

Women's Median Annual Earnings as a Percentage of Men's

Percentage of Women's to Men's Earnings (y-axis): 50, 55, 60, 65, 70, 75, 80. Year (x-axis): 1960, 1970, 1980, 1990, 2000, 2011.

compensation discrimination. When President John F. Kennedy signed the bill into law, he said that women often faced the difficult decision of accepting public assistance or taking a job at a much lower pay rate than men. Ironically, though women's participation in the labor force had risen to 57 percent by 2011, they still made only 77 cents for every dollar earned by men.

Expanded presence in pink-collar jobs and new industry

6   Women were closed off from many employment avenues in the 1950s, yet they steadily entered the workforce, albeit in new ways from the manufacturing-era push of the war. After the war, when women left their jobs or were demoted or fired by employers, many turned to lower-level service roles, such as secretarial work, food service positions, clerical work, and other "pink-collar" jobs. Women also expanded the workforce by starting home enterprises, such as selling Tupperware or Mary Kay cosmetics out of their homes, largely to other women. These types of jobs worked well for women who continued to be homemakers, which was the case for most women, particularly in the 1950s.

> **CULTURE NOTE**
> *Pink-collar jobs* are low-paid jobs that are usually service-oriented and typically held by women. Examples include secretaries, nurses, and teachers.

> **CULTURE NOTE**
> *Tupperware* is a brand of plastic food storage containers developed by Earl Silas Tupper in 1946. It was common for women to throw "Tupperware parties" in their homes where they sold Tupperware to their friends and family and kept a percentage of the sales.

7   Women's participation in the workplace has risen since World War II, and the reasons for this trend appear to be long lasting. Women continue to gain access to higher-level positions in the workforce, and the economic need for a job remains strong. The 1950s, when women's involvement in the workforce was limited, is often idealized as a time of innocence and family values, but it is also viewed as a period of repression of women. The 1960s and beyond saw a steady change toward women's increasing participation in the workforce. The women's rights movement greatly contributed

> **CULTURE NOTE**
> *Mary Kay cosmetics* is a cosmetics line founded by Mary Kay Ash in 1963. Women called "beauty consultants" sold these products to women in their community and received a share of the sales.

to women's ability to choose such paths. Women's roles in the workforce will no doubt continue to evolve as they continue to seek opportunities to make equal contributions to society in both the positions they hold and the salaries they receive.

Source: Valerie Collier is a professor of women's studies at the University of Maryland, Baltimore. This essay was published in the *Journal of Gender Studies in America*, volume 29, pages 131–133 in August 2012. [Note: The source information is fictional and only for use in Exercise B.]

B. Answer the questions with a partner.

1. Write the citation in APA style.

   ....

   ....

2. Summarize the main idea in two or three sentences.

   ....

   ....

3. Evaluate the essay.

   a. What is the purpose? ....

       ....

   b. Who is the audience? ....

   c. What is the authority of the author? ....

4. What is a possible thesis you could support with this essay?

   ....

   ....

5. Reflect on how this essay could be used to support your thesis.

   ....

   ....

C. Write an annotated bibliography entry of the article, using the your responses from Part B. Be sure to begin with a properly formatted citation, followed by the annotation.

D. **PEER REVIEW.** Exchange your annotated bibliography entry with a partner. Respond to the questions to evaluate each other's work. For responses marked No, give feedback in the Notes column to help your partner revise.

	Yes	No	Notes
Is the citation accurate and properly formatted?	☐	☐	
Does the annotation include a brief summary, evaluation, and reflection?	☐	☐	
Does the writer accurately summarize the main idea?	☐	☐	
Does the writer include an effective evaluation of the essay?	☐	☐	
Does the reflection relate to the research topic?	☐	☐	
Does the reflection describe how the writer will use the source for his or her paper?	☐	☐	
Is the annotation well organized?	☐	☐	
Is the annotation concise?	☐	☐	

Go to MyEnglishLab to complete vocabulary exercises and skill practices and join in collaborative activities.

LANGUAGE SKILLS
EXPLORING VERB TENSES IN ACADEMIC WRITING

WHY IT'S USEFUL By being aware of how and why certain verb tenses are used in academic writing, you will establish the time of an action as well as understand specific textual functions in scholarly writing.

The three most frequently used tenses in academic writing are **simple present**, **simple past**, and **present perfect**.

Notes	Examples
Simple present is used to report current trends, general information, and findings or results of research. Summaries and abstracts included in an academic work tend to use the simple present.	The results of this study **indicate** that women **continue** to make up the majority of workers in low-wage jobs. As a result, the author **urges** companies to change their practices by promoting more women to higher-paid positions.
Simple past is used when reporting methods or procedures used in a study completed in the past. For this reason, simple past is commonly used in science writing when explaining steps in an experiment.	Smith **surveyed** the types of occupations women **held** during World War II and **recorded** how much they **were compensated** for this work.
Present perfect is used to show that a concept is still relevant and to describe ongoing processes that began in the past. It is also used to refer to completed events in the indefinite past and to refer to sources in ongoing debates. Present perfect can sometimes be used interchangeably with simple present. Present perfect is typically used in a conclusion to recap what has been stated earlier in a writing.	This study indicates that the effects of the increasing number of women in the workforce **have had** both positive and negative impacts on family life. Throughout the article, Campbell **has argued** that the positive effects **have** far **outweighed** any negative impacts on society.
Passive voice is another important aspect of tense and is frequently used in academic writing. Use the passive voice to emphasize the procedures or actions of the research instead of the writer.	 Transcripts of participants **were coded** and **analyzed** over a 2-month period.
Use the passive voice to include information that was introduced earlier, for better cohesion.	There are several explanations for the increase in women in the workforce. Labor shortages and financial necessity **are** the most frequently **given**.
Use the passive voice to avoid using a subject when it is not important or not known.	While the lack of women in certain positions in the workforce **is** sometimes **attributed** to the choices women make, documented patterns of discrimination against women provide a more accurate explanation.

EXERCISE 5

Read the passage. Circle the verbs, identify the verb tenses, and determine whether they use active or passive voice. Compare with a partner, and discuss why each tense was used.

Women's participation in the workplace has risen since World War II, and the reasons for this trend appear to be long lasting. Women continue gaining access to higher-level positions in the workforce, and the economic need for a job remains strong. The 1950s, when women's involvement in the workforce was limited, is often idealized as a time of innocence and family values, but it is also viewed as a period of repression of women. The 1960s and beyond saw a steady change toward women's increasing participation in the workforce. The women's rights movement contributed to women's ability to choose such paths. Today, women's roles in the workforce continue evolving as they seek opportunities for equality through contributions to society in both the positions they hold and the salaries they receive.

EXERCISE 6

Rewrite the active sentences in the passive voice.

1. World War II dramatically changed the landscape of women's participation in the labor force.

   ....

2. A small percentage of women made up the workforce.

   ....

3. The addition of women in the workplace affected both industry and society.

   ....

4. Rosie the Riveter inspired US housewives to join the war efforts.

   ....

5. Schools of law, medicine, and business did not accept women.

   ....

6. There was an intense drive for Americans to be apolitical during the atomic age.

   ....

7. Betty Friedan's 1963 book *The Feminine Mystique* launched the feminist movement in America.

   ....

8. The women's rights movement advocated equal rights and opportunities for women.

   ....

Go to MyEnglishLab to complete skill practices.

APPLY YOUR SKILLS

WHY IT'S USEFUL By applying the skills you have learned in this unit, you can successfully use the research writing process to narrow a topic, develop a research question, assemble an annotated bibliography, write a thesis statement, and create an outline for a paper.

ASSIGNMENT

Plan a research paper on an important event in your country's or culture's history that caused major social changes, specifically as they relate to the role of women. Look at issues connected to the economy, the workforce, and the family. Be sure to narrow down your topic, develop a research question, write a preliminary thesis, and create an outline.

BEFORE YOU WRITE

A. **Before you begin your assignment, discuss the questions with one or more students.**

1. What important event in your country or culture has caused major social changes for women?

2. How were women's lives impacted by this event?

3. How was the economy, workforce, and family life impacted as a result of this event?

B. **As you consider your assignment, complete the tasks below. Then share your ideas with another student. Get feedback and revise your ideas if necessary.**

1. Consider your purpose and audience. [Why are you exploring this topic for a paper? Why did you choose your topic? Who will read your paper?]

    a. Purpose: ....

    b. Audience: ....

2. Narrow down your topic. ....

3. Brainstorming: Create and complete a graphic organizer or freewrite for 5–10 minutes.

C. **Review the Unit Skills Summary. As you begin the writing task on page 27, apply the skills you learned in this unit.**

UNIT SKILLS SUMMARY

Narrow a topic and develop a research question.
- Identify an important issue that can be debated and analyzed.
- Create a research question that reflects the writing situation and assignment.

Write a preliminary thesis statement and create an outline.
- Develop a working thesis that responds to the research question.
- Create an outline that provides a framework of the ideas and organization of a research paper.

Assemble an annotated bibliography.
- Use an annotated bibliography to develop a thesis and keep track of sources.

Explore verb tenses in academic writing.
- Be aware of how tenses function in academic writing.

THINKING CRITICALLY

As you consider your assignment, discuss the questions with another student. Get feedback and revise your ideas if necessary.

1. What are the arguments against the position you have taken on an event that has impacted women in your country or culture?
2. Would most women in your country or culture agree with your position? Why or why not?
3. Is the change you have chosen for your topic relevant and of interest in other cultures or countries?

THINKING VISUALLY

A. Look at the graph from the US Census Bureau. Write a summary of the information it conveys.

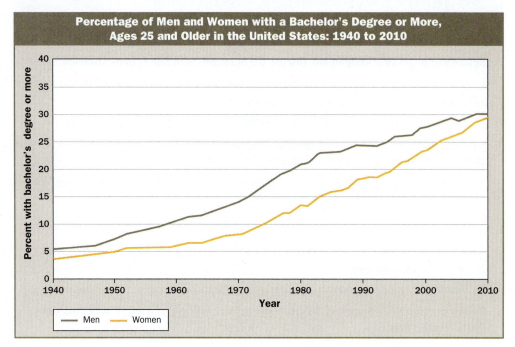

Percentage of Men and Women with a Bachelor's Degree or More, Ages 25 and Older in the United States: 1940 to 2010

B. Find (or create) another graph that provides information relevant to your assignment. Write

a citation for this source. ....

....

THINKING ABOUT LANGUAGE

Read the passage. Underline all of the verbs, identify the verb tenses, and determine whether they use active or passive voice.

Maureen Honey's systematic research of the strategies used by the government to preserve conventional ideas of women's roles in society, while at the same time encouraging them to enter the workforce, is the first of its kind. Unlike historian William Chafe, who believes that the war precipitated women entering the workforce, and Leila Rupp, who posits that the war had no effect on the number of women in the workforce, Honey believes that images of women in advertising and propaganda had an effect on their entry into and exit from the workforce.

WRITE

A. Revisit the writing assignment and your answers to the questions in Before you Write, Part B. Write a research question that reflects the audience and purpose of the assignment.

....

....

B. Research your topic. Search for preliminary sources, and create an annotated bibliography for at least two of the sources.

C. Develop a working thesis statement that responds to your research question.

....

....

D. Create a formal or informal outline of your research paper.

BEYOND THE ASSIGNMENT

Write a research paper. Think about an important event in your country's or culture's history that caused major social changes, specifically as they relate to the role of women. Look at issues connected to the economy, the workforce, and the family. Use all the skills you learned in this unit.

▶ Go to MyEnglishLab to listen to Professor Greenberg and to complete a self-assessment.

Individual choices impact the global economy.

ECONOMICS

Idea Development

UNIT PROFILE

There are many factors that influence people to buy certain products or choose a specific service over another. In this unit, you will read and write about topics related to consumer behavior, including common misperceptions about why people buy what they buy, the effectiveness of product placement as a marketing strategy, and the importance of decision simplicity.

Plan a research paper on the factors that influence a consumer's decision to buy certain products and services. Are there different factors that influence decisions to buy a particular product or service over another? Choose two products or services. Compare and contrast the drivers that impact decision making at the point of purchase.

OUTCOMES

• Conduct primary and secondary research
• Collaborate and share ideas
• Critically evaluate and organize research
• Summarize texts and incorporate summaries
• Use reported speech effectively

GETTING STARTED

▶ Go to MyEnglishLab to listen to Professor Clerici-Arias and to complete a self-assessment.

Discuss these questions with a partner or group.

1. There are many ways to get information about products and services now. How do you usually get your information? Do you place more value on the opinions of "experts" that you don't know or people that you do know?

2. Do you believe that we sometimes have too many choices as consumers? How can companies find the right balance between not having enough choices and having too many?

3. Professor Clerici-Arias suggests that understanding why people buy may not be as simple as we might think. Do you agree? Why or why not?

For more about **ECONOMICS**, see 2 3 . See also R and OC **ECONOMICS** 1 2 3

FUNDAMENTAL SKILL
IDEA DEVELOPMENT

WHY IT'S USEFUL By developing ideas, you can broaden your understanding of a topic, which allows you to craft a more interesting paper and make meaningful connections between your topic and research. Spending time developing clear ideas before you write will also make the writing process easier.

The starting point for any research paper is a **topic.** Academic writing assignments will usually include one of the following:

- a specific topic,
- a variety of topics from which to choose, or
- a general subject area within which to focus.

The instructor often adds (or it is up to you to add) a **focus** and a **genre** to the assignment. For example, if you are studying consumers' buying behaviors, your instructor might ask you to analyze the factors that influence consumers to buy a particular product or service. In this instance, your topic is *buying behaviors*, and the focus of your paper is explaining and analyzing the factors that influence consumers rather than arguing for or against a particular factor or way to influence consumers.

Topic: Buying Behaviors

Focus: Factors that influence consumers to buy a product or service

Genre: Expository essay

It is your job to then choose or find a specific aspect of the topic that interests you, to narrow the topic, and to develop a focused research question to guide you. You also want to consider your audience: who will read your paper—and your purpose: what you want to accomplish.

For instance, do you want to inform, to persuade, to help yourself discover ideas, or to demonstrate that you know the subject? All of this will affect not only the content of your paper but its structure, too. Finally, these decisions should be based on the time and resources available to you and be appropriate to your level of knowledge and experience.

With the topic, focus, and structure in mind, you are now ready for **idea development**. This stage is both daunting and liberating. It is challenging because you most likely have a lot to learn before you can begin to write well, but it is freeing as well because you are the author of the essay and can develop it as you like.

Many students feel overwhelmed by the research writing process, but a good way to begin is to explore what you already know. A good first step is **prewriting**, or generating ideas, and then organizing them. You can start by listing words and phrases related to the topic. Don't worry about being specific now; broad terms will be narrowed down later and will lead you to better sources. You might consider keeping a writing journal so all your ideas will be in one place.

NOTICING ACTIVITY

There are various prewriting techniques that can help you both generate ideas and show relationships between ideas. Look at the list of prewriting ideas. Which may be used to primarily generate many ideas? Which may be used to primarily show relationships between ideas? Mark each prewriting technique with *G* if it is primarily used to generate ideas or *R* if it shows relationships between ideas. Add other techniques you know of. Share your ideas with a partner.

Prewriting Techniques		
brainstorming	freewriting	making an outline
clustering	listing	
drawing a Venn diagram	making a flowchart	

Look at two examples of common prewriting techniques: **listing** and **cluster diagrams**. What differences do you see between the two techniques? When in the writing process would you use each?

Consumer behavior   Cost   Beliefs

Customer reviews   Big purchase or small   Age, gender

Product brand   Type of product or service Lifestyle

Product quality   Promotion   Occupation

Product features   Discounts   Advertising

Feelings and emotions   Reaction   Perception

Needs   Psychological factors   Benefits

Wants   Motivation   Culture

                                                     Experience

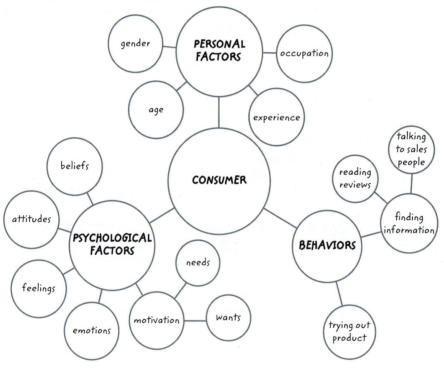

The next step in developing an idea for an academic paper is doing **research**. There are different types of research and a variety of ways to approach research:

- Conducting **secondary research** means gathering published information, typically from electronic and print sources, such as Internet sites, books, magazines, journals, and newspapers. It can include government reports and pamphlets from organizations and businesses. The information can also be audio or visual, such as radio or television broadcasts, documentaries, or films.
- Conducting **primary research** means interviewing people or having a first-hand experience of something—for example, observing people, an event, or a place.
- **Collaboration** is a kind of primary research and a practical means through which you test out your ideas. By sharing ideas with peers and others, you can glean valuable information and insight, and integrate that feedback into your work. This is a common practice in university courses, both at the graduate and undergraduate levels.

This chart lists examples of the three types of research sources. Add other sources you know of.

Primary Research	Secondary Research	Collaboration
interview	books (text, reference, non-fiction)	peers
survey	magazines, newspapers	classmates
observation	academic and trade journals	experts
analysis	Internet sites	instructor
experiment		librarians

Finally, after conducting research, the final step is to critically **evaluate** the information you've gathered and **organize** it. You will need to evaluate the sources by asking yourself if they are appropriate for your paper because they are relevant (pertain to your topic and focus), credible (are from a knowledgeable source), and reliable (provide trustworthy evidence or information to support a point). When you have done the necessary research and evaluated the sources, it is time to sort through the ideas to identify main ideas and supporting details and organize them in a way that will help you write your paper. You will read more about evaluating and organizing information in the next section.

Go to MyEnglishLab to complete a skill practice and join in collaborative activities.

SUPPORTING SKILL 1
DEVELOPING IDEAS THROUGH RESEARCH AND COLLABORATION

WHY IT'S USEFUL In research writing, it is essential to base your writing on something beyond your personal knowledge and opinions. By developing your ideas through research, your writing will have credibility and depth, and by collaborating with others, you can gather feedback that can be invaluable in shaping your ideas.

DEVELOPING IDEAS

When developing ideas for an academic writing assignment, whether you happen to be an expert or you have never heard of the concept, you must research the topic and seek answers to a research question. Keep an open mind and be willing to change your opinions if the research suggests this. You will want to examine, compare, synthesize, evaluate, and even challenge the ideas you find.

These preliminary steps are essential before you begin to conduct your research.

1. **Know your audience and your purpose.** If you are writing an assignment for a class, the instructor is most likely your audience. What is the purpose of this paper? (e.g., to demonstrate knowledge of the topic or to show that you can investigate a particular aspect of the course subject matter). Does the assignment include instructions like "explore" and "investigate"? The language used in the assignment may dictate the structure of your paper.

2. **Look carefully at the assignment guidelines your instructor has given you**. You will need to have a firm understanding of the assignment to understand what the instructor is asking you to produce. A multiparagraph essay? A longer research paper?

For more on assignment guidelines, see BIOLOGY, Part 1.

3. **Understand the topic.** Is there a particular focus? How should the paper be organized? What genre of essay should it be: analytical or argumentative?

4. **Do a prewriting activity to get your ideas and questions on paper.** For example, list key words and phrases to guide you in your search for appropriate sources. Write down as many questions and ideas as you can think of without worrying about grammar or spelling. Express and organize your thoughts in a graphic organizer. See X for examples.

5. **It is never too soon to jot down a preliminary thesis.** Remember a thesis statement presents the main idea (topic) and intention (focus) of an essay. It is your preliminary answer to your **research question** and will help you read research and evaluate its usefulness to your paper. You can and will revise it, so try not to put too much thought or detail into it at this point.

EXERCISE 1

A. Read the practice assignment. Think about topic, focus, purpose, and audience. Which verbs can help you figure out what your instructor is asking you to do? Work with a partner to answer the questions that follow.

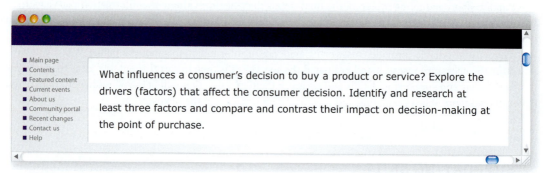

■ Main page
■ Contents
■ Featured content
■ Current events
■ About us
■ Community portal
■ Recent changes
■ Contact us
■ Help

What influences a consumer's decision to buy a product or service? Explore the drivers (factors) that affect the consumer decision. Identify and research at least three factors and compare and contrast their impact on decision-making at the point of purchase.

B. Prewrite by listing words or phrases you already know about the topic and at least two or three questions you have about the topic. Compare with a partner.

Words and phrases

1. ....

2. ....

3. ....

4. ....

5. ....

6. ....

Questions about the topic

1. ....

2. ....

3. ....

C. Create a cluster map like the one below. Add circles as necessary. Compare with a partner.

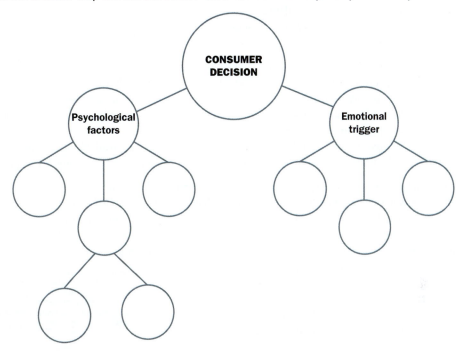

D. Revisit the assignment. Look at your questions and your notes in the cluster map. Write a preliminary thesis.

Preliminary thesis: ....

RESEARCHING IDEAS

Once you have a better idea of your topic and focus and have developed a preliminary thesis, the next step in developing ideas for an academic writing assignment is to **research** appropriate sources.

The most common source for research is **secondary sources**, meaning published information, typically from electronic and print sources such as Internet sites, books, magazines, journals, and newspapers. It can include government reports and pamphlets from organizations and businesses. Audio and visual sources are also secondary sources.

The easiest and fastest way to start your research is by going **online**. The key to successful online research is using good search terms (keywords) and being selective in the sites you visit.

- A lot of valid information can be found using a standard search engine, such as Google, Bing, or Yahoo. Specialty search engines that conduct searches of scholarly materials include Google Scholar, Academic Info, and RefSeek. In any case, avoid spending time on Internet sites whose authors or sponsorship cannot be determined. While Wikipedia can be a starting point in your Internet search, it is typically not an appropriate source to cite in academic work. However, you may find that some sources in Wikipedia's reference list are useful to you.
- For more verifiable, trustworthy, and scholarly information, use websites that are sponsored by universities, government agencies, or research journals. Reputable sites include:
  - online libraries such as The Library of Congress and the Internet Public Library
  - the scholarly journal clearinghouse site EServer Journals Collection
- When you find research that you may use, keep accurate and complete notes of where you found it and other details (e.g., URLs, dates, and authors). Remember: You will need to cite Internet sources in your bibliography just as you do printed materials.

After you have gained an understanding of the topic from online sources, the next stop should be a **library**. A reference librarian is an excellent resource in conducting secondary research, can save you time, and even help you refine your topic and focus.

When you get to the library:

- Explain your writing assignment to a reference librarian and ask what sources—online, print, audio, video, and so forth—the library offers. Libraries are uniquely valuable research resources in that they typically have access to other libraries' catalogs, subscription-based databases, and specialty online collections, such as art and maps, which cannot be found online. Ask the librarian for any recommendations for your specific topic.
- If there is a book or other item that you know of and want but isn't available at your library, find out if it can be borrowed through your school or public library, either electronically or physically.

Primary, or **original research** is information that you get first-hand. It is more labor-intensive than secondary research but is potentially more valuable in that it can be fine-tuned to a particular idea. There may be research topics for which primary research is not possible, but it is always good to include primary sources in your research whenever it is possible. For example, interviews with officials of institutions, historians, and experts in academia can offer unique insights on a topic. Experts can also provide you with suggestions for scholarly journals in the field to assist you in your search for secondary sources. Surveys can be designed to target specific aspects of your topic. Field observation and experiments can add first-hand knowledge of the topic and help confirm or refute your preliminary thesis.

> **TIP**
> ....
> *Writing good questions for a survey and finding respondents can be challenging. University writing centers are an excellent resource to help you get started.*

EXERCISE 2

A. Read the keywords and the hits from an online search. Which are most likely to provide reliable and relevant information? Rank the hits from most relevant (1) to least relevant (6) Compare and discuss your rankings with a partner.

Keywords: Consumer behavior, Drivers, and Optimization

Hits/URLs

.... "Six trends that will shape consumer behavior this year" *Forbes Magazine*

.... "Consumer Behavior" in Wikipedia

.... www.smartinsights.com marketplace

.... "How emotions influence what we buy" *Psychology Today*

.... "A study on mobile phone buying behavior using an image" sciencedirect.com

.... "What is buying behavior? Definition and Meaning" businessdictionary.com

B. Look back at your notes in Exercise 1, Part B. Identify keywords you can use in your online research. List them in the chart below. Then, use a search engine to type in your keyword(s). Review the hits on the first page of results. Which seem most likely to provide reliable and relevant information? Write the names of the hits (or save the URLs on your device).

Keywords	URLs

C. Think about the sources at your school or local library: books, magazines, newspapers, special databases, video, maps, and so on. Look at your list of questions in Exercise 1, Part B. Which of those sources would you like to use in your research? Make notes. Which questions are you still unsure about? Make notes about questions to ask a librarian.

Library sources

.... could answer my question about ....

....

....

....

....

....

Questions for a librarian ....

....

....

D. With another student, talk about how conducting primary research could help you develop your idea. List possible primary sources and a brief description of the information you hope to gain from those sources.

COLLABORATION

Another way to develop ideas for a writing assignment is through **collaboration**. Collaboration means exchanging ideas with peers, friends, instructors, and others. It can be formal or informal and in oral or written form. Collaboration provides a means to receive feedback as you develop and shape your ideas in this stage of the writing process.

EXERCISE 3

A. Look at the collaborative strategies and their descriptions. Check whether or not you have used each of the strategies. Add other strategies you have used or would like to use.

Collaborative strategy	I've tried it	I haven't tried it
Informal discussion Students describe ideas to friends, peers, or instructors, asking for opinions and advice. It's important to listen for feedback and take notes on any outstanding issues related to the ideas.	☐	☐
Group brainstorming A group of classmates or friends comes up with as many ideas as possible for an assignment, writing the ideas on a large piece of paper or the board. As the list is compiled, students ask questions and refine the ideas.	☐	☐
Review of documents Ask someone (a roommate, fellow classmate, or friend) to review the ideas you have in freewriting, listing, or a cluster diagram and suggest any other ideas.	☐	☐
Peer response A student asks another student for a formal written response to a paper (it can be a draft or outline of part or all of a paper). Peer review forms can be used to give more controlled feedback.	☐	☐

B. Share your chart with another student. Talk about the strategies you have used. Were they successful? Why or why not? Will you try some of the strategies you haven't used? Why or why not?

C. Use the informal discussion method of collaboration to share your ideas for your essay, including your preliminary thesis and the highlights of your research findings. Then ask your collaborator for feedback. Take notes.

My collaborator

Notes

Go to MyEnglishLab to complete skill practices.

SUPPORTING SKILL 2
CRITICALLY EVALUATING AND ORGANIZING RESEARCH

WHY IT'S USEFUL By evaluating and organizing your research, you will have a clear idea of the next steps you need to take as you begin to write.

EVALUATE SOURCES

As you gather research on your topic, it is critical to evaluate the information. Identify what's important, relevant to your purpose, and interesting to your audience; omit what is not.

As you evaluate sources for their appropriateness and usefulness to your research, consider the strength of the information or evidence. It should be:

- Accurate—The information presented is factual or clearly identified as opinion.
- Comprehensive—The sources present a full view of the topic.
- Convincing—The sources present supported arguments and address and refute opposing views.
- Credible—The sources are from a knowledgeable author and a reputable publisher.
- Fair—The sources present a balanced view of the topic.
- Relevant—All information is on topic.
- Reliable—The information presented is trustworthy and believable.
- Sufficient—The authors' ideas are adequately developed.
- Timely—The sources are from the right time period for the topic.

ORGANIZE IDEAS

After establishing that your sources are appropriate, it is time to organize your ideas. At this stage, you can add or delete ideas, as well as move ideas from one part of the information you have gathered to another. Ask yourself these questions:

- What background information do you need?
- What main idea should be discussed first, second, and third?
- What special terms that may be unfamiliar will you need to define or explain to your reader?
- What supporting (specific) ideas do you have for your main points?
- What (if any) conclusions have you reached?

This is a good time to do another prewriting technique, such as freewriting. After reviewing your research findings, freewriting is a great way to get your ideas out of your head and in a place where you can begin to organize them. Don't worry about proper essay format or language yet. You are just generating main ideas and supporting details for use later to develop your paper.

A final step in organizing your ideas is to put them into a form that helps you see how the ideas relate to one another. You can do this by creating an outline of your ideas and findings.

For more on outlining, see SOCIOLOGY, Part 1.

Once your research is in order, finalize the working thesis you created as part of developing your ideas. Your thesis needs to show that your paper has a clear point of view and will help the reader understand exactly what your paper is about. Your thesis will also reflect the reason you are writing about your topic. For example, your paper should not just compare the drivers of consumer buying behavior you researched. It should express the reason *why* you are comparing them. For example:

- Are you trying to find out which driver has the greatest impact on the buying decision? If so, you need to investigate why it has that impact.
- Do you want to compare the ways in which different drivers affect different types of purchases? If so, you need to find out why various drivers affect purchases differently.
- Do you want to compare ways businesses utilize the data on the drivers? If so, you need to note why businesses need to utilize data in different ways.

EXERCISE 4

A. Look back at Exercise 2 on pages 34–35. Organize your research in the chart. Include details about the sources where you found the material. Evaluate and list the sources in the order of their importance to your paper. You may need to look at the sources you found again to evaluate their usefulness.

(Topic) Buying Decisions	Main Ideas: Drivers That Affect Buying Decisions	Supporting Details	Source(s)
Other findings			

B. Review your research so far. Freewrite a response to this question: What are the drivers (factors) that affect a consumer's decision to buy a specific product or service? What is their impact on the decision making at the point of purchase and beyond? Write some notes below and add any additional information in a separate place.

_____

_____

_____

_____

_____

C. Finalize your thesis and put your main ideas and supporting details in order. Follow one of these models for organizing your essay.

Block Outline	Point-By-Point Comparison / Contrast Outline

I. Introduction
 Thesis:
II. Body
  A. Drivers that affect consumer decision to buy a specific product or service
    1. Supporting detail
    2. Supporting detail
    3. Supporting detail
  B. Comparison of the impact of drivers on decision making at the point of purchase and beyond
    1. Supporting detail
    2. Supporting detail
    3. Supporting detail
III. Conclusion
	I. Introduction
	 Thesis:
	II. Body (Points of Comparison / Contrast)
	  A.
	    1. Driver 1 and impact
	    1. supporting detail
	    2. supporting detail
	    3. supporting detail
	  B. Driver 2 and impact
	    1. supporting detail
	    2. supporting detail
	    3. supporting detail
	  C. Driver 3 and impact
	    1. supporting detail
	    2. supporting detail
	    3. supporting detail
	III. Conclusion

Go to MyEnglishLab to complete a skill practice.

READING-WRITING CONNECTION
SUMMARIZING TEXTS AND INCORPORATING SUMMARIES

WHY IT'S USEFUL By summarizing, you can better understand a text and connect your ideas with others' views on the topic. Summarizing also demonstrates how well you understand what you have read by presenting a brief overview of the main points.

In research essays or responses to essay exam questions, it is effective to support your ideas by referring to other research. When you refer to another text, it is necessary to summarize the key information from the research that supports the points you are making. By doing this, you connect your ideas to the conversation in the field and strengthen your argument. The same principles apply to summarizing both long and short texts:

- Refer to the source.
- Be brief and accurate.
- Write in your own words.
- Include only the key ideas.
- Exclude your opinion or analysis.

1. As you read a text, **make notes**: Mark section or chapter titles. Highlight the topic and main ideas of each section. Combined, these notes will give a good framework of what the text is about. Be sure to take notes in your own words. If you copy text directly from the original source, put quotation marks around what you've written and include a page number so you can easily identify it as a quotation.

2. **Make a list of the keywords** that you think are important to understand in the text. Note any content-specific or technical terms. Consider how these keywords might be incorporated into your summary. Be sure you can define any keywords you find in the text. Look them up if you aren't sure of their meanings.

3. Before you write a summary, **think how you would describe the text** conversationally to a friend. This will give you a snapshot of what your summary should contain.

4. **Create an outline** for your summary to help organize your thoughts before you write.

5. **Write your summary**.
   - Your first sentence should give the author's full name, the title of the article, publication information, and the topic of the text. You can format this information according to the style guidelines your teacher wants you to use (e.g., APA, MLA, or *Chicago Manual of Style*).
   - Clearly express all of the main ideas of the text. Use the keywords from your notes.
   - Use **transition cues** for coherence across sentences (e.g., *however, similarly, also, another*).
   - Use **reminder phrases** to refer back to the source (e.g., *The author goes on to say that …*).

6. **Review your summary** and be sure you have neither repeated any information, included details that are too minor, nor given your opinion. Remember, your summary should be shorter than the original text.

EXERCISE 5

A. Read the summary of Chapter 1 of *Buyology: Truth and Lies About Why We Buy.*

Buyology, Chapter 1 Summary

[1] In the first chapter of *Buyology* (2008, Doubleday), author Martin Lindstrom introduces his neuromarketing[1] study, in which he analyzed the brain activity of 2081 volunteers from around the world while they were shown images of different products in order to uncover what influences consumers' purchasing decisions. [2] Lindstrom embarked on this study because, as a global branding expert, he believes that traditional methods for analyzing what makes people want to buy a product, like surveys and focus groups, do not adequately predict the success of a product. [3] He reports that in the United States, only eight out of ten new products are successful.

[4] The first experiment in his study was conducted on 32 smokers. [5] He first interviewed them and asked if they thought the warning labels on cigarettes suppressed their desire to smoke. [6] All of the participants stated that the warnings did help to prevent them from smoking. [7] However, when Lindstrom used an fMRI (functional Magnetic Resonance Imaging) scanner to see how their brains reacted to warning labels and graphic images of health effects caused by smoking, he was shocked to discover that the images did not suppress their urge to smoke, but instead, stimulated "the craving spot" of the brain.

[8] Lindstrom goes on to describe other fields that use neuromarketing, such as politics, the entertainment industry, and law enforcement and describes how this research has been used to inform political campaigns and movie endings. [9] Lindstrom reveals that although the findings from his study would help companies save money, many of the corporations he approached would not fund it because they found it to be unethical. [10] They were concerned that brain-imaging was a form of manipulation or mind-control. [11] Lindstrom refutes this by saying that neuromarketing does not plant ideas into people's heads. [12] On the contrary, it simply exposes what is already there.

[1] *Neuromarketing* is the process of using brain-imaging to reveal what influences people to use a product or service.

B. Answer the questions.

1. Where in the summary do the title, authors, date, and publisher appear?

   ....

2. Where is the main idea of the chapter expressed? What is the main idea?

   ....

   ....

3. What information is expressed in paragraphs 2 and 3?

   ....

   ....

4. Which transition cues are used? Circle them.

   ....

   ....

5. How does the summary writer refer back to the source throughout the summary? Circle the words and phrases the writer uses to remind the reader that the original source is being referenced.

....

....

6. What do you think are the keywords from the reading? Does the summary writer define any of them for the reader?

....

....

EXERCISE 6

A. Read the article. As you read, highlight the main ideas of each section as well as keywords you think are important to understand the text.

MAKING DECISION SIMPLICITY WORK FOR YOU
STEVEN WRIGHT

1   Conventional wisdom once dictated that marketers should provide prospective customers with as much information as possible. In the digital age, this led many advertisers to desperately try to grab the attention of consumers through promotional campaigns, social media campaigns, loyalty discounts, and other similar programs. Consumers may love occasional discounts, but few of them stay "engaged" in the way marketers hoped.

2   Research has since determined that what customers really want isn't another newsletter or clever tweet but *decision simplicity*. Deciding on a purchase is a difficult task that requires serious analysis. In an age of information overload, customers need trusted sources they can easily navigate. These customers want to weigh their options more easily. Customers who find the process simple and direct buy more products. Customers who become overwhelmed or sidetracked along the way usually don't buy anything at all.

3   What's a marketer to do? Give customers what they want but in a carefully arranged way that leads them toward a purchase. To improve decision simplicity, a company must provide its customers with three things: 1) trusted sources of information, often in the form of other customers; 2) a way to easily navigate information about the product; and 3) a simple way for the customers to weigh their purchasing options based on information that is relevant to them.

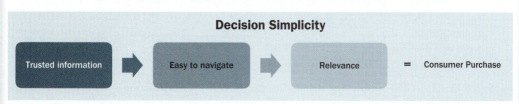

4   Improving decision simplicity requires a keen awareness of market trends and customer behavior. Data mining, search engine optimization research, and customer analysis are all a must. It's going to take a lot of careful analysis to figure out exactly what changes will be needed to streamline and simplify things for your customers. Here are a few rules to help you get started.

Continued

Rule 1: Improve consumer confidence by connecting customers with other customers.

5   This would have seemed terrifying a few decades ago. How do you control the message? You don't need to—at least not as much as you think you do. Happy customers talking to other happy customers will be better product advocates than any number of paid advertisements. Won't there be negative reviews right where everyone can see them? Yes, customers will point out problems, but this can be beneficial as long as you have a quality product.

6   Remember that customers are trying to decide if a product is or isn't right for them. Honest reviews from customers who wanted something different will actually help to sell your product if they provide the right kind of information. Is there a negative review, complaining about the complexity of your new home entertainment system sitting right on your user page? Great! Use it to pique the interest of customers who want complexity and lots of features.

7   What about the customers who want something simpler? Won't they find that product unappealing based on the review? Yes, but that's why you've built your website to guide them from that negative review to a positive review of your "easy-to-use, no-hassle" model from the same product line! When reviewers' opinions are trusted, they are useful even when they are negative. This is also a great starting point for thinking about how to guide your customers through information.

Rule 2: Guide your customers, helping them navigate the available information.

8   Imagine you are working for a computer company with great brand recognition. Potential customers visit your website, click on *products*, and are immediately greeted by 60 pictures of near-identical looking laptops with incomprehensible serial numbers. How are they ever going to find what they're looking for?

9   It's your job to simplify this process. Use search-engine optimization to help guide potential customers to appropriate product categories, based on their behavior. Use data analytics to categorize your products into similar, relevant, easy-to-understand groups. Provide information in a way that is immediately and easily comprehensible to your target market. Remember, consumers are only trying to learn enough to make what should be a simple decision. Don't lose them here.

Rule 3: Help customers weigh their decisions.

10   OK, so you've fixed your company's website, and now the prospective laptop buyers have been directed to your product line focused on user-friendliness. They're in the right neighborhood but need an easy way to make a final decision. Emphasize whatever it is that differentiates products at this final step of the decision-making process. Keep it streamlined. Keep it simple. If all of your products are option-rich and specifically targeted at certain needs, make it easy for consumers to understand their differences. Create search options and questionnaires that help customers figure out exactly what they're looking for, and let them do so, using the criteria they actually care about.

11   Remember the key to decision simplicity is to make the experience simple for the customers. For you, the marketer, it's going to mean a great deal of complexity and a lot more work. Don't let it discourage you—that work will dramatically improve the follow-through of your customers and put you well ahead of competition that is stuck using outdated strategies. That's why there's no time like the present to start with simplicity!

Source: Wright, S. (2013, Nov 5). "Making Decision Simplicity Work for You." *The Economy*, 18(3), 36–37. [Note: The source information is fictional and only for use in Exercise B.]

B. Complete the graphic organizer with the information you highlighted in the article. Compare with a partner and practice summarizing the text orally with each other.

Article title	
Author name	
Publication information	
Main idea of article	
Essential detail(s) that support main idea	
Keywords you will use in summary	

C. Write a 4–5 sentence summary of this article, using your notes.

D. <u>PEER REVIEW</u>. Exchange your summary with a partner. Respond to the questions to evaluate each other's work. For responses marked No, give feedback in the Notes column to help your partner revise.

	Yes	No	Notes
Does the summary include the title, author, date, and publisher of the original text?	☐	☐	
Does the writer clearly state the topic and main idea of the text?	☐	☐	
Does the summary include support for the main idea?	☐	☐	
Does the summary include only essential information?	☐	☐	
Does the writer repeat information?	☐	☐	
Is the summary well organized?	☐	☐	
Does the writer use transition cues well?	☐	☐	
Does the writer remind the reader of the source several times?	☐	☐	
Does the writer use keywords from the reading correctly?	☐	☐	
Is the length appropriate?	☐	☐	

Go to MyEnglishLab to complete vocabulary exercises and skill practices and join in collaborative activities.

For more about SUMMARIZING, see [R] ECONOMICS 1.

LANGUAGE SKILLS
USING REPORTED SPEECH EFFECTIVELY

WHY IT'S USEFUL By using reported speech, you can introduce a summary of what someone has said. Reporting verbs can indicate the author's point of view since different reporting verbs are used for different rhetorical purposes.

When you use **reported speech**, you do not use quotations. Instead, you summarize what someone has said by using a noun clause introduced by a reporting verb.

1. When reporting a statement, most reporting verbs are followed by a *that* clause:

    The author **claims that** using social media is not helpful for marketing a product.

2. Some reporting verbs are followed by an indirect object plus a *that* clause:

    She **informs us that** simplifying advertisements can increase customer loyalty.

3. Other reporting verbs are followed by a direct object:

    The study **supported** the **opinion** that customers want decision simplicity.

Reporting verbs have different rhetorical purposes:

- Expressing agreement
- Making a claim
- Making a suggestion
- Questioning or disagreeing
- Making a recommendation
- Making a neutral observation

It is important to use a reporting verb that accurately reflects the point of view of the author you are summarizing. This will show your reader that you have understood what you read. It is also important to use the correct verb tense. As explained in the Language Skills section in Sociology, Part 1, simple present is most commonly used to report general information and findings or results of research. Simple past is used when reporting methods or procedures used in a study completed in the past. For this reason, simple past is commonly used to explain steps in an experiment.

EXERCISE 7

A. Identify the rhetorical purpose of the reporting verbs in the chart. Write *agreement, claim, suggestion, disagreement, recommendation,* or *neutral observation.* Then compare your answers with a partner and discuss any differences.

Reporting Verb	Rhetorical Function	Reporting Verb	Rhetorical Function
acknowledge	*agreement*	express*	
agree		illustrate*	
argue		imply	
assert		inform***	
believe		insist	
call for*		maintain	
caution		observe	
claim		present*	
comment		question**	
conclude		recommend	
contend		refute*	
contradict*		reject*	
demand		report	
deny		reveal	
describe*		state	
discuss*		stress	
dispute		suggest	
emphasize		support*	
encourage*		think	
endorse*		urge***	
examine*		warn***	

TIP

The reporting verbs with an asterisk (*) are usually followed by a direct object. A question has two asterisks (**) and is usually followed by if / whether or a question word. Inform, Urge, and Warn have three asterisks (***) and are followed by an indirect object.

B. Choose five reporting verbs from the chart and use them to write sentences about "Making Decision Simplicity Work for You." Compare your sentences with a partner. Consider which tense is best for your sentences, and use the correct noun clause for the reporting verbs. Use a direct or indirect object when necessary.

EXERCISE 8

A. Underline the reporting verbs in the summary. Write a replacement reporting verb in the margin. Be sure the grammar is correct and the rhetorical purpose is the same.

[1] In the first chapter of *Buyology* (2008, Doubleday), author Martin Lindstrom introduces his neuromarketing study, in which he analyzed the brain activity of 2081 volunteers from around the world while they were shown images of different products in order to uncover what influences consumers' purchasing decisions. [2] Lindstrom embarked on this study because, as a global branding expert, he believes that traditional methods for analyzing what makes people want to buy a product, like surveys and focus groups, do not adequately predict the success of a product. [3] He reports that in the United States, only 8 out of 10 new products are successful.

[4] The first experiment in his study was conducted on 32 smokers. He first interviewed them and asked if they thought the warning labels on cigarettes suppressed their desire to smoke. [5] All of the participants stated that the warnings did help to prevent them from smoking. [6] However, when Lindstrom used an fMRI (functional Magnetic Resonance Imaging) scanner to see how their brains reacted to warning labels and graphic images of health effects caused by smoking, he was shocked to discover that the images did not suppress their urge to smoke, but instead, stimulated "the craving spot" of the brain.

[7] Lindstrom goes on to describe other fields that use neuromarketing, such as politics, the entertainment industry, and law enforcement and describes how this research has been used to inform political campaigns and movie endings. [8] Lindstrom reveals that although the findings from his study would help companies save money, many of the corporations he approached would not fund it because they found it to be unethical. [9] They were concerned that brain-imaging was a form of manipulation or mind-control. Lindstrom refutes this by saying that neuromarketing does not plant ideas into people's heads. [10] On the contrary, he insists it simply exposes what is already there.

B. Scan the summary of "Making Decision Simplicity Work for You" that you wrote in Exercise 6. Look for the reporting verbs.

1. Circle the reporting verbs and identify their rhetorical function.
2. Try substituting different reporting verbs for the ones you used.
3. If you didn't use any reporting verbs, rephrase some of your sentences to include some.
4. When finished, review your summary with a partner and check to make sure you each have used reporting verbs correctly.

Go to **MyEnglishLab** to complete skill practices.

APPLY YOUR SKILLS

WHY IT'S USEFUL By applying the skills you have learned in this unit, you can successfully develop ideas by conducting research, collaborating and sharing ideas, evaluating and organizing research, and summarizing texts.

ASSIGNMENT

Plan a research paper on what influences a consumer's decision to buy certain products and services. Are there different factors that influence decisions to buy a particular product or service over another? Choose two products or services. Compare and contrast the drivers that impact decision making at the point of purchase. Be sure to conduct research, collaborate and share ideas, and evaluate and organize your research.

BEFORE YOU WRITE

A. **Before you begin your assignment, discuss the questions with one or more students.**

1. What influenced your decision to buy a particular product recently?

2. What factors might influence a consumer's decision to buy different types of products?

3. How do you get information about a product or service that you are considering buying?

B. **As you consider your writing assignment, complete the tasks below. Then, share your ideas with another student. Get feedback and revise your ideas if necessary.**

1. What products or services have you chosen to research? Describe them.

   a. Brainstorming: What techniques will you use to generate ideas about factors that influence a

   decision to buy the product or service? ....

   b. What graphic organizers will help you organize your ideas?

   ....

2. List keywords and use them and your research question to find sources for your topic.

3. Write a preliminary thesis and outline to organize the information from your research.

C. Review the Unit Skills Summary. As you begin the writing task page 49, apply the skills you learned in this unit.

UNIT SKILLS SUMMARY

Develop ideas
- Review the assignment. Do you understand the topic? The focus? Who is your audience, and what is the purpose of the assignment?
- Do a prewriting activity to get your ideas and questions on paper. Start to formulate a thesis.

Research ideas
- Determine your sources and conduct the research you need.
- Use keywords from your brainstorming activities to research your questions online.
- Time allowing, do additional research at the library or do primary research.
- Choose a collaboration strategy and share your ideas with others. Note their feedback and adjust your plans accordingly.

Evaluate and organize research
- Summarize texts that you have researched and will be using in your paper.
- Critically evaluate your research sources and decide the strength of the evidence for your paper.
- Organize your research and evidence.
- Decide on your main ideas and list the evidence from your research to support those ideas. Include the sources of your information as you go along.
- Freewrite to get some ideas on the page.
- Finalize your thesis and write an outline of your paper.

Use reported speech effectively
- Use reporting verbs to summarize a text and to indicate the author's point of view.

THINKING CRITICALLY

As you consider your writing assignment, discuss the questions with another student. Get feedback and revise your ideas if necessary.

1. What might be some of the challenges of researching consumer behavior? How would you overcome them?
2. Is it ethical to do psychological studies to determine why consumers make buying decisions? Is this influencing consumers or exposing their reasons for buying?
3. Is the number of options in products and services affecting buying behavior in positive or negative ways? Justify your response with examples.

THINKING VISUALLY

A. Look at the graphic. Then write a summary of the information it conveys.

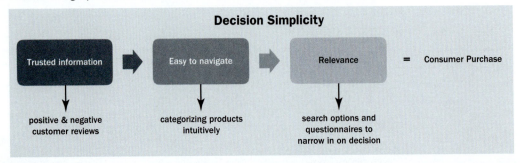

B. Read the passage. Create a graphic or chart that conveys the information.

Shoppers were asked three questions about the research they did when buying a car:

1. Did you feel anxious about your purchase?

2. Did you do any research after you bought the car?

3. Compared to five years ago, do you do more or less research for major purchases?

> The results show that 81 percent of car buyers feel anxious about their purchase, and 32 percent reported that they did some post-purchase research to make sure that they made the right choice. When asked if they do more or less research than five years ago, 5 percent reported that they do more now, compared to 55 percent who said they do less. Forty percent of car buyers noted that they do about the same amount of research. Overall, these findings indicate that although car buyers do less research today, the majority of them feel anxious about whether or not they made the right choice.

THINKING ABOUT LANGUAGE

Read the passage. Underline the reporting verbs. Then discuss with another student what rhetorical purpose they express.

Research reveals that people of all ages in Britain love electronics and are making informed decisions about the technology they buy. Economists report that consumers are also using more resources than in the past when deciding what to purchase. They claim that the greatest influences on buyer behavior are friends and relatives, followed by customer reviews, expert reviews, and online forums.

Researchers also assert that brand loyalty is at an all-time low. They warn that economies are in danger of depending on gadgets as a commodity, and price is becoming the overall factor in determining which products consumers choose. Therefore, economists stress the importance of using innovative communication strategies. They maintain that the second biggest driver for tech purchases is the need to replace broken or outdated products.

WRITE

A Revisit the writing assignment and your answers to the questions in Before You Write Part B. Write a research question that reflects the audience and purpose of the assignment.

....

B. Research your topic. Use both secondary and primary sources. Collaborate by sharing ideas with others.

C. Develop a working thesis statement that responds to your research question.

....

D. Evaluate your sources and organize your research. Finalize your thesis.

....

BEYOND THE ASSIGNMENT

Write a research paper. Think about the factors that influence a consumer's decision to buy certain products. Are there different factors that influence decisions to buy one product or service over another? Choose two products or services. Look at the drivers that impact decision making at the point of purchase and beyond. Use all the skills you learned in this unit.

▶ Go to MyEnglishLab to listen to Professor Clerici-Arias and to complete a self-assessment.

Exploring the secret lives of viruses.

BIOLOGY

Extended Writing

UNIT PROFILE

Viruses spread quickly and have the potential to do great harm. In this unit, you will read and write about biological and computer viruses. Specifically, you will learn about characteristics and properties of both types of viruses, including whether computer viruses can be considered a form of artificial life, and some noteworthy examples of the damage both can do.

UNIT ASSIGNMENT

Write a short paper analyzing similarities and differences between biological viruses and computer viruses. Use a general-to-specific organizational pattern and include appropriate cohesive devices to guide your reader. Revise your paper for coherence and cohesion.

OUTCOMES

- Create coherence and cohesion
- Revise writing
- Analyze organizational patterns
- Use language to add cohesion

GETTING STARTED

▶ Go to MyEnglishLab to listen to Professor Siegel and to complete a self-assessment.

Discuss these questions with a partner or group.

1. The common cold is caused by a virus. What are viruses? What are some viruses you are aware of? How are they treated? Can they be cured?

2. Has your computer ever been affected by a virus? What are computer viruses? How are they fixed? Can they be stopped altogether?

3. What makes the topic of viruses so complex? How might you organzie an essay on viruses to make it coherent for your reader?

For more about **BIOLOGY**, see ② ③. See also ⬜R and ⬜OC **BIOLOGY** ① ② ③.

FUNDAMENTAL SKILL
EXTENDED WRITING

WHY IT'S USEFUL By completing an extended writing assignment, you will use writing and critical thinking skills to draft a paper that reflects appropriate choice and narrowing of a topic, research and integration of sources, and organization and development of ideas in an appropriate rhetorical mode. Writing multiple drafts and revising effectively will help you achieve a cohesive and coherent paper that fully develops your ideas.

As the name suggests, **extended writing** means a longer paper, but in addition to length, extended writing needs to have depth and breadth of research and thought. Extended writing typically involves research, critical reading for ideas and information, and integration of evidence in support of a well-developed thesis. It assumes critical thinking and original ideas to present a well-justified and substantiated case that may propose possible hypotheses and future courses of action.

Extended writing is common in academic settings because it helps students develop high-level critical and creative reasoning and problem-solving skills and encourages them to explore connections and relationships between ideas. It is a means for students to work independently to gather and use evidence from diverse sources to support their ideas as they examine a complex topic more deeply, understand interrelationships better, and generate their own creative response to a research question.

Because extended writing is time-consuming and involves a heavy workload, it typically takes place over an extended period of time, requiring the writer to manage use of time and resources to meet a deadline. A common problem is misjudging how much time to spend on each part or how much research is necessary, either doing too little research, resulting in insufficient or incomplete evidence, or doing so much that there isn't enough time to think and write about the topic, revise, edit, and meet the deadline.

Extended writing assignments often include requirements or opportunities to collaborate with others through discussion and peer review and feedback during the drafting and revision process. The assignments culminate in a product that showcases not only the writer's knowledge of the discipline, but also the writer's communication skills and ability to effectively convey ideas in writing appropriate to the discipline. Finally, to successfully complete an extended writing assignment, the writer needs to fully understand the assignment. Pay close attention to specific instructions and guidelines provided and ask for clarification if something is unclear.

> **TIP**
> Like other academic writing, extended writing tasks vary based on rhetorical context and academic discipline. For example, in sociology the extended writing task might be an advocacy paper arguing in favor of a position on an issue supported by evidence; in economics, an analysis of a theory or statistical model; in humanities, a literary analysis with citations from texts; in science, a case study report; or in engineering, a research report on an experiment.

NOTICING ACTIVITY

A. Read the example of an extended writing assignment. Look for answers to these questions.

1. What is the **purpose** of this paper? (e.g., to demonstrate knowledge of the topic, to show that you can investigate a particular aspect of the course subject matter, etc.)

2. Who is the **audience** of the paper?

3. What is the **topic**?

4. What is the particular **focus**? (or will you decide on the issue?)

5. What **type of paper** is it? How should the paper be **organized**? What **genre** should it be: analytical or argumentative? (The language used in the assignment may indicate the structure of your paper.)

6. What are the expectations for finding and integrating ideas from **sources**?

7. How should the paper be **formatted**?

8. What is the **due date** and what are the **grading criteria?**

9. What **additional information** is provided in the assignment?

CASE REPORT ASSIGNMENT

Case reports are used in the health professions to report on specific cases involving one or more patients. Case reports are used at scientific and medical conferences, and published in medical journals. A case report provides data and observations (e.g., a new disease, disease presentation, diagnostic method, treatment, etc.) but should also include a conclusion or lesson derived from the case. Good case reports provide original material that adds to what is known and may present or support a hypothesis or stimulate further research. They should briefly introduce the problem, present the details of the case, and draw an important conclusion.

The purpose of this assignment is to introduce you to this form of writing, which requires logic, attention to detail, and clarity and is useful in many professions. The format is generic; different publications may require slightly different formats.

The assignment

Read the case reports provided as examples. Write a case report based on a (fictional) patient that has your chosen infectious disease. Look up details of the symptoms of the disease or use a real patient or study, but do not plagiarize an actual case report. Include enough information or evidence to support your conclusion.

Format

Your case report should contain the following parts. You may include figures and tables, real or fabricated, to support your point.

Title: Succinctly explain what the case is about and indicate why it's important, relevant, or new. Include the disease, type of patient, treatment, and other relevant details.

Structured abstract: Offer a brief summary of the most important information of the paper in section headings: Introduction, Case Report, Discussion, and Conclusion. Although it appears after the title, the structured abstract is written last.

Introduction: Provide context or background on the disease with references if needed, and indicate the importance of the case study without stating results.

Case Report: Describe the patient, including progress and outcome, what was observed and done, and further investigative studies or treatment. Be complete, so that the observations and treatment could be reproduced, but avoid irrelevant details.

Discussion: Provide an explanation of observations, reasons for decisions, suggestions or hypotheses to explain outcomes of the case or lessons learned, and comparison to past cases or knowledge (with references).

Conclusion: Give a few important points that this case demonstrates without repeating what's already been said.

References: Create two sections. In the first, include references you refer to in your case report. The second section is a bibliography. Here, list references used to find out information about your disease and its symptoms, patients, and so on, whether or not you referred to them in the text. You can use any format, but your references must be complete.

Grading criteria

Grading will be based on how clear and logical your case report is and whether it presents necessary information to support its points.

The case report is organized, follows the assigned format, and is written objectively in a professional style and tone appropriate to the audience and purpose. Words are appropriate and well chosen. Avoid jargon. Don't make mistakes in grammar, spelling, and mechanics. Use appropriate verb tenses for scientific writing (present tense to report facts, past tense to report what you did, observed, etc.).

B. With a partner, complete the chart with information from the assignment. Is all the information you need provided? What questions would you need to ask about the assignment to complete the table?

Understanding an extended assignment: Instructions and guidelines	
Purpose	
Audience (other than instructor)	
Topic and focus	
Type of paper	
Sources—number, type, specific requirements (in-text and reference page)	
Formatting requirements—sections, use of visuals, integrating sources, length, citation style	
Due date(s) and grading criteria	
Additional information	

C. Discuss your reaction to this assignment: Would you know how to begin? How would you break this assignment up so that it's manageable to complete? What would you do first, second, and so on?

COMPOSING AND DRAFTING AN EXTENDED PAPER

Composing an extended paper, like any skill in the writing process, presents both challenges and opportunities. Idea development doesn't end with the planning stage in the writing process. Composing is thinking. As you begin writing your ideas, you may learn new things and find connections you didn't see before as you combine your ideas with the notes from your research and critical reading. **Creating coherence and cohesion** by connecting the ideas in a logical order and **revising** your **writing** are critical aspects of the drafting process.

Facing a blank paper or screen as you begin the **first draft** is daunting, but while you are looking at a blank page, remember that your mind is full. You have your preliminary thesis to guide you along with all the information you've gathered and evaluated in your research. The process is messy, so do not expect to get all your ideas down in the first draft.

TIP

There is no one best way to handle the first draft, so experiment and determine what works best for you. You may find it easier to write the body paragraphs before you write an introduction. You may find that you work best if you set a time limit or write and then leave what you have written for a while and return with fresh eyes. You may find that getting your ideas down first and then adding in your evidence from research in a later draft is best for you.

Remind yourself of your **purpose** and **audience**. Think about the **rhetorical context** and the best ways to develop and organize your ideas. For example, to present your ideas you may need to provide definitions, examples, explanations, reasons, causes and effects, or solutions to a problem. You may support your points by summarizing or paraphrasing information from a source, providing a personal narrative or description, or comparing and contrasting points. Using a variety of ways to develop and support your ideas will make your paper more interesting and convincing.

Gather and review all your **notes**, your **annotated bibliography**, your **research question**, your **thesis**, and your **outline**. Your outline provides the **main ideas** that you plan to develop in your paper. For each main idea, write a topic sentence. This sentence should connect logically to the topic and focus of your paper and restate the main idea, in different words if the idea was listed in your thesis statement. Then, for each topic sentence, choose the ideas you want to use to support the main idea and write them down as quickly as possible.

In the first draft, focus on developing your ideas. Set a time limit if this helps you. If you can't remember the details of a particular piece of evidence or idea you want to integrate in support of your idea, note the idea and move on. You can add details later. Do not worry about grammar or other mechanics at this point.

TIP

If you experience writer's block, a feeling that you have no ideas and can't write, try rereading what you have written or talking to someone about your topic to see if that generates new ideas. Choose another section of the paper to work on or take a break from the writing if time allows.

Once you have a first draft, plan to revise the draft to further develop, organize, and clarify your ideas. You may need to elaborate further on a point or integrate (more) evidence from your sources. This is a good time to ensure you have integrated your source information smoothly and have acknowledged your sources to avoid plagiarism. The second draft may involve some structure revision for clarity, cohesion, and coherence. You may need to add, remove, replace, or move ideas in this draft. At this stage, getting feedback is very helpful.

Go to MyEnglishLab to do a vocabulary exercise and a skill practice and join in collaborative activities.

SUPPORTING SKILL 1
CREATING COHERENCE AND COHESION

WHY IT'S USEFUL By creating both coherence and cohesion in your text, you will present your ideas in a logical order that flows smoothly and connects them in ways that help your reader understand how ideas relate to each other.

Good research, great ideas, and strong evidence will not help a paper that is hard to read. Writing multiple drafts is one way to improve readability, but another key element is having a keen awareness of **coherence** and **cohesion**. These two aspects of writing are closely related, and in fact, many writing texts treat them as the same thing, but there are important differences.

Coherence means the connection of ideas at the text level. It is more closely tied to the rhetorical aspects of writing in developing, organizing, and clarifying ideas. A coherent text is easy to read and understand because it follows a logical and systematic organization, and ideas flow smoothly. Ideas in each sentence relate to those in previous sentences and lead to the next new idea, and the train of thought at the end of each paragraph is picked up at the beginning of the next. A coherent text has unity, which means all the ideas in each paragraph deal with the one main idea of that paragraph, and all the paragraphs are about the topic of the paper.

Cohesion means the connection of ideas at the sentence level. Cohesion deals with the lexical and grammatical aspects of writing. A cohesive text is easy to read because there are clear connections between ideas within and between sentences and paragraphs. A cohesive text has sentence unity—all ideas in the sentence are related to each other and the topic.

Here are some ways to achieve coherence in a text.

- Arrange ideas in a **logical** order so they flow smoothly. Ideas might be developed in chronological order, in order of importance, in blocks, or point by point.
- Use **parallel structure** by maintaining consistent form when listing more than one idea.
- Use these **cohesive devices**:
  - Link old and new information by connecting ideas with sentence patterns, placing old information in the first part of the sentence followed by new information in the later part of the sentence. Passive voice (common in academic writing) is useful for this.

    > For more on parallel structure, see HUMANITIES Part 2.

  - Transition signals guide the reader from one idea to the next: addition (similar idea), contrast, (opposite idea), examples, further explanation (*in other words; put another way*), reasons, results, and conclusions. Transitions can be words, phrases, or even sentences, and there are different types: subordinators, coordinators, adverbs, adjectives, and prepositions.
  - Repetition of key words or related words for clarity and lexical chains or synonyms restate points without repeating nouns or noun phrases.
  - Consistent pronouns signal that an idea is connected to a previously mentioned one by maintaining the same person and number. Don't change from *he* to *you* (person) or *he* to *they* (number), and avoid using pronouns when the meaning is unclear. When a pronoun and the word that it refers to (the referent) are not clearly linked, cohesion breaks down.
  - Demonstratives (*this / that* and *these / those*) are used to connect current ideas to previous ones.
  - Consistent verb tenses should be used in one time frame; make it clear when switching to another with a signal word or time phrase (simple present is most common, followed by simple past).

This paragraph, while fully developed, lacks coherence.

> Before addressing whether computer viruses can be classified as an artificial life form, it is important to arrive at a definition of viruses. It should be acceptable to most computer scientists. Computer viruses are segments of machine code that copy themselves into a larger host program when activated. When the affected program runs, the viral code is executed and the virus spreads. The term *virus* was introduced in 1983. Computer scientists disagree on what a virus is and what it is not. Are all viruses bad? One definition suggests there are good viruses. Are viruses alive? Is it useful to classify them as a form of artificial life? The term *virus* derived from the biological virus. *Virus* in Latin means "poison." Fred Cohen, PhD, coined the term and devoted much of his work to studying computer viruses. He proposed that a virus was any program capable of reproducing itself. There could be good viruses and bad viruses according to his definition. Others disagreed. Some definitions included the requirement that viruses be able to attach themselves to other programs, files and so on.

Notice how reordering the sentences and making adjustments to improve the cohesion makes the paragraph more coherent. Some sentences were moved, others removed, and still others combined to make the paragraph more readable. Changes are in red.

> Before addressing whether computer viruses can be classified as an artificial life form, it is important to arrive at a definition of these viruses that is acceptable to most computer scientists. Computer viruses are segments of machine code that copy themselves into a larger host program when activated, so that when the affected program runs, the viral code is executed and the virus spreads. The term *virus*, which means "poison" in Latin, was derived from the biological virus and was introduced in 1983. Fred Cohen, PhD, coined the term and devoted much of his work to studying computer viruses. He proposed that a virus was any program capable of reproducing itself. Computer scientists disagree on what a virus is and what it is not. Some definitions include the requirement that viruses be able to attach themselves to other programs, files, and so on. Are viruses alive? Is it useful to classify them as a form or artificial life? Are all viruses bad? There could be good viruses and bad viruses, according to his Cohen's definition. Others disagree.

One way to improve coherence is to use a **reverse outline**. This technique is especially helpful in extended writing assignments where there is a lot of data to integrate and ideas are complex. It helps you analyze the structure and organization of your paper and make decisions about how to logically arrange information. It gives you a much clearer idea of what is in your paper, how much space you have given to each point, and how it is currently organized.

To create a reverse outline, write the main idea of each paragraph in a short clear statement. If you have drafted your paper by writing topic sentences for each main idea, you may already have a good start on your reverse outline. Next, verify that each topic sentence is connected to your thesis statement. Any that are not may need revision. Then, read all the sentences in each paragraph and ask yourself if they address the topic and if they are arranged in a logical order.

A reverse outline can be written as brief annotations in the margins of the draft by writing the topic of each paragraph in the left-hand margin and a brief statement of how the topic connects to the thesis statement and supports it in the right-hand margin.

TIP
....
A reverse outline can also be written on a separate page, especially if you are using it to more fully outline a text.

These annotations will help you see if each paragraph is unified, focused on the topic, clear, and logically ordered, and if the paragraph fits into the overall organization of the paper.

When rereading your draft, if you are not able to complete your reverse outline for each paragraph and summarize the topic and its connection to your thesis in a few words, the paragraph may need revising. Your annotations may also show you a better organization or reordering of ideas for flow.

Notice how the writer annotated the paragraph using the reverse outline technique.

an acceptable definition of computer viruses

Before addressing whether computer viruses can be classified as an artificial life form, it is important to arrive at a definition of these viruses that is acceptable to most computer scientists. Computer viruses are segments of machine code that copy themselves into a larger host program when activated, so that when the affected program runs, the viral code is executed and the virus spreads. The term *virus*, which means poison in Latin, derived from the biological virus. The term virus was introduced in 1983. Fred Cohen, PhD, coined the term and devoted much of his work to studying computer viruses. He proposed that a virus was any program capable of reproducing itself. Computer scientists disagree on what a virus is and what it is not. Some definitions include the requirement that viruses be able to attach themselves to other programs, files, and so on. Are all viruses bad? There could be good viruses and bad viruses according to Cohen's definition. Others disagree.

connection to thesis—whether viruses are an artificial life form

EXERCISE 1

A. **Read the practice assignment. Then read a student's first draft of a paragraph for the assignment and answer the questions that follow.**

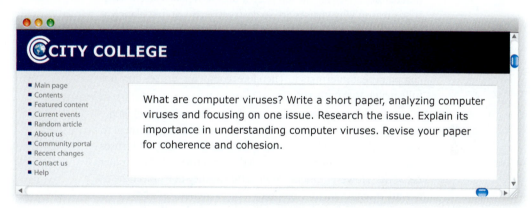

CITY COLLEGE

- Main page
- Contents
- Featured content
- Current events
- Random article
- About us
- Community portal
- Recent changes
- Contact us
- Help

What are computer viruses? Write a short paper, analyzing computer viruses and focusing on one issue. Research the issue. Explain its importance in understanding computer viruses. Revise your paper for coherence and cohesion.

Before delving into computer viruses as artificial life forms, it is important to look at how they have evolved. This evolution is often described as generations of viruses. The first generation of computer viruses is simple viruses. The viruses keep reinfecting programs so they are often detectible by size. Self-detecting viruses are code with signatures written in by programmers. They make it easier to detect the viruses. Third-generation viruses are stealth viruses whose code is harder to detect. Thus the name "stealth." Then came armored viruses. They are named for the confusing and often unnecessary code that makes detection harder by antivirus software. They are harder to attack by antivirus software. They appeared in 1990 and are larger and more complex. The last generation is called polymorphic, which, as the name suggests, can make modified versions of themselves to make them even harder to detect. They were self-mutating. The evolution has occurred primarily as a result of efforts to prevent detection. This was done by programmers.

B. Rewrite the paragraph to make it more coherent.

C. Compare your ideas for improving the coherence of the paragraph with a partner.

EXERCISE 2

A. Read the thesis and the body paragraphs. Create a reverse outline using annotations in the margin. Write the topic (main idea) of each paragraph on the left. On the right, briefly state its connection to the topic and focus of the paper.

Thesis: While computer viruses may have some of the properties associated with artificial life, this is not a useful way to classify them after considering a definition of computer viruses acceptable to most computer scientists, their history since inception, and an examination based on properties required of organisms to meet the basic requirements of artificial life.

1 In order to determine if viruses are a form of artificial life, it is necessary to know what artificial life is and then examine the properties of viruses to see if they match those of artificial life. One property always associated with life is that of self-reproduction in itself or a related organism, including information storage of a self-representation. This is one of the main characteristics of viruses. Viruses reproduce themselves or a version of themselves. The code that defines a virus is the template it uses to replicate itself. This is one reason why viruses are so destructive. So, at first glance, it would seem that computer viruses meet these criteria. However, the virus code is not the agent of its reproduction. The computer is. Basically, it is not the code that is causing the change but the computer that interprets it. Therefore, computer viruses may not fully match this property.

2 Life forms evolve over time, and they grow and expand, and once again, computer viruses appear to meet this requirement to be considered artificial life. No one questions that computer viruses have grown over time and expanded over entire global computer networks. However, under closer scrutiny, they don't meet the evolution requirement. Computer viruses mutate, but these mutations are not evolutionary; they are caused by the programmer, not the virus itself. Some may argue that there have been strains of viruses that have interacted with each other, but the resulting strains have been sterile and can't reproduce themselves.

3 A final property worth including in this examination of artificial life and whether we can say that computer viruses are a form of artificial life is the requirement that living organisms have interdependence of parts. Viruses, like living organisms, can't be arbitrarily divided and then made whole again, so their parts are interdependent. However, unlike living things, they can be reassembled and will function again. This makes them more like simple machines than living organisms. Once again, computer viruses fail to completely match the properties of artificial life.

Go to **MyEnglishLab** to complete a vocabulary exercise and a skill practice and join in collaborative activities.

SUPPORTING SKILL 2
REVISING WRITING

WHY IT'S USEFUL By revising your paper, you will more fully develop your content with sufficient evidence and support and order it in a logical way that convinces your reader of the strength of your ideas. Revising improves the content, coherence, and cohesion of your paper.

Before revising, it is helpful to review the assignment you were given. Did the assignment include guidelines on style or characteristics associated with effective writing in your discipline? Were you provided with samples or exemplars? Reread those and ask yourself if your paper matches them.

For example, notice how this additional information from the case report assignment addresses expectations about the writing.

Grading criteria

The case report is organized and follows the assigned format. Paragraphs are organized, unified, and coherent. Each paragraph has a controlling idea (which may be expressed in a topic sentence). Transitions help the paper flow smoothly.

Revising, like drafting, can be done in different ways. Revising focuses on rereading and rethinking what you want to communicate as much as it focuses on writing. Consider your own writing habits and style and revise in ways that work for you. You might write a lot and then cut down and organize your ideas. You might sketch out your ideas briefly and then add content to expand and more fully develop your ideas. Experiment with adding additional support, deleting parts that are not relevant or that repeat ideas, replacing what you have removed, and moving around ideas. Save earlier drafts so that you can return to them if you change your mind on later revisions. You might treat revising like a game or puzzle, piecing together your ideas in different ways until you achieve a good order and flow.

One of the first considerations when revising a paper is content. Revising for content means rethinking your paper and verifying that your ideas achieve your purpose, are presented clearly and effectively, and are fully supported. Multiple drafts with attention to coherence will help the readability of a text, but if a paper doesn't fully develop and support ideas, the paper will not be interesting or convincing to your reader.

As a reminder, to fully develop your ideas, you may need to provide another definition, more examples, further explanations, reasons, causes and effects, or solutions to a problem. A narrative or description can more fully develop your content. You may also need to add more evidence from your sources.

Feedback from an instructor or peer can provide another point of view and is advisable when possible. In an academic setting, both instructor feedback and peer feedback are often built into assignments and even required. Peer feedback, both received and given, is another way of thinking. In reading peer's work, you often see ways to improve your own writing, just as you can from the comments that a peer gives you on your work.

You can and should provide feedback to yourself. Reading your paper out loud is a good tool to use to show how smoothly your ideas flow. Using a reverse outline helps you see if your main ideas are clear and identify problems with your claims and evidence. Asking yourself questions is a good way to determine if you have provided the evidence and support to fully develop your ideas.

Continued

To improve the content of your draft ask yourself these questions.

- Does the content achieve your purpose?
- Is there sufficient background information in your introduction to help your audience understand your paper?
- Is there a clear thesis that states the topic and focus of the paper and suggests how you will develop your ideas about the issue?
- Are main ideas clearly presented and linked to the topic and focus of the paper?
- Is the support for each main idea sufficient, specific, clear, and relevant to the paper?
- Is the information from sources integrated smoothly into your paragraphs and cited correctly, and does it support rather than replace your ideas so that there is a balance of your ideas and ideas from the source?
- Is the discussion of the main ideas balanced, and have you said everything you want to say?
- Are the ideas presented in a logical order and connected to each other?
- Is there a conclusion that is clearly connected to the paper?

EXERCISE 3

A. **With a partner, read another paragraph from the practice essay. Discuss your suggestions for revising the paragraph.**

While it is interesting to examine computer viruses and there may be value in studying their properties, it is important to remember the damage these viruses cause. Research into computer viruses is of interest to scientists. There are many aspects of viruses that scientists can study. The problem with this research is the threat viruses pose to all computer users. Viruses are often the work of unethical programmers. Even when there isn't an intention to do harm, viruses can cause major damage. Researchers need to find safe ways of controlling computer viruses if they continue to study them.

B. **Answer Questions 1–4 using sentences from the paragraph. Then write a sentence that adds support to each of the sentences you chose. Then answer Question 5.**

1. Where would examples help support a point being made? ....

   ....

2. Where would the paragraph benefit from further explanations? ....

   ....

3. Where would adding effects or results improve the paragraph? ....

   ....

4. What statements could be supported by evidence from a source? ....

   ....

   ....

   ....

5. What other types of support might work in the paragraph? Narrative? Description?

   ....

   ....

C. With a partner, read these two drafts of paragraphs from the practice assignment. Each connects two properties of artificial life. Which is more coherent? Which is more fully developed? In the most logical order? Discuss the changes the writer made.

Two other important properties of artificial life are that living organisms have a metabolism that converts matter and energy and that they have functional interactions with the environment. Computer viruses would again appear to match these properties. First, they use energy from the computer, which is metabolism. However, having a metabolism also suggests that an organism expends energy, and computer viruses do not expend energy. This is done by the computer. Thus, computer viruses have only partially met this requirement. Second, they have functional interactions with the environment, as they must interact with the computer in order to continue to exist. Once again, computer viruses have only partially met the requirement to be considered artificial life.

Life, including artificial life, has functional interactions with the environment and is stable under perturbations of that environment. Computer viruses have interactions with the environment as they interact with the computer in order to replicate, which is critical to their continued existence. They can examine memory and alter addresses to hide themselves. Unfortunately, they frequently alter their environment accidentally due to "bugs" or mistakes in their code. Much of the damage done by computer viruses is due to these interactions. Additionally, computer viruses have proven themselves to be very stable as they can run on a variety of computers systems and often successfully avoid or thwart detection by antivirus software and attempts to remove them or stop them from spreading.

D. Reread the paragraphs in Exercise 2. Where would the paragraph in Part C above best fit? What other revisions would improve this draft? What suggestions do you have for an introduction to this assignment? Discuss your ideas with a partner.

Go to MyEnglishLab to complete a vocabulary exercise and a skill practice and join in collaborative activities.

READING-WRITING CONNECTION
ANALYZING ORGANIZATIONAL PATTERNS

WHY IT'S USEFUL By analyzing organizational patterns, you will better understand how writing is structured to achieve a purpose. Using appropriate organizational patterns ensures that your intended purpose is conveyed and your reader understands the information being presented.

The organizational pattern used in your writing depends on the rhetorical context (genre, purpose, audience) of the writing task. There are predictable patterns of organization for some writing genres and purposes. For example, a medical case report would follow this organizational pattern: 1. Title; 2. Abstract; 3. Introduction; 4. Case description; 5. Discussion; 6. Conclusion. In contrast, a problem-solution paper would normally begin with background information about the situation and would be followed by a description of the problem, solutions, and an evaluation of the solutions. In any writing situation, the writer must be aware of the established organizational patterns for the genre. When writing in a particular discipline, it is helpful to analyze the patterns used in scholarly articles within the field.

In addition to the influence genre and purpose have on a text's organization, the audience has an impact on the overall flow of information. For example, if the reader is not familiar with the topic, you will likely need to provide more background information and definitions of specialized terms before focusing in on specific ideas or arguments.

There are many ways to organize academic texts. General-to-specific and Specific-to-general are common organizational patterns across many disciplines.

General-to-specific, the most frequently used pattern, is used in both short and extended writing tasks, such as essay exam responses, introductory paragraphs, background paragraphs in a research paper, and argument papers. Whether you are discussing problems and solutions, comparing and contrasting ideas, showing causal relationships, or classifying information, the general-to-specific pattern is a clear and effective way to organize your writing. This organization uses a direct approach because it starts with a general statement that leads into more specific details. This pattern is referred to as a *deductive* approach because it follows a top-down organization that leads to a logical accurate conclusion:

Broad statement about the topic: fact, statistic, definition, or generalization

Elaboration

Examples data

Thesis or Concluding Statement

The **Specific-to-general** pattern begins with a specific observation and is followed by an exploration of that observation from which a general conclusion can be made. Writers use this pattern to encourage readers to use *inductive* reasoning to discover the conclusion by analyzing the details first. For this reason, Specific-to-general is prevalent in medical case reports and legal case notes where a patient's symptoms or details in a legal case are examined in order to arrive at a general conclusion, theory, or hypothesis.

TIP
The specific-to-general pattern is also used in the disciplines of art and art history to describe an artistic movement or work of art.

Specific observation

Elaboration

Description of the larger context

Thesis or Concluding Statement

Here are some tips for analyzing organizational patterns:

- Read through the introduction section or introductory paragraph of the text and determine whether or not it uses a general-to-specific or specific-to-general pattern. Although several organizational patterns may be used throughout a paper, general-to-specific or specific-to-general is usually used in the introduction of a paper. Sometimes the introduction will also include a purpose statement that states the aim of the paper along with a summary of how the text will be organized.

- Skim through the text for subheadings to get a sense of how the thesis or hypothesis will be explored and supported. Note whether the general-to-specific or specific-to-general pattern is used throughout the entire text.
- Create a simple reverse outline that notes the type of information included in each section of the text and think about what purpose it serves. Here is an example:

> Introduction section: Background about scientific study of satellite viruses. Starts with rationale of study and ends with hypothesis.
>
> Methods section: Describes how study was conducted. Explains how variables were tested.

- Identify which rhetorical modes (also referred to as *modes of discourse*) are used in the text. Rhetorical modes represent the different ways in which information can be communicated and for what purposes. Each paragraph will likely use one mode, but an entire paper may use several. These are the most commonly used modes of discourse:
  - Argumentation—Is the writer making a claim and trying to persuade the reader?
  - Cause / Effect—Is the writer describing the reasons for something and the results?
  - Classification—Is the writer breaking the subject up into parts or categories?
  - Comparison / Contrast—Is the writer comparing and contrasting two subjects?
  - Description—Is the writer describing the subject?
  - Extended definition—Is the writer defining the subject and providing details about it?
  - Chronological Narrative—Is the writer recounting events in the order in which they happened?
  - Process Narrative—Is the writer explaining how to do something?
- Think about why the author organized the information in this order:
  - Does the text begin with a lot of background information or definitions of specialized terms?
  - How is the author meeting the needs of the audience by presenting the information in this order?
  - Is the author using a general-to-specific or specific-to-general organizational pattern? Why do you think this pattern is used?
  - Which rhetorical modes are used in the text and what purpose do they serve? For example, an author may use classification to explain a complex system that has many parts.

EXERCISE 4

A. Read the example paragraphs. Identify which paragraph uses general-to-specific organization and which paragraph uses specific-to-general organization. Write a reverse outline for each paragraph. You do not need to use complete sentences.

Paragraph 1

The Internet is becoming increasingly dangerous. New destructive viruses and other forms of computer malware are detected every year. Even more concerning is that these viruses are spreading across cyber networks at an increasing rate. Some computer scientists have turned to the field of biological immunology to study the natural immune systems' response to viruses and to research whether similar responses could be engineered in commuter systems in order to combat malware. Computer scientists concede that it is unlikely that they will be able to develop virus protection software that exactly imitates the body's natural immune system; however, they believe that computer immune system research could lead to advances in building more robust security systems. With the help of biology, computers may soon be able to respond to viruses more effectively.

Paragraph 2

In August 2014, a 36-year-old epidemiologist contracted the Ebola virus disease in Sierra Leone. He began experiencing symptoms on the second day of his infection. His symptoms included fever, nausea, vomiting, abdominal pain, and diarrhea. On day 10 of the infection, he was airlifted to a facility in Hamburg, Germany where he received intensive treatment. Within the first 72 hours at the treatment facility, he experienced several complications including a bacterial blood infection, respiratory failure, and brain malfunction. Aggressive treatment measures were taken, including high-volume fluid resuscitation, broad-spectrum antibiotic therapy, and ventilatory support. As a result of this treatment, the patient was able to fully recover. This case illustrates that even extreme and highly contagious diseases like Ebola can be treated effectively with routine aggressive care in an isolated environment.

General-to-Specific _____   **Specific-to-General** _____

B. Answer the questions.

1. Why do you think the authors used these organizational patterns in each paragraph?

....

....

....

2. What does the organization of Paragraph 1 tell you about the audience? ....

....

....

3. Does the author of Paragraph 2 define specialized terms? What does this tell you about the

intended audience? ....

....

....

4. What rhetorical mode(s) are used in Paragraph 1? Identify areas of the text that exemplify this

mode of discourse. ....

....

....

5. What rhetorical mode(s) are used in Paragraph 2? Identify areas of the text that exemplify this mode of discourse. ....

....

....

EXERCISE 5

A. Read the essay.

THE DESTRUCTIVE POWER OF VIRUSES

1   The word *virus* refers to two different types of pathogens: the biological variety and computer malware. Biological viruses evolve through mutation and survive by using a living organism as a host. Despite advances in vaccines, which have transformed the way medical professionals manage many viral illnesses, it is impossible to predict the ways in which viruses will evolve. Computer viruses behave with similar, irregular patterns and can be difficult to contain, even for experts. Biological viruses and computer viruses can both be swift, unpredictable, and damaging to anyone who comes in their path. This essay will first discuss biological viruses and the most virulent and damaging cases found in modern history. We will then examine computer viruses, the way they function, and the hazards they create for society.

Biological Viruses

2   Biological viruses are microscopic infectious agents that contain nucleic acid[1] that is enclosed in a protein coating. Their physical shapes differ, but all viruses have essentially the same function, which is to establish a parasitic relationship with a living organism and reprogram cells in the host to replicate virus particles. First, after entering the body, the virus attaches itself to a host cell. Once the cell is infected, the virus copies its DNA or RNA[2] into the cell. After coding the cell to its liking, the virus uses the cell to replicate copies of itself and send out viral particles to more cells in the body. Most viruses follow this pattern, though exceptions exist, such as "satellite" viruses, which require a helper virus to transmit data when they infect. Whenever a virus is introduced to the human body, the immune system recognizes the viral particles in the body as antigens, or intruders, and deploys white blood cells to fight them off. However, if the virus is too strong for the body, the immune system can become overpowered. If a person's immune system is overwhelmed, the virus can cause severe symptoms or even death.

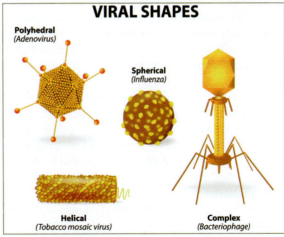

VIRAL SHAPES

Polyhedral
(*Adenovirus*)

Spherical
(*Influenza*)

Helical
(*Tobacco mosaic virus*)

Complex
(*Bacteriophage*)

Four main types of virus shapes can be identified. In all four, a capsid of either helical, icosahedral, or a combination of both is present.

---

[1] Nucleic acid is a complex organic substance inside living cells that consists of complex organic acids linked in a long chain.

[2] Deoxyribonucleic acid (DNA) and ribonucleic acid (RNA) are molecules that carry an organism's genetic code and are essential for life.

Continued

3   The worst viruses are incredibly efficient at destabilizing their hosts. These pathogens strike quickly, without warning, and leave thousands dead in their wake. In a prime example of a lethal virus of the past, the Spanish flu of 1918 infected up to 40 percent of the world's population. In 2014, the World Health Organization estimated that seasonal influenza strains kill approximately 250,000 to 500,000 people annually. By comparison, the 1918 strain of flu killed 50 million people. Vaccines and antiviral drugs have dramatically reduced the number of individuals affected by these types of catastrophic illnesses. However, the nature of mutating viruses always leaves humans guessing, and consequently, outbreaks continue to occur. In a more recent example, the Ebola virus, which has no vaccine, exploded in a global pandemic that killed more than 10,000 people. The virus re-emerged in the summer of 2014, primarily affecting people from nations already plagued by poor health care systems.

Computer Viruses

4   Computer viruses are software codes that replicate themselves once they gain entry into a computer program. Once in the system, the virus proceeds to infect entire networks. Computer viruses are designed by people specifically intending to infect systems in a network. The software they create is given the classification *malware*, coined from the Latin *mal*, meaning "bad." Malware includes viruses, worms, Trojans, and bots. The most common types of malware are viruses and worms. Viruses propagate themselves when someone inadvertently opens a file with the malware

Some studies estimate that computer viruses cost businesses hundreds of billions of dollars a year.

attached, and once it infects one computer, it goes on to spread to other computers. In contrast, worms are more insidious and copy themselves to a new host via information-sharing features or other security holes in a system. While worms tend to spread more quickly, viruses are often more detrimental because they are specifically designed to destroy or steal information. Other pernicious software includes Trojan horses, which are malware hidden within what appears to be safe information, and bots, which are malware that gives the code writer control over the computer the virus has accessed.

5   Computer viruses do not directly cause physical pain or suffering, but they can inflict financial troubles and security breaches. Several computer viruses are noteworthy for their extensive data and system-disabling capabilities. One such worm, launched in 2008 and titled "Conficker," targeted Microsoft Windows programs. After breaching networks, the worm was able to disable anti-malware software and break through firewalls. In the end, the worm caused $9.1 billion in damage and affected national security programs in several nations. In France, for example, the worm grounded some French Navy planes after officials could not download their flight plans. In another instance, in England, 75 percent of the Royal Navy Fleet's systems were affected by the virus.

6   Viruses of both types, the biological variety and the computer coding, can create destabilization within their hosts. In this brief examination of the two types of viruses, we have left some issues undiscussed. These matters include the broader social question of how economic wealth—or poverty—influences the prevalence of viruses in a society. Also worth noting in a discussion of viruses is the history of virus types and how they have developed, improved, and changed over the past century since the arrival of modern medicine and the digital age.

B. **Create a reverse outline of the essay.**

Paragraph 1: ....

Paragraph 2: ....

Paragraph 3: ....

Paragraph 4: ....

Paragraph 5: ....

Paragraph 6: ....

C. **Answer these questions about the organization of the essay.**

1. Which organizational pattern (general-to-specific / specific-to-general) is used? Why do you think the author chose this pattern?..

....

....

2. Does the author define specialized terms? How much background information is provided? What does this tell you about the intended audience? ....

....

....

3. Why do you think the author includes this sentence in paragraph 3?

   In 2014, the World Health Organization estimated that seasonal influenza strains kill approximately 250,000 to 500,000 people annually.

....

....

4. Why do you think the author states, *Computer viruses do not directly cause physical pain or suffering,* in paragraph 5? ....

....

5. What rhetorical mode(s) are used in each paragraph? ....

....

....

Go to MyEnglishLab to complete a vocabulary exercise and a skill practice and join in collaborative activities.

LANGUAGE SKILLS
USING LANGUAGE TO ADD COHESION

WHY IT'S USEFUL By using cohesive devices to make connections between sentences and parts of a text, you will improve the coherence of your ideas and your readers' understanding of your writing.

As stated in Supplemental Skill 1, cohesion refers to the connection of ideas at the sentence level. **Cohesive devices** are the strategies writers use to create cohesion across and within sentences. The most important cohesive device is the **old to new information pattern**. When using this pattern, information that is already known is given before information that is being introduced for the first time. Notice in the example how the new information (in blue) refers back to the old information (in red) that came earlier in the text.

> New destructive viruses and other forms of computer malware are detected every year. Even more concerning is that these viruses are spreading across cyber networks at an increasing rate. Some computer scientists have turned to the field of biological immunology to study the natural immune system's response to viruses and to research whether similar responses could be engineered in computer systems in order to combat malware.

Here are some effective cohesive devices when using the old to new information pattern.

Cohesive Devices	Examples
Repetition of key words using different forms of the word or synonyms.	The doctors were not able to contain the virus. This inability to prevent the spread of the disease caused millions of people to become infected.
Reference to previous information by using one of the following: Demonstrative determiners (**this, that, these, those**) Comparatives (**another, the other, others,** number + **other(s), such**) Pronouns (e.g., **he, them, me**) Possessive pronouns (e.g., **your, their, hers**) Relative pronouns (e.g., **which, who, whose**)	The doctors were not able to contain the virus. This inability to prevent the spread of the disease caused millions of people to become infected. There are many other types of malware besides viruses. Worms, bots, and Trojans are three others. In August 2014, a 36-year old epidemiologist contracted the Ebola virus disease in Sierra Leone. He began experiencing symptoms on the second day of his infection.
Cohesive nouns preceded by a referent. These types of nouns can summarize many words using just one noun (e.g., **these arguments, these advantages, these solutions, such difficulties, this method, those procedures**).	As a result of this treatment, the patient was able to fully recover. Their methods were successful in treating the virus.
Topic introducer followed by a referent and a noun or noun phrase (e.g., **concerning, regarding, in reference to, as for, in regard to, related to**).	In regard to other types of malware, worms are much more insidious than viruses. Concerning the symptoms he experienced, they have not had any long-term effects on his health.
Logical connector followed by a referent and a noun phrase (e.g., **because of, due to, as a result of, based on, given, in light of, regardless of, despite, like, similar to, in contrast to, in comparison to, unlike, in addition to**)	In contrast to the computer's immune system, a natural immune system has the ability to continue functioning after it has been infected with a virus. Given these findings, isolated facilities should remain open.

TIP
....
If old-to-new patterns are not used, linking adverbials can create cohesion between sentences (e.g., In addition, Therefore, However). See HUMANITIES Part 1 for more examples of linking adverbials.

EXERCISE 6

A. Read the excerpt. Underline all the cohesive devices. Compare your answers with a partner and identify and discuss each device.

[1] Computer viruses are software codes that replicate themselves once they gain entry into a computer program. [2] Once in the system, the virus proceeds to infect entire networks. [3] Computer viruses are designed by people who specifically intend to infect systems in a network. [4] The software they create is given the classification malware, coined from the Latin *mal*, meaning "bad." [5] Malware includes viruses, worms, Trojans, and bots. [6] The most common types are viruses and worms. [7] Viruses propagate themselves when someone inadvertently opens a file with the malware attached, and once it infects one computer, it goes on to spread to other computers. [8] In contrast, worms are more insidious and copy themselves to a new host via information-sharing features or other security holes in a system. [9] While worms tend to spread more quickly, viruses are often more detrimental because they are specifically designed to destroy or steal information. [10] Other pernicious software includes Trojan horses, which are malware hidden within what appears to be safe information, and bots, which are malware that gives the code writer control over the computer the virus has accessed.

B. Answer the questions about the cohesive devices in Part A.

1. What do the words *themselves* and *they* in sentence 1 refer back to? ....

....

2. What phrase in sentence 3 echoes information from sentence 2? ....

....

3. What does the word *they* in sentence 4 refer back to? ....

....

4. What does the word *types* in sentence 6 refer back to? ....

....

5. What synonyms for the word *virus* are used in the paragraph? ....

....

6. What noun do the two pronouns, *it*, in sentence 7 refer back to? ....

....

7. What is a synonym for the word *host* in sentence 8? ....

....

8. What word earlier in the paragraph does *code writer* refer to in sentence 10? ....

....

A. Rewrite the sentences using appropriate cohesive devices.

1. There have been advances in vaccines. It is still impossible to predict the ways in which viruses will evolve. ....

....

2. This essay will discuss biological viruses and the most damaging viruses found in history. We will examine computer viruses and the hazards viruses create for society. ....

....

....

3. Whenever a virus enters the body, the immune system recognizes the virus in the body as an antigen or intruder, and deploys white blood cells to fight the virus off. ....

....

....

4. Once a cell is infected, the virus copies the cell's DNA or RNA. The virus uses the cell to replicate copies of the virus and send the virus to more cells. Most viruses infect a cell and make copies of the virus, which send the virus to more cells. ....

....

....

5. Several computer viruses are noteworthy for the virus's extensive data and system-disabling capabilities. There was a worm that targeted Microsoft Windows programs. ....

....

....

6. New destructive viruses are detected every year and are spreading across networks at an increasing rate. Programmers are concerned that they will not be able to stop the viruses from spreading.

....

....

7. Some computer scientists have turned to the field of biological immunology. Computer scientists are studying the natural immune systems' response to viruses and are researching how to make computer systems have a strong response to viruses. ....

....

....

8. Aggressive treatment measures were taken. The patient was able to fully recover. ....

....

....

Go to MyEnglishLab to complete skill practices.

APPLY YOUR SKILLS

WHY IT'S USEFUL By applying the skills you have learned in this unit, you will be able to understand an assignment and achieve a well-developed and organized final paper that, through multiple drafts, has been revised for content, coherence, and cohesion.

ASSIGNMENT

Write a short paper analyzing the similarities and differences between biological viruses and computer viruses. Use a general-to-specific organization pattern as well as a variety of cohesive devices to help guide your reader. Revise your paper for coherence and cohesion when you are finished.

BEFORE YOU WRITE

A. **Before you begin your assignment, discuss these questions with one or more students.**

1. How concerned are you about the spread of viruses? Do you do anything to try and prevent getting viruses?

2. Have you had problems with a computer due to a virus? How did you fix it? Do you have a better understanding of how to prevent viruses?

3. What do you think scientists should be doing to manage both biological and computer viruses? Should governments be involved or should viruses be contained by private companies?

B. **As you consider your assignment, complete the Venn diagram to organize the similarities and difference between computer and biological viruses.**

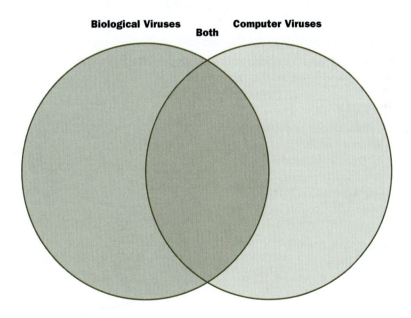

Biological Viruses   **Both**   Computer Viruses

C. Review the Unit Skills Summary. As you begin the writing task on page 73, apply the skills you learned in this unit.

UNIT SKILLS SUMMARY

Creating coherence and cohesion
• Arrange ideas in a logical order to create a smooth flow.
• Understand how cohesive devices enhance the coherence of a text.

Revising writing
• Reread a draft and add, delete, replace, or move ideas.
• Develop content fully with specific and concrete support.

Analyzing organizational patterns
• Understand how organizational patterns achieve different purposes.
• Use organizational patterns effectively to help readers understand your message.

Using language to add cohesion
• Use cohesive devices to make connections between sentences and parts of texts.

THINKING CRITICALLY

As you consider your assignment, discuss the questions with another student. Get feedback and revise your ideas, if necessary.

1. People who unleash computer viruses are criminals, but they also have a deep understanding of how complex computer systems work. Is it ethical for a government or company to hire a person like this to advise them on how to prevent future cyber-attacks?

2. Which poses the greater risk to people's safety and security—computer viruses or biological viruses?

3. Will both types of viruses be better controlled in the future, or will they become impossible to contain? Explain why you feel this way.

THINKING VISUALLY

A. Look at the visual showing how the biological immune system works. Then find (or create) a visual that shows how a computer security system protects computers from viruses. Include a citation for your source.

B. Write a paragraph comparing and contrasting the natural immune system with a computer security system.

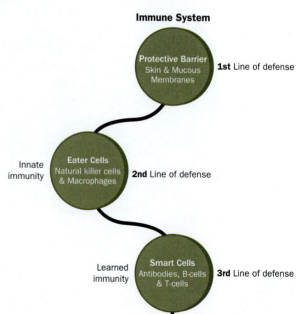

Immune System

Protective Barrier
Skin & Mucous Membranes — **1st** Line of defense

Eater Cells
Natural killer cells & Macrophages — **2nd** Line of defense

Innate immunity

Smart Cells
Antibodies, B-cells & T-cells — **3rd** Line of defense

Learned immunity

THINKING ABOUT LANGUAGE

Read the excerpt. Underline all the cohesive devices. Identify each type of device.

The worst viruses are incredibly efficient at destabilizing their hosts. These pathogens strike quickly, without warning, and leave thousands dead in their wake. In a prime example of a lethal virus of the past, the Spanish flu of 1918 infected up to 40 percent of the entire world. In 2014, the World Health Organization estimated that seasonal influenza strains kill approximately 250,000 to 500,000 people annually. By comparison, the 1918 strain of flu killed 50 million people. Vaccines and anti-viral drugs have dramatically reduced the number of individuals affected by these types of catastrophic illnesses. However, the nature of mutating viruses always leaves humans guessing, and consequently, outbreaks continue to occur. In a more recent example, the Ebola virus, which has no vaccine, exploded in a global pandemic that killed more than 10,000 people. The virus re-emerged in the summer of 2014, primarily affecting those from nations already plagued by poor health care systems.

WRITE

A. Revisit the assignment and the similarities and differences you included in Before you Write Part B. Which similarities and differences are the most significant?

B. Take notes about how you will organize the information using a general-to-specific organizational pattern. ....

....

....

....

....

....

C. When you are finished composing a first draft, create a reverse outline to ensure that the flow of ideas is coherent. Revise your text for coherence and cohesion.

BEYOND THE ASSIGNMENT

Write a research paper on how concepts from biological immunology could be used to solve today's computer security problems.

▶ Go to MyEnglishLab to listen to Professor Siegel and to complete a self-assessment.

Education teaches you to love the world.

HUMANITIES

Rhetorical Context

UNIT PROFILE

For centuries, people have sought opportunities for education that have led to possibilities for technological advancement. In this unit, you will read and write about the connection between knowledge acquisition and technology. Specifically, you will learn about views held by several classical and modern philosophers, including Aristotle, Plato, Heidegger, and Marx.

Write a 1–2 page analysis of the rhetorical context for a source that explores how technology impacts acquisition of knowledge. Identify the rhetorical purpose, audience, genre, style (including voice and tone), and the language that the author uses to connect ideas and provide examples to support your analysis.

OUTCOMES

- Make stylistic choices
- Control voice and tone
- Analyze the rhetorical context
- Use appropriate adverbials to fit the rhetorical context

GETTING STARTED

▶ Go to MyEnglishLab to listen to Professor Harrison and to complete a self-assessment.

Discuss these questions with a partner or group.

1. What role has technology played in your education? Do you think it has helped or hindered your learning? Give examples.

2. Do you think people read more or less because of technology? Does technology influence the types of things people read as well as how much they read? Explain your answer.

3. What types of technologies do you think were being debated in the days of Plato?

For more about **HUMANITIES,** see ② ③. See also R and OC **HUMANITIES** ① ② ③.

FUNDAMENTAL SKILL
RHETORICAL CONTEXT

WHY IT'S USEFUL By understanding rhetorical context, you will make appropriate writing choices, knowing what writing style and structure is most suitable for the situation.

The word *rhetoric* is defined as the art of communicating effectively through speaking or writing. When we write, we are constantly making rhetorical choices, whether we're texting a friend, drafting a cover letter for a job application, or writing a paper for an English class. In any writing context, it is critical to consider the reason for writing (purpose), the reader (audience), and the form of text (genre) to ensure that you communicate your message successfully. These three elements work together to form the rhetorical context.

Rhetorical purpose: There is always a general purpose for writing. The concept of *rhetorical purpose* goes deeper in that it requires writers to consider how they want their audience to think about a topic. Consider how a writer's message changes depending on the rhetorical purpose: **to express, to explore, to inform, to analyze, to persuade**, or **to entertain or give aesthetic pleasure**. What is your rhetorical purpose if you are writing a script for a play? Drafting a manual of policies and procedures for your workplace? Investigating the background of a candidate in the next election?

Audience: Knowing your audience helps you to determine how much background information is necessary to include and what style (e.g., formal or informal) is appropriate. If your reader knows less than you, this likely means that your rhetorical purpose is to inform or explain, so you need to include more background information. If your readers know more than you, usually the case for academic writing, your rhetorical purpose will likely be to analyze or to persuade.

Genre: Types of writing that have similar style, approach to subject matter, and structure are referred to as *genres*. Examples of nonfiction genres are essays, case studies, laboratory reports, news articles, blogs, and scholarly articles. Examples of literary genres include novels, short stories, and poetry. Writing in any given genre requires the writer to follow certain conventions—that is, rules or agreed-upon practices—to meet readers' expectations. For example, a potential employer would probably not consider an applicant for a position if the cover letter didn't follow appropriate conventions of the genre.

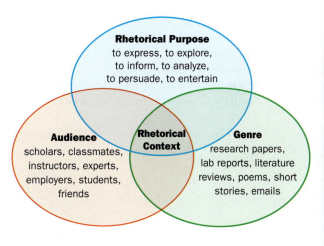

Purpose, audience, and genre are interrelated and influence one another: The reason for writing dictates the genre a writer should use; the rhetorical purpose is influenced by the reason for writing and the audience; the audience determines the content and style that is appropriate; and the genre dictates the overall form of the writing and limits the content and style. **Making appropriate stylistic choices** by ensuring that the language, sentence structure, and diction, fit the rhetorical context in addition to **controlling voice and tone** will help you to communicate your ideas effectively to your readers.

Consider the relationship between rhetorical purpose, audience, and genre in this everyday situation and writing scenario:

> You need to contact a friend to let him know that you will be late. You send him a text message. Here, your rhetorical purpose is to inform your friend about something he does not know. Because your audience is a friend, the writing style is informal and has a familiar tone. The genre requires that you write no more than a couple of short sentences, which may include acronyms and abbreviations to communicate efficiently.

NOTICING ACTIVITY

Read the writing tasks. Think about the questions below as you analyze the rhetorical context for each task.

Writing Task 1. Write a 2–3 page reflective essay on how technology has had an impact on your learning throughout your life.

Writing Task 2. Write an op-ed piece about Facebook founder Mark Zuckerberg's goal to change the world through technology and discuss why some people are uneasy about this.

Writing Task 3. Write an email to your professor, letting her know that you do not understand an assignment and would like to meet with her after class to discuss further.

- What is the reason for writing and what is the rhetorical purpose? / Is the reason for writing an assignment for a class? Or something else? Is the rhetorical purpose to inform, to persuade, or something else?
- What genre does the writing task call for? Is it a letter, a poem, a memo?
- Who is your target audience? Your friends? Your professor? Scientists? Liberal / conservative readers?
- How might the rhetorical purpose and audience influence the content? If your rhetorical purpose is to give aesthetic pleasure, will the content include a lot of descriptive detail? If your audience is someone who knows you well, do you need to provide more or less information?
- How will your audience influence the style of your writing? Is an informal tone appropriate? Should your sentences be concise or descriptive?
- To what extent does the writing task limit the style and content of your writing? Does the genre dictate the organization of the text or the amount of information that is acceptable?

Go to MyEnglishLab to complete a skill practice and join in collaborative activities.

SUPPORTING SKILL 1
MAKING STYLISTIC CHOICES

WHY IT'S USEFUL By understanding how to shape the style of your writing so that it has the intended effect on your audience, you can influence how readers respond to your ideas.

In addition to thinking about rhetorical purpose, audience, and genre, writers also need to consider *how* they should say something. **Style** refers to the way writers use language to influence how readers perceive information. For instance, consider how these two examples paint very different images about the authors and their relationship to you as the reader.

> "Technology has fooled us into thinking that we are smarter, more sophisticated beings because it provides us with quick access to information. It's true that you can find an answer to almost any question by searching the Internet, but does this make you smarter? Information and knowledge are not the same things."

> "Those who oppose technology warn that it will have adverse, unintended consequences on society, such as prizing specific knowledge and technological understanding in the sciences above intellectual development in the arts and humanities."

The first example has an informal, conversational style, which brings us closer to the author. In contrast, the second example uses an academic, impersonal style, which gives the author a voice of authority. Both examples show how different styles elicit very different reactions from readers. It's important that you use a style that is appropriate for the rhetorical purpose, genre, and audience. For example, a professor would most likely find the style used in the first example to be unacceptable in a research paper.

Making stylistic choices can be difficult because there is no simple way to check whether or not a particular style is appropriate. Is it acceptable to use *I* or *we* in an academic paper? How should a professor be addressed in an email? Here are some common factors writers should consider about style.

Elements That Affect Style	
Concise / Wordy Language	• Is it better to write efficiently and provide only necessary information to convey information or elaborate on ideas and include a lot of detail?
Sentence Structure	• What kinds of sentences should dominate the writing: simple / complex, main / reduced clauses, normal / inverted word order, many modifiers / few modifiers? • Is it better to use parallel structures or fluctuate between long and short sentences? • Are contractions (*I've, she's,* etc.) appropriate?
Diction	• What types of words should be used: simple / elaborate, technical / general, formal / slang, scientific / flowery, abstract / concrete, unusual / ordinary? • Do the words have positive or negative connotations (implied meanings), for example, *assertive* vs. *domineering*?
Point of View	• What point of view is appropriate: first person (*I, me, mine, we, us, ours*), second person (*you, yours*), third person (*he, she, it, they*)?
Voice	• What image of the writer should be projected: expert / amateur, scholar / student, comedian / romantic, liberal / conservative?
Tone	• What attitude should be projected to the audience about the subject matter: personal / impersonal, humorous / serious, literal / ironic, threatening / pleasant, optimistic / pessimistic, objective / subjective?

Students often want to know what style is appropriate for academic writing. Because style conventions can vary across disciplines, it is important to analyze research articles or papers from your discipline and examine how style elements are used. You can ask your professor or college writing center for model papers to analyze. You may also ask a librarian for help in locating examples of published papers within the discipline and field you are writing.

Although style can vary across disciplines, here are some general stylistic features of academic writing:

- Language is efficient and concise to increase clarity.
- Sentences are usually dense and include:
  - Long noun phrases (e.g., *The absence of any sense of purpose along with any idea of what the outcome might be is concerning.*)
  - Single verbs instead of phrasal verbs (e.g. *research* instead of *look into*)
  - Parallel structures (e.g., *The absence of any sense of purpose along with any idea of the outcome is concerning.*)
  - Few to no contractions (e.g., *she's, it's, etc.*)
- Vocabulary tends to be from the Academic Word List, is discipline-specific, and is formal. Slang and colloquial expressions should not be used. Using online corpora, such as the British National Corpus or the Compleat Lexical Tutor, can be helpful for finding common academic vocabulary and phrases.

> **TIP**
> ....
> *The Academic Word List was developed by Averil Coxhead as her MA thesis at the School of Linguistics and Applied Language Studies at Victoria University of Wellington, New Zealand. The list contains 570 word families selected based on range, frequency, and uniformity of frequency in academic writing. The list does not include words that are in the most frequent 2000 words of English.*

- Point of view tends to be in third person, although first person is acceptable in some genres and disciplines. For example, reflective essays are commonly written in first person.
- The tone is usually impersonal and objective in order to give the writer a voice of authority. Emotive language should be avoided unless the rhetorical purpose of the writing is to entertain, express feelings, or relate to a personal experience. Voice and tone are discussed in greater detail in Supporting Skill 2.

Regardless of the style you use for a writing task, it's important that it be consistent throughout and that it is appropriate for the rhetorical purpose, audience, and genre.

EXERCISE 1

A. Rewrite the sentences in a formal, academic style.

1. The positive feedback gave our team the courage to continue our study about the effects of technology on learning. ....

....

....

2. The web was created in 1989, and this started the Information Age. ....

....

....

3. You can clearly see how this study gave us new information about how children learn. ....

....

....

4. When I need a question answered or am researching just about anything, my first stop is the Internet. ....

....

....

5. The researchers weren't worried about the different results. The differences between the control and experimental groups actually told them a lot. ....

....

....

6. If your only friends exist online, you're using technology as a substitute for meaningful relationships. ....

....

....

7. We found tons of examples of how technology has changed how kids learn in school. ....

....

....

8. Technology helps those of us far from home have considerably less homesickness. ....

....

....

EXERCISE 2

A. Use the chart on p. 77 to identify the stylistic choices the writer makes in the paragraph.

(1) When I started working twenty-five years ago, the Web did not exist. (2) When I had a work-related question, I found answers by meeting with people or by researching information in bookstores and libraries. (3) Now, when I need a technical question answered or am researching just about anything, my first stop is the Internet. (4) Seeking out people and books for specific knowledge and information has been replaced by online video tutorials and search engines. (5) I still interact with people, but it is usually through the virtual world of online video sharing.

B. Write a five-sentence paragraph about how technology affects the way you acquire knowledge. Match the styles of each sentence to those in the paragraph from Part A, using similar sentence structure, type of vocabulary, point of view, voice, and tone.

C. <u>PEER REVIEW</u>. Exchange your paragraph with a partner. Respond to the questions to evaluate each other's work. For responses marked No, give feedback in the Notes column to help your partner revise.

	Yes	No	Notes
Is the writing concise?	☐	☐	
Does each sentence use the same grammar structures as Part A?	☐	☐	
Does the writer use first person narrative consistently?	☐	☐	
Is the vocabulary general?	☐	☐	
Is the tone personal and conversational?	☐	☐	
Is the overall style informal?	☐	☐	
Does the writer successfully follow the style of the paragraph in Part A?	☐	☐	

Go to MyEnglishLab to complete a skill practice.

SUPPORTING SKILL 2
CONTROLLING VOICE AND TONE

WHY IT'S USEFUL By controlling voice and tone, your writing will have the intended effect on the reader.

Tone is the quality in your writing that projects your attitude about your topic and audience. Whether or not your writing is formal or informal is a matter of tone. Some other examples of tone are personal / impersonal, humorous / serious, literal / ironic, threatening / pleasant, optimistic / pessimistic, and objective / subjective. What other examples of tone can you think of?

Voice is similar to tone in that it is connected to how writing is perceived. But it goes even further because the voice that is expressed in a piece is uniquely that of the writer's. Altering style and tone helps writers show their true voice to the audience. Some examples of voice are: expert / amateur, scholar / student, comedian / romantic, and liberal / conservative. Can you think of other examples of voice?

Tone and voice are conveyed to the reader through word choice. Well-chosen words create a courteous and confident tone in an email and strengthen your voice as a professional, or create an objective and impersonal tone in an academic essay and convey a scholarly voice to your readers. Sentence structure and how information is organized can also help to reinforce tone and voice. Look at these examples of text choice reinforcing tone and voice:

Sentence structure: Densely packed sentences with long noun phrases reinforce an academic tone.

> The absence of any sense of purpose along with any idea of what the outcome might be is concerning.

> The notion that the technological age has positively influenced the development of thought in society by opening pathways to learning and by providing health, efficiency, and global connection to individuals is a view held by many.

Denotation and connotation of words: The denotation of a word is its meaning. The connotation of a word is a word's implied meaning, which can be positive, negative, or neutral. It is important to choose words that connote your intended meaning.

> The speaker was *notorious* in certain areas of the world. (Negative connotation)

> The speaker was *famous* in certain areas of the world. (Positive connotation)

Diction: The use of contractions, slang, and imprecise words project an informal tone.

> The meeting *isn't happening* today.

> The researchers had a *rough time* conducting the study.

> Less human interaction is one *thing that will happen* if people spend too much time on electronic devices.

Active vs. passive voice: Passive voice softens the tone by making a sentence sound less accusatory since the focus is on the object, not on the subject.

> You are not permitted to wear jeans at the office. (Active)

> Jeans are not permitted at the office. (Passive)

Single verbs vs. phrasal verbs: Single verbs give writing an academic tone, whereas phrasal verbs are informal and conversational.

> Kids should *cut down on* their screen time.

> Children are encouraged to *reduce* their screen time.

> The police have been *looking into* the issue for several weeks.

> Scientists have been *investigating* the problem for several years.

Point of view: Pronoun choice indicates the writer's relationship with the reader. Using first person *I* or second person "you" creates a more personal connection to the reader. Using third person "it" is more common in academic writing, especially science writing, because the focus should be on the research, not the researcher.

> Technology has fooled *us* into thinking that *we* are smarter, more sophisticated beings because it provides *us* with quick access to information.

> The *effects* of technology on critical thinking were measured over an eight-year period in a longitudinal study. In the study, *it* was recommended that teaching strategies be reevaluated.

The tone and voice should also be appropriate for the genre, audience, and rhetorical purpose of the text. For example, when writing an editorial in a local newspaper, using a tone that expresses anger at a recent law may be appropriate and achieve the purpose. In contrast, in an academic article, an angry tone would be inappropriate; an objective tone conveys a scholarly voice. Look at the tone and voice used for each rhetorical context. Note the type of language features that best express the writer's intentions.

Genre	Email	Argument Essay	Statement of Purpose
Audience	co-workers	professor	college admissions counselor
Rhetorical Purpose	to inform about a new dress code policy	to persuade that technology improves one's capacity to learn	to express your goals and personal attributes
Style	conversational	academic	narrative
Voice	professional	scholarly	ambitious
Tone	confident	objective	motivated
	respectful	impersonal	passionate
Language Features	• Short sentences to emphasize ideas • Compound / complex sentences to give details • General vocabulary • Contractions • First and second person point of view	• Complex sentences that are densely packed • Academic and topic-specific vocabulary • Few to no contractions • Hedges and boosters to qualify claims • Third person point of view	• Descriptive sentences to tell your story • Natural sounding language • No slang or "text speak" • Few to no contractions • First person point of view

EXERCISE 3

A. Read the practice assignment. Then read a student's first draft of a paragraph for the assignment and answer the questions that follow.

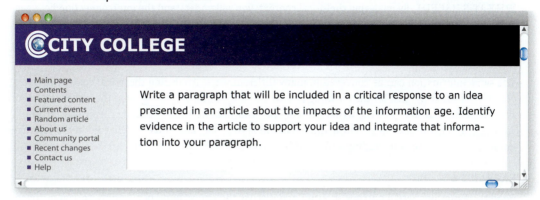

CITY COLLEGE

- Main page
- Contents
- Featured content
- Current events
- Random article
- About us
- Community portal
- Recent changes
- Contact us
- Help

Write a paragraph that will be included in a critical response to an idea presented in an article about the impacts of the information age. Identify evidence in the article to support your idea and integrate that information into your paragraph.

The author thinks that advertisements are telling us that we'd better stay connected to our electronic devices at all times, or else! The author ridiculously believes that our lives are so overrun with technology that we are in danger of not being able to connect deeply with loved ones, books, or even our thoughts. I think this is totally absurd and shows that the writer is stuck in the Middle Ages. In my opinion, technology has increased our ability to connect with people, especially those who live far away. Computers and tablets also give us greater access to books by allowing us to download them off the Internet. Last, technology broadens the range of information that is available to us on a daily basis, and I believe that this diversifies what we think about.

B. Read the paragraph closely for voice and tone. Do you see any issues with either? Discuss with a partner.

C. Rewrite the paragraph using appropriate voice and tone.

D. <u>PEER REVIEW</u>. Exchange your paragraph with a partner. Respond to the questions to evaluate each other's work.

What is the tone and voice of the original paragraph?	
What is the tone and voice of the revised paragraph?	
What language from the original paragraph did your partner change?	
Is the tone of the revised paragraph appropriate?	
Is the tone of the revised paragraph consistent throughout?	

Go to MyEnglishLab to complete a skill practice.

READING-WRITING CONNECTION
ANALYZING THE RHETORICAL CONTEXT

WHY IT'S USEFUL By analyzing rhetorical context, you will understand the interconnection between genre, audience, and purpose in how ideas are presented. You will also be aware of how style, voice, and tone affect language choices. This understanding will enable you to make appropriate choices in your writing.

The same information can be conveyed in many different ways. Analyzing rhetorical context requires you to read a text not just for the meaning but for why the author is writing, who the writer is directing the information to, and how the writer presents the information. Understanding rhetorical purpose, audience, and genre and the resulting differences in **style, tone**, and **voice** as reflected in the **language choices** will improve your reading skills and help you become a better writer.

EXERCISE 4

Read the examples with a partner. Identify and discuss the genre, audience, and rhetorical purpose.

Email Message

From: John Lee
To: The Superintendent of the Jefferson County, CA school district
Subject: Summer Reading Program

As a parent of a student in the district, I really must protest the recent decision to cut funding to the Summer Reading Program in order to put more money into new computers for the schools. I read recently that reading for pleasure has declined and some young people don't even read at all. Quite frankly, this is shocking. Cutting the reading program is just wrong. How can we expect students to develop imagination and creativity if all they do is play video games and do whatever it is they all seem to be doing on their phones whenever I see them? Technology is changing our schools and not in good ways. I am mad, and I know other parents are, too. I can only hope that the school district will do what they are supposed to do and encourage kids to read. In my opinion, kids have plenty of chances to use technology on their own. The schools should spend their money on programs that encourage our kids to read.

Sincerely,

A concerned parent

---

1. Genre: ....

2. Audience: ....

3. Rhetorical purpose: ....

The role that technology should play in teaching and learning is a topic of high interest in education. As you would expect, many studies have made valuable contributions to deciding the role of technology. However, there is still a need for more studies that target the impact of technology on specific skills. The purpose of this study is to examine the role of technology in the perceived decline in critical thinking skills of high school graduates in Jefferson County, California. As the use of technology has increased, skills in critical thinking and analysis have declined, according to Patricia Greenfield, UCLA professor of psychology. Greenfield analyzed more than 50 different studies on learning and technology, including research on the use of computers, the Internet, video games, and multitasking and contends that learners have changed as a result of exposure to technology. This more recent study, using a problem-solving video simulation administered to seniors in the four district high schools, while limited in scope, adds to the body of evidence from past studies that suggests that technology may be impacting students' ability to think critically, especially to analyze and synthesize abstract ideas and apply them.

1. Genre: ....

2. Audience: ....

3. Rhetorical purpose: ....

ANALYZING RHETORICAL CONTEXT

The previous two examples are different **genres**: a letter and a research report. Both are nonfiction, and both have as their broad topic the use of technology in a particular school district. But each genre, one academic and the other not, approaches and addresses the topic in very different ways.

One **audience** for the letter is clearly the specific person to whom it is addressed, the superintendent, but this type of letter is often sent to a newspaper's editorial page, so the audience may be much broader, including parents, students, teachers, and other interested people in the school district. This audience is, therefore, general, but localized.

The research study will most likely be read by a very different audience. The researchers are speaking to a specific audience of other educators and researchers, including students in the field of education. So in this sense, it is more specific, but it will also be read by a wider audience spread much farther than the local school district in which the study took place.

Each has a different **rhetorical purpose**. The letter to the superintendent of the schools is expressing a strong opinion and arguing against a decision, "*I really must protest the recent decision to cut funding to the Summer Reading Program in order to put more money into new computers for the schools.*" In contrast, the research study is informing the reader and as is a common convention in academic genres, the purpose is clearly announced, "*The purpose of this study is to examine the role of technology in the perceived decline in critical thinking skills of high school graduates in Jefferson County, California.*"

While both texts are on a similar topic, the differences in genre, purpose, and audience, result in differences in style, voice, and tone. The letter expressing an opinion is in a less formal and more personal **style**. It is direct and blunt in expressing an opinion, "*This is wrong.*" It does not offer the support for its claims that is expected in academic work. "*I read recently that reading for pleasure has declined.*" In contrast, the research article is more formal and neutral in style and expresses its claims more cautiously: "*suggests that technology may be impacting students' ability to think.*" In addition, it supports its claims by citing an authoritative source, Patricia Greenfield, and refers to an existing body of research on the topic, "*more than 50 different studies on learning and technology.*"

In each text, the writer's **voice** comes through. Both writers establish themselves as credible, but in different ways. The writer of the letter maintains an informal style while stating immediately that he is a parent of a student in the district.

The author of the research study uses his voice, that of a reasoned and thoughtful researcher, to establish his credibility as someone who can be believed.

The **tone** of each piece comes through clearly. Direct and clear statements and the choice of idiomatic language set the tone of the letter as angry and clearly of a single opinion, "*I protest …*" "*I am mad,*" and "*The schools should spend their money on programs that encourage our kids to read.*"

The tone of the research article also comes through clearly. Supported statements and language that softens the stance give this text a more neutral tone that persuades through evidence: "*perceived decline,*" and "*This study, while limited in scope, adds to the body of evidence that suggests that technology may be impacting students' ability to think critically ….*"

While style, voice, and tone can vary across genres and reflect the individuality of the writer, the conventions of each genre result in some generalizable style, voice, and tone choices.

EXERCISE 5

A. Read the three opinion pieces.

The technological age has positively influenced the development of thought in society by opening pathways to learning and by providing health, efficiency, and global connection to individuals. As Aristotle stated in his *Metaphysics* treatise, all people have an innate desire for knowledge. Modern technology, which offers nearly limitless information to anyone at any time, is arguably the logical conclusion of this human yearning. Scientists and philosophers who studied Aristotle, such as eminent Western scientist Isaac Newton, contributed to the evolution of scientific thought by developing the scientific method, which has ushered in the digital age. Therefore, an important aspect of the development of modern technology, and one that would have likely been championed by socialist and philosopher Karl Marx, is that technology has become an equalizer. Rather than scholarship for only a privileged few in a society, today's academia offers knowledge to everyone, including women and marginalized groups, and offers it at an individual's own pace of learning. Technology has also given individuals the blissful expectation of a long life, efficient work, and an enormous breadth of knowledge.

Like any development, however, modern technology includes inherent consequences. For example, in Plato's writings, his character King Thamus criticizes the god Theuth's gift of the technology of writing, warning that writing would lead to a lapse in memory and to wisdom that is only recorded but not comprehended. Similarly, neo-Luddites[1] warn that technology will have adverse, unintended consequences on society, such as prizing specific knowledge in the sciences and technical understanding above intellectual development in the arts and humanities. Furthermore, critics argue that there is no guarantee of knowledge acquisition being unique, since learning in the same way—through technology—can cause education itself to fall into a standardized, and thus limited, path. German philosopher Martin Heidegger, who critiqued

Academic Text

---

[1] Luddites were 19th century English textile workers who protested against new technologies they feared would be the end of their trade. Neo-Luddite refers to those who are antitechnology or opposed to technological innovation now.

the technology of the early 20th century, warned of such pitfalls when he argued that humanity was limiting itself through dependence on technology. However, as it may be argued that literacy is clearly more beneficial to members of society than not knowing how to write, the benefits of modern technology far outweigh its disadvantages.

How society is shaped after being immersed in the technological age seems to be one of the biggest philosophical questions of the time, raising emotions that range from curiosity and marvel to fear and dread. The question is not new. Plato philosophized about rudimentary technology in ancient times, and thousands of inventions along the path of history to modernity have found themselves on other philosophers' chopping blocks. The latest inventions—from the rise of personal computers and cellular phones in the 1990s to driverless cars of the mid-2010s—are of course at the forefront of our scrutiny. The great question of *What will this technology do to us?* has been bandied about for ages without any definitive answer.

Perhaps we are our own best evidence. Think about what humans can accomplish now that they could not at the time scholar Isaac Newton was laying the groundwork for the scientific revolution of the 1700s, or even what humans can accomplish now compared to

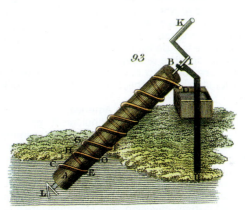

Rudimentary technology in ancient Greece included the use of steam to operate machines, gears, locks, odometers, and alarm clocks, and equipment for building cranes and winches. This is an illustration of Archimedes' screw, which transfers water from low-lying areas to higher ground.

75 years ago. Immunizations and advancements in modern medicine have saved millions of lives, the Human Genome Project has mapped the genes of human beings, and astrophysics has helped humankind not only walk on the moon, but chart untold portions of the galaxy. Such growth can definitely be attributed to the technological age. Beyond the rewarded accomplishments of the age, however, there exists an underlying intellectual development that did not exist before, and that is access. People with learning challenges, people without money, women, and minorities all would have been dismissed in earlier times. The hope that this gives to individuals is no small step in society's advancement.

That education is immediately accessible does not mean it is solving all of society's problems. Social ills and economic woes still plague all nations, and whether this is due to society's transitioning to a knowledge-based

Continued

economy rather than an industrial economy cannot be known. Nor can it be deduced that if society went backward and gave up technology such social problems would be resolved. Instead, we must focus attention on areas of learning that are the most vulnerable in the technological age, including creativity in the sciences, development of critical thinking skills in individuals, and commitment to the arts.

TechNow

YOUR VIEW WORLDVIEW CONNECT MORE

Blog Comments Tags

Blog to match Academic Text and News Magazine

Let me guess how you spent your morning.

First, you woke to light a fire, which was followed by chopping wood and walking four miles in the cold to your single-room schoolhouse. Then you talked to a boy your age who is in mourning because his little brother died of typhoid several weeks ago. Sad, but not uncommon. There is little light when it is dark outside, little talking to anyone beyond those you know in your family and neighborhood, and on the whole, little prospect beyond becoming a shopkeeper, as your father is.

> **Did you know?**
> Typhoid is a serious and potentially fatal disease spread by contaminated food and water. It is still common in many parts of the world but is far less prevalent than it was in the past.

That's because it's the year 1825 in America.

Compared to this life, the modern technological age, for all its downsides, has given people in developed nations an immense cushion of comfort. Before such technology, death was more common than a paper cut in an English class. Opportunity was limited. So, to go starry-eyed when recollecting life before the advent of the technological age is falsely assuming that a quaint, old-fashioned lifestyle, if you can call it that, was easier and better before modern education, medicine, and communication systems. It is possible that life was easier, but it is not probable.

Of course problems exist in our technological society. Really, if your only friends exist on Snapchat and Facebook, you're using technology as a false substitute for meaningful relationships. If you copy an essay off Wikipedia, you're plagiarizing and cheating yourself by not taking the time to learn and synthesize information.

But while those scenarios could easily happen—and do—for many people, our overall society benefits immensely from technology. It brings the world closer and spurs empathy, as evidenced by global efforts to help other nations during crises. Technology helps those of us far from home have considerably less homesickness because our families and friends are only a Skype call or a text away. Older people, as well, probably benefit from life in a technological age. Those making a career switch or reentering the workforce can explore new career options and interests through online or

> **Did you know?**
> There are over 74 million Skype users, with approximately 124 million monthly log-ins?

distance-learning programs. I guess all people have the desire to learn and discover, and technology offers the vehicle to easily reach those goals.

The 1800s can keep its quaintness—not surprisingly, I'll take the comfort, efficiency, and opportunity of the technological age.

B. Answer the questions.

1. What is the rhetorical purpose of each text? Is it the same or different for the three pieces? Underline the sentence in the text where the purpose is stated.

   Academic text ....

   News magazine ....

   Blog ....

   ....

2. Who is the intended audience for each piece? What assumptions is the writer making about the audience? Which text would be read by a more specific audience? A geographically limited audience? More people in general? What evidence in the texts supports these assumptions about the audience?

   Academic text ....

   News magazine ....

   Blog ....

   ....

3. How many outside sources are mentioned or cited in the text? List them. What does this tell you about each genre?

   Academic text ....

   News magazine ....

   Blog ....

   ....

4. What examples of technology are mentioned in each piece? Why do you think there are differences?

   Academic piece ....

   News magazine ....

   Blog ....

   ....

5. Which text uses rhetorical questions? Write the questions here. ....

   ....

   ....

6. Which text sounds like a conversation with you? Give examples. ....

   ....

   ....

7. Which texts address opposing ideas? Explain how and give examples. ....

   Academic text ....

   News magazine ....

   Blog ....

   ....

8. What is the style of each text? Use your answers in questions 3–7 and the information in the supporting skills to analyze the style of each text and write two or three sentences describing it.

   Academic text ....

   ....

   ....

   News magazine ....

   ....

   ....

   Blog ....

   ....

   ....

9. How would you describe the tone and voice of each text? Give examples of words and phrases that support your opinion.

   Academic text ....

   News magazine ....

   Blog ....

   ....

10. How does each text conclude? How does each conclusion fit the conventions of the genre?

    Academic text ....

    News magazine ....

    Blog ....

    ....

C. Compare your answers in Part B with a partner. Did you agree? Did you have the same examples from the text to support your answers? Discuss any differences in your opinions.

EXERCISE 6

A. Pick one of the genres in Exercise 5: academic, news magazine, or blog. Write another paragraph on the topic of technology and learning in that genre. You can add information or counter information in the text. For example, you might address the accessibility of information today or the difference between information and knowledge. Consider style, tone, and voice. Use appropriate language for the genre, rhetorical purpose, and audience.

B. Exchange paragraphs with a partner. Analyze the rhetorical context of your partner's text using the chart.

	Analysis	Evidence / Examples from Text
Genre		
Purpose		
Audience		
Style		
Tone		
Voice		

C. Discuss your chart with your partner. Does your partner agree with your analysis?

Go to MyEnglishLab to complete a vocabulary exercise and a skill practice and join in collaborative activities.

For more about RHETORICAL CONTEXT, see R and OC HUMANITIES 1.

LANGUAGE SKILLS
USING APPROPRIATE ADVERBIALS TO FIT RHETORICAL CONTEXT

WHY IT'S USEFUL By using adverbials that fit the rhetorical context to link ideas and express a stance, you will maintain a consistent and appropriate style in your writing.

Adverbials are words or phrases that function as adverbs and are an important part of writing in all rhetorical contexts. Here is some information about adverbials:

- They create textual cohesion.
- They have many **semantic roles** and express a variety of meanings such as location, reason, concession, time, agency, and attitude.

For more on cohesion, See BIOLOGY, Part 1.

- They take a wide range of **syntactic forms**, from single-word adverbs to prepositional phrases and clauses, with adverbs and prepositional phrases being the most common.
- They occur in **various positions** in clauses—initial, medial, and final.
- **More than one** adverbial can occur in a single clause.
- They are most often **optional**.
- They serve different **functions**, including linking and stance (expressing the writer's feeling, opinion, or judgment.)

Explanation	Example
Linking adverbials are used by writers to show the relationship between units of discourse—clauses, sentences, or longer pieces of text. They connect rather than add information. They occur most often in initial position.	**Therefore**, an important aspect of the development of modern technology, and one that would have likely been championed by socialist and philosopher Karl Marx, is that technology has become an equalizer. [Clause]

Let me guess how you spent your morning. **First,** you woke to light a fire, followed by chopping wood and walking four miles in the cold to your single-room schoolhouse. [Sentences]

Of course problems exist in our technological society. If your only friends exist on Snapchat and Facebook, you're using technology as a false substitute for meaningful relationships. If you copy an essay off Wikipedia, you're plagiarizing and cheating yourself by not taking the time to learn and synthesize information.

But while those scenarios could easily—and do—happen for many people, our overall society benefits immensely from technology. [Text offering a contrast to the previous paragraph] |
The relationship can be: **Contrast / concession** (*however, in contrast, nevertheless, though, besides, anyway, but, yet, still*)	That education is immediately accessible, **however**, does not mean it is solving all of society's problems.
Enumeration and addition (*first, second, finally, for one thing, for another thing, in addition, similarly, next, then*)	**In addition**, technology has given individuals the expectation of a long life.
Summation (*furthermore, moreover, to summarize, in conclusion, overall, all in all*)	**Overall**, the benefits of modern technology far outweigh its disadvantages.
Apposition (*in other words, for example, for instance, specifically, which is to say, such as, namely*)	**For example**, in Plato's writings, his character King Thamus criticizes the god Theuth's gift of the technology of writing, …
Inference/result (*consequently, therefore, as a result, hence, thus, so*)	Learning in the same way, through technology, can cause education itself to fall into a standardized, and **consequently** limited, path.

Academic writing	
Academic writing uses linking adverbials most frequently and with great variety. Because academic writing presents and supports explanations and arguments, ideas need to be connected overtly.	Like any development, **however**, modern technology includes inherent consequences. [Argument]
The most common linking adverbials in academic writing are result / inference, apposition, and contrast / concession, which all help structure arguments and explanations. Enumerative / summation is also found more in academic writing than other registers.	**Similarly**, neo-Luddites warn that technology will have adverse, unintended consequences on society, **such as** prizing specific knowledge in the sciences and technical understanding above intellectual development in the arts and humanities. [Enumeration and apposition]
Common linking adverbials in academic writing are *however, thus, therefore, for example, first, finally, furthermore, rather, yet, for instance, in addition, on the other hand, that is.*	**Furthermore**, critics argue that there is no guarantee of knowledge acquisition being unique, since learning in the same way—through technology—can cause education itself to fall into a standardized, and **thus** limited, path.
Other nonfiction writing	
Nonfiction genres use less linking and rely more on implicit connection.	The question is not new. Plato philosophized about rudimentary technology in ancient times, … [Apposition not directly stated] That education is immediately accessible does not mean it is solving all of society's problems. [Contrast not directly stated]
Common linking adverbials in informal writing are *so, then, though,* and *anyway.*	Opportunity was limited. **So,** to go starry-eyed when recollecting life before the advent of the technological age is falsely assuming that a quaint, old-fashioned lifestyle was easier and better before modern education, medicine, and communication systems.
Coordination with *but* is more common in nonfiction genres and less common in academic writing.	It is possible that life was easier, **but** it is not probable.
And serves a different role in different genres—in nonacademic writing, it is used at clause level whereas in academic writing, it is most often used at phrase level.	All people have the desire to learn and discover, **and** technology offers the vehicle to easily reach those goals. [Clauses] Technology has also given individuals the blissful expectation of a long life, efficient work, **and** an enormous breadth of knowledge. [Phrases]

Explanation	Example
Stance adverbials comment on the content or style of a clause.	
They overtly mark the writer's attitude.	The 1800s can keep its quaintness. **Not, surprisingly**, I'll take the comfort, efficiency, and opportunity of the technological age. [Attitude]
Single-word adverbs are the most common form.	**Perhaps** we are our own best evidence. [Single word]
They can focus on a particular element or the clause.	*Modern technology*, which offers nearly limitless information to anyone at any time, is **arguably** the logical conclusion of this human yearning. [Focus on a particular element—modern technology]
	Therefore, *an important aspect of the development of modern technology, and one that would have **likely** been championed by socialist and philosopher Karl Marx, is that technology has become an equalizer.* [Focus on the entire clause]
They occur in all positions and with same meaning; medial is most common. They are always optional. Note: Stance can also be conveyed with noun phrases: *the fact that*, modals: *may*, and verbs: *seems.*	**Perhaps** we are our own best evidence. [Initial position] We are, **perhaps**, our own best evidence. [Medial position] We are our own best evidence **perhaps**. [Final position] **(Perhaps)** we are our own best evidence. [Optional]

Continued

Explanation	Example
Academic writing vs. other nonfiction writing	
Stance adverbials are relatively common in academic writing. Academic writing addresses the certainty of information and provides evidence, both of which are accomplished with stance adverbials.	**As** Aristotle stated in his Metaphysics treatise, all people have an innate desire for knowledge. [Provide evidence] However, as it may be argued that literacy is **clearly** more beneficial to members of society than not knowing how to write, the benefits of modern technology far outweigh its disadvantages. [Address certainty]
News has the lowest frequency of stance adverbials.	Social ills and economic woes still plague America ... [Not marked for stance]
Choice of stance adverbial is affected by rhetorical context—genres, audience, and purpose. For example, *I guess*, while common in informal writing, is rare in academic writing.	**I guess** all people have the desire to learn and discover, and technology offers the vehicle to easily reach those goals. [Choice affected by genre]
There are three categories of stance adverbials: epistemic and attitude, which comment on ideas, and style, which comments on manner. **Epistemic**	
Judges the truth of information; show the viewpoint, express limitations of the truth value.	Modern technology, which offers nearly limitless information to anyone at any time, is **arguably** the logical conclusion of this human yearning. [Academic]
Note: Stance adverbials listed here are ordered from most common in academic and formal writing to most common in least formal writing (and speaking).	Therefore, an important aspect of the development of modern technology, and one that would have **likely** been championed by socialist and philosopher Karl Marx, is that technology has become an equalizer. [Academic]
	The latest inventions—from the rise of personal computers and cellular phones in the 1990s to driverless cars of the mid-2010s—are **of course** at the forefront of our scrutiny. [News]
Certainty or doubt *Perhaps, arguably, undoubtedly, most likely, of course, probably, maybe, I think, I guess, I suppose, who knows*	Older people, as well, **probably** benefit from life in a technological age. [Blog]
Actuality or reality *in fact, actually, truly, really*	**Really,** if your only friends exist on Snapchat and Facebook, you're using technology as a false substitute for meaningful relationships.
Source of knowledge *according to X, as X states, reportedly, evidently, apparently*	As the use of technology has increased, skills in critical thinking and analysis have declined **according to Patricia Greenfield**, UCLA professor of psychology.
Limitation *generally, in most cases, in most instances, on the whole, mainly, typically*	There is little light when it is dark outside, little talking to anyone beyond those you know in your family and neighborhood, and **on the whole** little prospect beyond becoming a shopkeeper, as your father is.
Viewpoint or perspective *from our perspective, to my knowledge, in our view, in my opinion (Note the use of a possessive pronoun.)*	**In my opinion**, kids have plenty of chances to use technology on their own.
Imprecision hedges *so to speak, if you can call it that, sort of, kind of*	So, to go starry-eyed when recollecting life before the advent of the technological age is falsely assuming that a quaint, old-fashioned lifestyle, **if you can call it that**, was easier and better before modern education, medicine, and communication systems.
Attitude Tells writer's evaluation, expectation, assessment, or judgement of importance *(un)fortunately, as you'd expect, predictably, importantly, naturally, (not) surprisingly, as you might guess, to my surprise, hopefully*	**As you would expect**, many studies have made valuable contributions to deciding the role of technology.
Style Manner of writing or voice *(More) simply put, in short, in a word, figuratively speaking, (quite) frankly, truthfully, if I may say so, honestly*	**Quite frankly**, this is shocking.

Stance adverbials are also used in all rhetorical contexts to emphasize a point. For example, "Such growth can definitely be attributed to the technological age," and, "I really must disagree. ..."

EXERCISE 7

Choose the best linking or stance adverbial for the genre.

Academic essay

Technological innovations have (1) (indeed / really) affected billions of people all over the world.
(2) (According to the Pew Research Center / Reportedly the Pew Research Center says) 64 percent of US
citizens owned a smart phone in 2015, (3) (and / moreover) almost half of those owners reported that
they couldn't live without it. Robert Pogue Harrison, in his article, "The Children of Silicon Valley," says
this has turned the last four decades into a series of "before and after" divides—before and after personal
computers, Google, Facebook, iPhones, and so on. He claims that the often heard motto of the silicon
age of "change the world" (4) (in fact / really) translates to new and more ways to make our smart phones
our only means to access "reality." He (5) (further / also) argues that technology hasn't so much changed
the world as changed us and how we interact with others. He suggests that, contrary to Thoreau's
notion that we crave reality, we (6) (actually / just) prefer to trade reality for the screen of a smart phone.
(7) (Undoubtedly / Actually) this has been profitable for the technology industry. (8) (Perhaps / I guess)
the most disturbing notion is Harrison's suggestion that it "corrodes the core of [our] worldly humanity,
leaving [us] increasingly worldless."

In-class discussion on a learning management system

Wow. To my surprise, I (9) (really / thoroughly) enjoyed the article about Silicon Valley by Robert Pogue
Harrison. It made me think about how I use my smart phone. I am in that half of owners who can't live
without their phones, (10) (nevertheless / but) I didn't really realize how much of my time I spend on it
and how little time I spend (11) (in fact / really) hanging out with friends in real time. (12) (I suppose /
arguably) I thought I was living in reality but (13) (most likely / maybe) I'm not since I do seem to
(14) (so to speak / sort of) relate to the world via my phone. (15) (In my opinion / I guess) I'm what
he calls assimilated since I consider my friends on Facebook a part of my social circle. (16) (And /
moreover), I always am in line to buy the latest smart phone, so I am making Silicon Valley richer.
(17) (However / Anyway), it's pretty shocking to think that my world is the screen of my phone and
that might mean I'm losing my humanity! I definitely want to look for more information about this
on my phone.

EXERCISE 8

**Choose one paragraph in each genre. Rewrite the paragraph. Add adverbials that fit the genre and tone
of the paragraph. Use at least three linking adverbials and two stance adverbials.**

Academic—Paragraph in the discussion section of a research article

A review of the studies indicates that a balanced approach that uses technology along with
more traditional techniques such as reading, lecture, and discussion is best. As we saw in
Greenfield's review of 50 studies, technology in education has both benefits and costs in terms
of skill development. Studies have shown that visual media help students process information.
A visual presentation can enhance a lecture. It is real time. It doesn't allow time for reflection or
deep thought.

Studies have shown that reading develops analytical skills and imagination, as well as
vocabulary. Reading for pleasure has a place in the curriculum at all levels. A study found
that multitasking, frequent in the use of technology, prevented people from getting a deeper
understanding of the material. In some professions, skill at multitasking is beneficial. A study
indicated that video games improve multitasking. Taken together, the studies, including our own
results, suggest that technology be added to other educational practices to provide students with
opportunities to develop a range of skills.

News article—Paragraph in the conclusion of an article in a news magazine

What is the place of technology in our classrooms? How much should schools use new technology versus older techniques like reading and discussion? Technology is both good and bad. We must find a balance. Wiring classrooms for technology does not enhance learning. Television, movies, and video games help students catch on and understand quickly. They don't develop deep thinking.

Reading does develop deep thinking, according to experts. It seems children don't read much anymore. Kids should read for fun, and schools should allow time for them to do that. Video games and other devices like smart phones and tablets help children multitask and improve hand-eye coordination. They don't help them understand ideas. Books can. Technology is here to stay. We must integrate it into our schools. We shouldn't replace old but tried and true methods like reading and talking about ideas with others. There's a place for both in our classrooms.

Go to **MyEnglishLab** to complete a skill practice.

APPLY YOUR SKILLS

WHY IT'S USEFUL By applying the skills you have learned in this unit, you will make appropriate choices in your writing to fit the rhetorical context and convey your ideas using the style, tone, voice, and language that will have the intended effect on your readers.

ASSIGNMENT

Find a source describing how technology impacts how people acquire knowledge. Write a 1–2 page analysis of the rhetorical context. Be sure to identify the rhetorical purpose, audience, genre, style (including voice and tone), and the language that the author uses to connect ideas. Provide examples from the text to support your analysis.

BEFORE YOU WRITE

A. Before you begin your assignment, discuss these questions with one or more students.

1. What are the different ways people acquire knowledge?

2. How does technology help or impede people in acquiring knowledge?

3. What is something that is better learned without technology? Why?

B. As you consider your assignment, analyze the rhetorical context of your source by completing the chart. Then, share your ideas with another student. Get feedback and revise your ideas, if necessary.

	Analysis	Evidence / Examples from Text
Genre		
Purpose		
Audience		
Style		
Tone		
Voice		

C. Review the Unit Skills Summary. As you begin on the writing task on page 99, apply the skills you learned in this unit.

UNIT SKILLS SUMMARY

Make stylistic choices
- Understand the elements that affect style.
- Be aware of the stylistic features used in academic writing.

Control voice and tone
- Understand how to use textual features to control voice and tone.
- Identify tone and voice in different rhetorical contexts.

Analyze the rhetorical context
- Understand the interconnection between purpose, audience, and genre in how ideas are presented.
- Be aware of style, voice, and tone differences in text and how they affect language choices.
- Convey your ideas using an appropriate style and voice.

Use appropriate adverbials to fit the rhetorical context
- Use adverbials that fit the rhetorical context to link ideas and express a stance.

THINKING CRITICALLY

As you consider your assignment, discuss the questions with another student. Get feedback and revise your ideas, if necessary.

1. What is the difference between information and knowledge?
2. What are some of the ethical issues in making technological advancements that may have unforeseen consequences?
3. Is technology changing how people acquire knowledge? If so, how? If not, why not?

THINKING VISUALLY

A. Look at the bar graph. Write two or three sentences describing what it expresses about the ways different age groups use their smart phones.

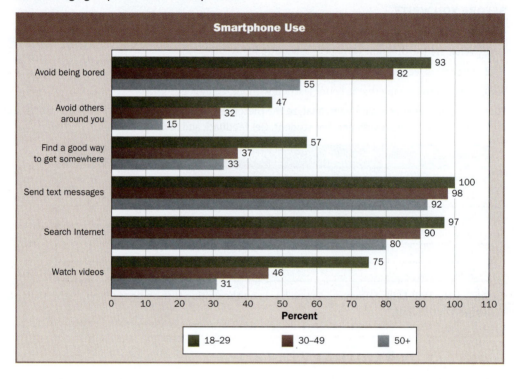

B. Are you surprised at the statistics? If so, which ones and why? Do these statistics have any bearing on the argument that technology has changed the way we interact with others? Discuss with a partner.

THINKING ABOUT LANGUAGE

Rewrite the paragraphs as either a blog entry or an excerpt from a popular technology magazine. Change the underlined adverbials to more appropriate ones and make other changes necessary to fit the genre.

One classroom study Greenfield analyzed showed that students who were allowed to use the Internet during a lecture did not process it as well as students not using the Internet. <u>Moreover</u>, when students were tested on the lecture, those without Internet access, <u>in fact</u>, performed better.

According to Greenfield in another study, college students who watched news with just the news anchor on the screen remembered more facts than students who watched the news on a screen with a news crawl across the bottom with additional information about the stock market and weather. <u>Undoubtedly</u>, the news crawl was <u>clearly</u> a distraction.

These studies indicate that multitasking most likely prevents students from understanding information fully. <u>As a result</u>, it seems advisable not to allow students to use laptops and other technology during classroom activities. Lectures <u>definitely</u> require a student's full attention.

WRITE

A. Revisit the assignment and the answers to the questions in Before You Write Part B. Examine how the stylistic choices, including voice and tone, reflect the genre, purpose, and audience of the text.

B. Identify at least three stylistic choices made by the author.

C. Write about three important stylistic choices the author made. Include examples from the text.

BEYOND THE ASSIGNMENT

Write a research paper on learning and knowing and how technology has helped or hindered this. Support your ideas by referencing classical and modern philosophers on the subject of knowledge acquisition. Use all the skills you learned in this unit.

▶ Go to MyEnglishLab to listen to Professor Harrison and to complete a self-assessment.

Sound design creates a healthier world.

ENVIRONMENTAL ENGINEERING

Publishing

UNIT PROFILE

Air quality has a wide range of effects on the health of humans and the environment. In this unit, you will read and write about topics related to air pollution and its impact on respiratory health. Specifically, you will learn about common air pollutants, how factors such as coal removal contribute to respiratory diseases, and the role of air-quality monitoring devices.

Prepare a manuscript for publication on the influence of air pollution on respiratory health. Research a case study focusing on how air pollution has affected a population in a particular area. Summarize the aim and results of the study, create a visual, and edit all of your material.

OUTCOMES

• Use visuals to present information in writing

• Edit text and visuals

• Relate visuals to text

• Examine sentence structure and subject-verb agreement

GETTING STARTED

▶ Go to MyEnglishLab to listen to Professor Hildemann and to complete a self-assessment.

Discuss these questions with a partner or group.

1. Do you, or anybody you know, suffer from health issues related to the environment? Do medications help or is a change in environment essential?

2. What do you know about government regulations regarding air pollution? Since different countries have different regulations, what can realistically be done to combat air pollution globally?

3. What engineering solutions do you know of that have had a positive impact on air quality or respiratory health?

For more about **ENVIRONMENTAL ENGINEERING**, see **2** **3**. See also **R** and **OC** **ENVIRONMENTAL ENGINEERING** **1** **2** **3**.

FUNDAMENTAL SKILL
PUBLISHING

WHY IT'S USEFUL By using visuals and editing your text to prepare your manuscript for publication, you enhance your work and create a polished and professional-looking document. Incorporating visuals allows you to convey information concisely and support arguments. Editing the text and design of a document improves both the quality of your content and the overall look and feel of your work.

It is critical that all of your academic writing is accurate and engaging and that it follows any guidelines you were given by your instructor. In some cases, your instructor will be the only person who sees your work, while in others, you may be posting to a class website or sharing your material with others in any number of ways, including having your work published. Whether you are turning in an assignment for a class or submitting a manuscript for publication, it is important that your writing have a polished and professional look. This means that your writing should be clear of spelling or grammatical errors, and the overall design should enhance your message. Visuals should be incorporated to support the text and illustrate information that would be difficult to understand using text alone.

Writers can **use a wide range of visuals to present information**, including images, such as photographs and illustrations; and graphics, such as graphs, charts, diagrams, maps, and tables. These visuals are commonly used in academic writing to clarify meaning, illustrate key ideas, highlight specific information, support arguments, and present data. In fact, the more data your material has, the more important it is that you have clear, simple visuals to illustrate the information.

Using visuals to persuade readers is referred to as *visual rhetoric*. Photographs, illustrations, and animations are especially useful for influencing how readers perceive information. Deciding when and what kind of visuals to use in your writing are important rhetorical choices you need to consider. These questions can help you determine when and what kind of visuals to incorporate into a paper:

- What is the purpose of the visual: to clarify, to highlight important information, to present data, or to persuade?
- What information should be presented visually?
- Will this visual help communicate that information? Will it enhance the point it is meant to support?

Once you have chosen your visuals, you must look at them with a critical eye, as you do with text. In Biology Part 1, you learned techniques for revising a paper to clarify and strengthen ideas. Unlike revising, **editing text and visuals** addresses sentence-level errors and overall design. Editing focuses on spelling, grammar, punctuation, or word choice errors and also includes making changes to the overall design and layout of the paper so that it is easy to navigate and follows the style conventions of the discipline and genre. In academic writing, the design is usually functional, not artistic. However, it is still important to consider the fonts, spacing, headers and footers, and the placement and colors of your visuals.

The appearance of a document enhances the clarity and strength of your message and also conveys your level of professionalism. When editing the design of your paper, consider these questions:

- Does the document's appearance follow the style conventions of the genre and discipline?
- Do the headings and subheadings provide a helpful framework for my argument or key points?
- Are the visuals positioned and labeled correctly?
- Does the design show that I am knowledgeable about the genre? Does this add to my credibility?

NOTICING ACTIVITY

You are studying the links between air pollution and respiratory diseases such as asthma and chronic obstructive pulmonary disease (COPD), both of which obstruct airflow making it difficult to breathe. You are writing a paper that examines the link between air pollution and respiratory diseases in a particular geographic area and presents solutions to mitigating this problem.

You narrow your research to studying the negative health effects of mountaintop coal removal in Appalachian mining communities. Look at the photo. Would it be useful to your paper? Discuss this with a partner. Can you think of another photograph that would support your claims about the negative health effects? Describe it to your partner.

Figure 1 Coal miners are exposed to many different hazards.

Look at the headings used in a paper about the negative effects of mountaintop coal removal in Central Appalachia. Notice how the headings frame the argument. From these headings, can you identify the writer's claim? Do you think the headings effectively outline the writer's argument? What do you notice about the design of the headings? Why is the first heading different from the others?

THE HUMAN COST OF MOUNTAINTOP REMOVAL COAL MINING:
Mapping the science behind health and economic woes of Central Appalachia

High Incidences of Cancer

Lung Cancer and Respiratory Diseases

Cardiovascular Disease and Heart Attacks

Shortened Lives and Preventable Deaths

Population Change and Socioeconomic Struggles

Go to MyEnglishLab to complete a skill practice and join in collaborative activities.

SUPPORTING SKILL 1
USING VISUALS TO PRESENT INFORMATION IN WRITING

WHY IT'S USEFUL By understanding how visuals are used across academic disciplines, you can see how readers' understanding of a text is enhanced and how the writer's thesis or hypothesis is supported. Visuals also provide readers with a clear overview of research findings and reduce the need for lengthy explanations or descriptions.

Research writing, especially in the sciences, requires reporting a large amount of quantitative information. Most writers choose to illustrate this type of information with graphs, charts, maps, or tables because **visuals** offer a clear and concise way to present data. Each type of graphic has a specific purpose, so the writer must determine the visual that best represents the information. Here are the most commonly used visuals for reporting data.

Bar graphs contrast two or more quantities and are useful for making quick comparisons. The title must include all information relevant to understanding the data. Notice how the vertical and horizontal axes represent different information and how the legend explains the shading of the groups being compared.

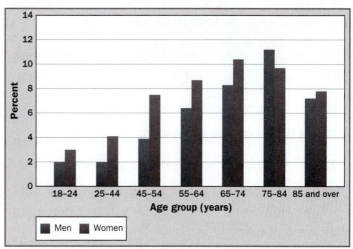

Figure 2 Prevalence of COPD among adults aged 18 and over, by age group and sex: United States annual average 2007–2009.

Line graphs show trends over time. The horizontal axis normally shows the time span in sequential increments, and the vertical axis includes the variable that fluctuates and provides the important information. Line graphs can include one entry or multiple entries for comparison. Notice here how women are at a greater risk for acquiring COPD than men.

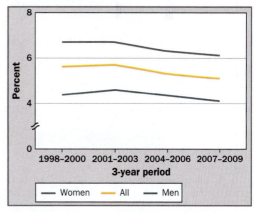

Figure 3 Prevalence of COPD among adults aged 18 and over: United States, 1998–2009.

Pie charts show percentages of a whole, explaining how a total is divided into "slices" of different sizes. Pie charts are especially effective if one part of the pie is disproportionately larger or smaller than the other parts. Notice here how on-road gasoline and diesel are the largest sources of nitrogen oxide emissions recorded in New England in 2011.

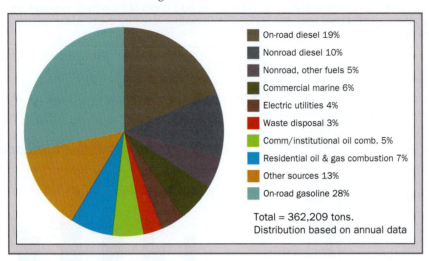

Legend:
- On-road diesel 19%
- Nonroad diesel 10%
- Nonroad, other fuels 5%
- Commercial marine 6%
- Electric utilities 4%
- Waste disposal 3%
- Comm/institutional oil comb. 5%
- Residential oil & gas combustion 7%
- Other sources 13%
- On-road gasoline 28%

Total = 362,209 tons.
Distribution based on annual data

Figure 4 NOx Emissions in New England, 2011.

Maps show a specific geographic area and use shading, lines, or other illustrations to highlight differences in measurement. Maps should always include legends that explain what is being compared. Notice here how shading is used to separate different geographic areas of the United States. Which areas have the highest numbers of COPD cases and which areas have the lowest?

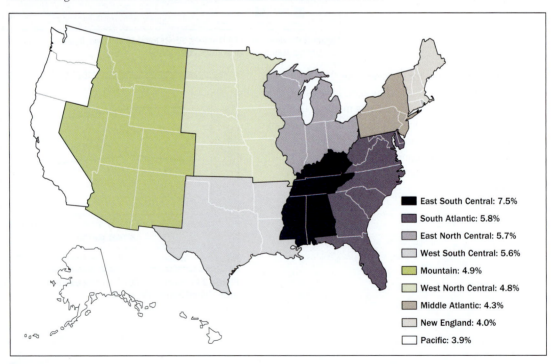

Legend:
- East South Central: 7.5%
- South Atlantic: 5.8%
- East North Central: 5.7%
- West South Central: 5.6%
- Mountain: 4.9%
- West North Central: 4.8%
- Middle Atlantic: 4.3%
- New England: 4.0%
- Pacific: 3.9%

Figure 5 Prevalence of COPD among adults aged 18 and over, by United States Census Division: United States annual average 2007–2009.

Tables show relationships between several variables. They are effective for explaining data that is too complex to explain through text. Tables consist of rows and columns, with clear labels for each. What variables are being compared in this table?

TABLE 1 Metro Area Per Capita Mortality Risk (2010 est.)

Rank	Metro Area	Total Mortality (Annual)	Mortality Risk per 100,000 adults
1	Johnstown, PA	30	25.5
2	Cumberland, MD-WV	17	20.8
3	Steubenville-Weirton, OH-WV	21	20.7
4	Altoona, PA	21	20.6
5	Sandusky, OH	12	19.8
6	Wheeling, WV-OH	23	19.3
7	Youngstown-Warren-Boardman, OH-PA	85	18.6
8	Mansfield, OH	18	18.4
9	Springfield, OH	20	18.0
10	Pittsburgh, PA MSA	340	17.9

CREATING VISUALS

In order to create a clear graphic, the data you collect during your research will need to be synthesized by classifying totals or calculating averages. You should then determine the most effective graphic to present the data or information to support your claims. You can create your graphics using spreadsheet or presentation programs such as Excel or PowerPoint. There are many tutorials online for using these programs. Here are some guidelines for creating visuals:

1. In academic papers, graphics should be labeled, numbered sequentially, and titled.

2. The title must clearly and concisely indicate what the graphic is about and relate to the other labels within the graphic.

3. Most citation styles require that tables are labeled "Tables," while all other visuals are labeled "Figures." Refer to the citation style for your discipline to ensure that you are labeling visuals correctly.

4. A good graphic is able to stand on its own, without needing to refer to the text it is supporting.

5. It is unethical to misrepresent an image by cropping out elements or leaving out data that is contrary to your claims. Don't manipulate the data to suit your claims or obscure data by using charts or graphs that are so complex that the relationship to your point isn't clear.

6. Check if you need permission to use information from a visual, even if you found it online. Cite the source(s) below the visual.

EXERCISE 1

A. Read the practice assignment. Work with a partner to answer the questions that follow.

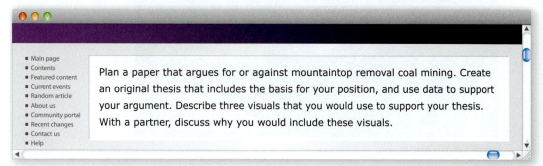

- Main page
- Contents
- Featured content
- Current events
- Random article
- About us
- Community portal
- Recent changes
- Contact us
- Help

Plan a paper that argues for or against mountaintop removal coal mining. Create an original thesis that includes the basis for your position, and use data to support your argument. Describe three visuals that you would use to support your thesis. With a partner, discuss why you would include these visuals.

B. Answer the questions about the use of these visuals for your paper.

1. How would you use Figure 1 to argue *against* using coal as a major energy source?

2. From the opposite viewpoint, how could a writer use Figures 2 and 3 to argue *for* coal mining as a major energy source?

Figure 1 Mountaintop coal removal.

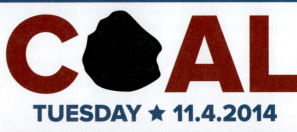

Figure 2 Election sign in support of coal mining.

Figure 3 Miners hard at work.

C. Write an original thesis that includes your position. Then find several sources that include data that would support your argument. Create an original graphic using this data. List all the data sources below your visual.

D. <u>PEER REVIEW</u>. Exchange your thesis and original graphic with a partner. Respond to the questions to evaluate each other's work. For responses marked No, give feedback in the Notes column to help your partner revise.

	Yes	No	Notes
Is the visual labeled correctly as a table or figure?	☐	☐	
Does the title clearly and concisely indicate what the graphic is about?	☐	☐	
Does the title relate to the other labels within the graphic?	☐	☐	
Is the visual relevant to the writer's thesis?	☐	☐	
Is the graphic appropriate for the type of data the writer is presenting?	☐	☐	
Is the graphic easy to understand?	☐	☐	

Go to MyEnglishLab to complete a skill practice.

SUPPORTING SKILL 2
EDIT TEXT AND VISUALS

WHY IT'S USEFUL By editing your text and visuals, you enhance your work's overall appearance and strengthen the clarity and credibility of your ideas. Readers will better understand your work and will find you to be a credible source if you present them with a polished and professional-looking document.

Editing is the final step in the writing process and should not be overlooked. It is important to read your paper one last time to correct any errors you may have missed in earlier revisions. Take your time and systematically look for one type of error at a time. Don't rely on spelling and grammar checkers as they often miss errors and may not correct them accurately. The goal of your edit is to achieve:

- Accuracy: Find and correct minor errors in spelling, grammar, and punctuation.
- Consistent tone: Is your paper formal? Informal? Persuasive? Make sure your overall tone is consistent and reflects your intention.
- Appropriate word choice: Find and correct redundant or unnecessary words and phrases. Also, be sure to review for correct use of gendered and gender-neutral language.
- Logical flow: Make sure that ideas within and between paragraphs and sections of the paper flow logically.

In addition to editing the text, it is also important to review the overall **design**, including visuals. Design elements highlight, emphasize, clarify, or support the text. Look at the list of design elements that will help you produce a clear, professional-looking document.

Color—Using color emphasizes important information by making the information stand out. It is common for writers to use color for headings, text boxes, graphics, and illustrations. When using color, consider these points:

- Do not use too many different colors; this can confuse the reader.
- Use colors sparingly; the more you use them, the less effective they are for emphasizing key information.

- Use colors that complement one another, like red and green or blue and orange. The colors will appear brighter and will draw attention to the information.
- Make sure the colors are visible in both electronic and printed documents.

Repetition—Repeating design elements such as color, headings, columns, and fonts enhances the organization of your document and can help readers understand your ideas. For example, it is helpful to use the same font style and parallel grammatical structures for the same level headings. Notice how these headings are all noun phrases:

- High Incidences of Cancer
- Lung Cancer and Respiratory Diseases
- Cardiovascular Disease and Heart Attacks
- Shortened Lives and Preventable Deaths
- Population Change and Socioeconomic Struggles

Alignment—Placement of text, visuals, and text boxes are alignment considerations that writers need to make. Text can be left- or right-justified or centered and may appear in one, two, or three columns. For papers with a dense amount of text, using columns will increase readability. Left-justified margins are commonly used for academic papers. Text boxes can be useful for highlighting key quotations or adding additional information to the main text.

Placement and Appropriateness of Visuals—Visuals should be sized properly, positioned close to the text they refer to, and labeled and numbered correctly. Graphics should have a title, and images should have captions, both clearly describing the content of the visual. Titles are normally positioned above graphics, whereas captions are listed below an image. In the final reread of your paper, consider whether or not the visuals function appropriately or whether different types of visuals are needed. It is helpful to get a fresh perspective by testing your visuals on someone who is not familiar with your paper. Your visuals should be polished and professional looking.

TIP

Remember to follow the style conventions of the genre and discipline. For example, academic research papers, which tend to have a functional design, will look quite different from a news article on a website.

Notice how the design elements in this paper help to guide the reader.

Internal Combustion Engines and Air Quality

1   Internal combustion engines in vehicles consume petroleum and other liquids such as gasoline, diesel, and fuel oil, and they produce exhaust emissions that result in environmental degradation. As shown in Figure 1, the most common internal combustion engine in automobiles is the four-stroke engine, which completes a four-part cycle of intake, compression, combustion, and exhaust. A crankshaft turns a piston to draw in an air-fuel mixture in the first step, as is illustrated in the diagram. In Step 2, the engine compresses the mixture, causing Step 3, the firing of a spark plug. Finally, as is presented in the diagram, the exhaust valve opens, resulting in the release of exhaust gases into the air through the vehicle's tailpipe.

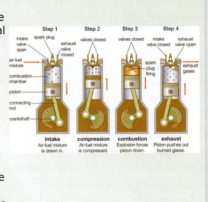

EXERCISE 2

A. Read the passage for general understanding. Then find the sentence-level errors and correct them. Edit the design by adding headings and grouping information appropriately. Compare your edits with a partner and discuss your choices.

Thousands of people die from asthma-related deaths each year. Air pollution, allergens, stress, or chemicals can causes airways to narrow making it difficult for a person to breath. It isn't exactly known why asthma affects some and not others however, researchers and health care professional are helping to alleviate some of the hardships of asthma, making it easier to live with the disease.

The CDC national asthma control program funds programs that help to monitor the prevalence of asthma, training health care professionals, provide self-care education to people with asthma, and educate the public about the disease

As a result of this efforts, asthma data has collected at the state and national levels. Nationally, observation data includes asthma prevalence, activity limitations, work or school absenses due to asthma, medication use, self-care education, doctor and emergency department visits, hospitalizations, and asthma-related deaths. At the state level, asthma observation data contains asthma prevalence in both child and adults.

To maintain this progress, the following critically work must continue: tracking asthma cases, strengthening the capacity of public health offices; training health care professional; implementing interventions; continue to conduct research; and increasing awareness and understanding of the disease.

Through a coordinated effort, the burden of asthma can be alleviated and americans can breathe easier.

B. Look at this graphic. What edits would you make to it? Discuss your choices with a partner.

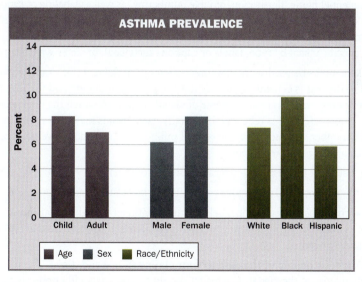

Go to MyEnglishLab to complete a vocabulary exercise and a skill practice.

READING-WRITING CONNECTION
RELATING VISUALS TO TEXT

WHY IT'S USEFUL Writers and researchers in all academic disciplines use visuals to support their theses and ideas. By analyzing the relationship of visuals to text and how writers refer to visuals, you will be able to create appropriate visuals to support your ideas and refer to them in ways that help your reader understand them and their purpose in your text. You will also be able to avoid using irrelevant visuals that are not related to your ideas.

ANALYZING THE RELATIONSHIP OF VISUALS TO TEXT

The goal of using visuals is to **develop ideas** and **display data** in a way that supports and is consistent with a writer's purpose and the claims being made. Analyzing how the visuals relate to the text in a research article will help you successfully incorporate visuals into your own work. Part of reading critically requires analyzing and taking notes on the visuals to determine if the data they contain is **relevant**, **appropriate**, and **useful** as support of the ideas in a research paper.

Visuals, when used well, supplement support; they are not a substitute for support. Visuals enhance understanding; they don't detract from it. Visuals expand or demonstrate a point made in the text or convey abstract ideas presented in the text more clearly. They simplify and organize numerical data and provide evidence in a compact form. However, the relationship between the visuals and the text must be clear.

Visuals don't usually speak for themselves. They require an explanation, analysis, or interpretation to show how they relate to, inform, and support ideas. Examples of appropriate ways to refer to visuals are giving background information; interpreting complex numerical data; explaining the connection between illustrations, images, abstract concepts, and text; and analyzing how data supports or refutes an argument.

REFERRING TO VISUALS

In most cases, unless the relationship between the text and the visuals is very clear, academic writing uses consistent sequential figure, illustration, or table numbering, as well as labeling or captioning each visual. Visuals should be placed as close to the text they relate to as possible, but when this isn't possible, a clear relationship must be established in the text. The reference to the visual can be direct when the writer refers to the specific visual by type, labels or captions the visual, or states what the reader will see.

Visuals can sometimes be used without a direct reference in the text, for example, when the relationship of the visual to the text is evident or the visual is not needed to understand the idea in the text. Photographs or other images are an example of visual support in which the relevance may be clear, and therefore, no direct reference is required. Informally used visuals may or may not include a figure, table, or illustration number, depending on the type of publication. They do, however, typically have a label or caption, especially in a research paper.

When using visuals, it is essential to refer to them appropriately.

1. Make the **purpose and main idea** of the visual clear to the reader.
2. Be as **accurate** as possible. The labels and text that refer to your visuals must correctly represent the relationship of the visuals to your points or claims. If the relationship isn't clear, the visual may be misinterpreted.
3. Make the **relationship of the data to your claims** simple and direct. The reader starts with the text, then looks at the visual. The reader should be able to quickly understand the visual and why it was included.
4. Address the **reliability** of the data in the visuals. The source of the data should be credible, and the reader should know when the data was collected and when the visual was created.
5. Use a **title or caption** that identifies each visual. This information also helps the reader determine the visual's usefulness in supporting the point being made in the text.

6. **Label and number** visuals sequentially and place the visuals as close to the text that refers to them as possible so your reader can quickly find them when relating them to the text.

7. **Cite the source** of the data and / or visual. Credit must always be given to the source(s) of the visual just as you would for print sources. Use an appropriate document style for your discipline and follow the guidelines for labeling and describing visuals.

EXERCISE 3

A. Read the article. Note the use of visuals to support the ideas. Evaluate their relationship to the ideas in the text.

The Effect of Environmental Air Pollution Triggers on Respiratory Illnesses

[1]Epidemiological studies show that poor air quality can greatly exacerbate respiratory illnesses such as asthma and chronic pulmonary disease (COPD) by increasing inflammation and airway constriction in patients. Asthma and COPD sufferers manage these conditions, when possible, by avoiding environmental triggers that cause symptoms and by taking appropriate medication. In addition, new home healthcare devices enable patients to scan the air for critical information about air purity and to gather diagnostic information relevant to assess and prevent acute episodes.

PREVALENT RESPIRATORY ILLNESSES

[2]Asthma, a chronic, noncommunicable respiratory disease characterized by bronchoconstriction and lung passage inflammation, leads to decreased airflow and oxygenation impairment. The disease afflicts some 235 million Americans and is prevalent among children. The illness is influenced by inherent genetic features as well as external environmental exposure to respirable particles and other triggers that irritate the airways and cause an allergic response. Some studies show

evidence of air pollution causing the onset of asthma in addition to being a trigger for it, but research remains inconclusive. Among minority groups and lower socioeconomic groups, asthma is more prevalent, and the cause for this disproportionate relationship also remains unclear. What is evident is the number of cases in children, which has doubled over the past 30 years despite the substantial air pollution-mitigating efforts of the Clean Air Act. The childhood rate of asthma has risen from 3.6 percent in 1980 to 7.5 percent in 1995, and it has climbed further in the 2000s and early 2010s to reach 8.3 percent in 2013 (see Figure 1).

[3]Another lung disease that inhibits breathing is chronic obstructive pulmonary disease (COPD), which occurs when airborne irritants permanently damage lung tissue. The disease manifests as emphysema[1] or chronic bronchitis,[2] and it kills several million people

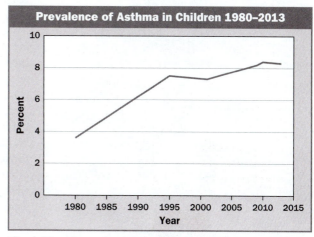

Figure 1 Prevalence of asthma in children 1980–2013.

Continued

---

[1] *Emphysema* is abnormal enlargement of the alveoli with loss of pulmonary elasticity that is characterized especially by shortness of breath.

[2] *Bronchitis* is an inflammation of the bronchial tubes, resulting in chronic coughing.

each year. Chronic obstructive pulmonary disease is preventable, and while the primary cause of the disease is smoking and secondhand smoke, chemical fumes and air pollution are also culpable agents. Both asthma and COPD are found worldwide, and deaths from the illnesses occur disproportionately more in poorer nations where treatment is not readily available.

RESPIRATORY DISEASE TRIGGERS

[4]Numerous studies show a link between exposure to environmental triggers and the exacerbation of asthma and COPD. When episodes of this type are triggered, cells in the respiratory system become inflamed, and airway passages constrict, leaving individuals wheezing, gasping for breath, and in need of medications that open the air passages and reduce inflammation. Figure 2 illustrates the manifold environmental triggers for respiratory illnesses, including cigarette smoke, wood-burning smoke, fumes from common household products, dust mites, mold, pet dander, pollen, and air pollution. Among ambient air pollutants, respirable particulate matter, sulfur dioxide (SO_2), nitrogen oxides [nitric oxide (NO) and nitrogen dioxide (NO_2)] , and tropospheric ozone—or ground-level ozone (O_3)—play a role in exacerbating attacks.

Figure 2 Respiratory disease triggers.

Such pollution originates from combustion engine vehicle exhaust, coal-fired power plants, and other sources.

[5]Epidemiological studies show a correlation between exposure to ground level ozone and inflammatory responses in individuals with respiratory illnesses. In one such study, researchers monitored more than 800 asthmatic children from eight urban areas during peak ozone levels in the summer and found that the children had an increased prevalence of respiratory illness symptoms in the mornings after days during which the ozone level had been higher. Other similar studies show corroborating results, leading major governmental health agencies—including the Environmental Protection Agency and the World Health Organization—to include air pollution in the list of triggers for asthmatic and COPD patients.

[6]While the negative effect of ozone and other air pollutants on respiratory illnesses is conclusive, the fundamental cause for diseases like asthma remains the subject of research and debate. In one of the largest studies on the subject, scientists revealed a causal relationship between long-term exposure to air pollution and the development of COPD. Researchers followed more than 50,000 participants, taking into account their residential addresses and their proximity to heavy traffic over a 35-year period. They found a positive association between higher levels of air pollution at participants' residences and the incidence of COPD. Researchers also took into account factors such as occupation, education level, body mass index, smoking habits, and diet, but still found a positive correlation between proximity to traffic pollution exhaust and the occurrence of COPD, particularly for those who were exposed to greater amounts of air pollution over a longer period of time. Other studies have not been able to draw such a strong causal relationship.

MANAGEMENT AND MONITORING

[7]While residential proximity to air pollution may not be a controllable variable for a patient with a respiratory illness, other environmental triggers may be managed. Simple steps can be

taken to improve air quality in the home, like regularly changing furnace filters, choosing pump sprays instead of aerosol, using natural products without harsh chemicals, eschewing fragrances, and installing a high-efficiency particulate air filter. In addition, a number of new monitors and sensors have been developed to help patients manage their conditions. Handheld, portable nanotube sensors can detect an individual's nitric oxide and oxygen levels to both identify and prevent attacks. Similarly, portable room-monitoring devices can detect air-polluting volatile organic compounds that could trigger an attack. Portable devices, shown in Figure 3, monitor breathing conditions and other physiological conditions of asthmatics and individuals with COPD to help educate both patients and physicians.

[8]Advancements in research and the development of effective screening devices can assist individuals suffering from asthmatic and other respiratory conditions. While individuals often have no control over ambient air-quality conditions, they can monitor environmental air pollution triggers to help avoid respiratory distress. Preventative asthma therapy and improved treatment options aid the goal of reducing the overall disease mortality rate.

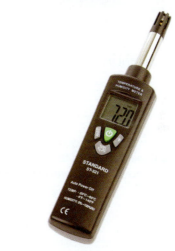

Figure 3 Air-pollution monitoring devices. The top photograph shows a wearable device; the bottom photo shows a portable, hand-held device.

B. Answer the questions.

1. What point is Figure 1 supporting? Find the text that refers to the graph. What information does the text provide to help the reader understand the data in the graph? Do you think the graph supports the point? Could the text explain the information better than the graph does? Is there a better visual for the purpose?

   ....

   ....

   ....

2. What point is being made in Figure 2? Find the text that refers to the illustration. How is the illustration introduced in the text? Do you think the illustration enhances the reader's understanding of environmental triggers of respiratory illnesses?

   ....

   ....

   ....

3. What point is Figure 3 supporting? Find the text that refers to the photos. How are the photos introduced in the text? Are the photos necessary to the reader's understanding of monitoring equipment? Are there different photos that would serve the same purpose?

....

....

....

4. The article doesn't include a table. Do you see a place for a table that would help the reader see a point that wasn't illustrated in Figures 1, 2, or 3? Write a brief reference to the table.

....

....

....

5. Is there a visual that doesn't add anything to the ideas in the article? Explain.

....

....

....

C. **What visual could be added to further support an idea in the article? Briefly describe the visual and write a reference to it. Note where you would add it to the text.**

....

....

....

D. **Discuss your answers in Part B and share your idea for a visual in Part C with a partner.**

EXERCISE 4

Read the visuals for general understanding. Then answer the questions.

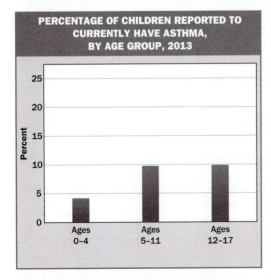

PERCENTAGE OF CHILDREN REPORTED TO CURRENTLY HAVE ASTHMA, BY AGE GROUP, 2013

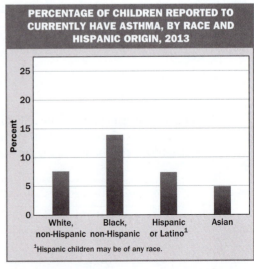

PERCENTAGE OF CHILDREN REPORTED TO CURRENTLY HAVE ASTHMA, BY RACE AND HISPANIC ORIGIN, 2013

[1] Hispanic children may be of any race.

TABLE 1 Percentage of children, ages birth through 17, who were reported to currently have asthma: 2001–2013

	2005	2007	2009	2011	2013
Total	8.9	9.1	9.6	9.5	8.3
Gender					
Male	10.0	9.7	11.3	10.2	9.3
Female	7.8	8.5	7.9	8.8	7.3
Race and Hispanic origin[1]					
White one race, non-Hispanic	7.9	7.3	8.5	7.8	7.6
Black one race, non-Hispanic	13.1	15.4	17.0	16.3	13.9
Hispanic or Latino	8.6	9.3	7.7	9.6	7.4
American Indian or Alaska Native	13.6	7.7	7.1	8.1	4.9
Asian	6.5	7.4	7.7	7.0	4.9
Age group					
Ages 0–4	6.8	6.8	6.3	6.9	4.2
Ages 5–11	9.9	8.8	10.7	9.9	9.8
Ages 12–17	9.6	11.4	11.2	11.4	9.9
Poverty status					
Below poverty	11.2	11.7	13.7	12.6	11.8
100%–199% above poverty	9.0	10.6	9.5	10.4	8.2
200+% above poverty	9.1	8.2	8.4	8.0	7.1
Region					
Northeast	10.1	10.9	11.1	11.4	9.3
Midwest	8.5	9.3	10.9	8.3	7.3
South	9.2	9.0	9.8	9.7	9.1
West	7.9	7.8	7.1	8.6	7.4

[1] Hispanic children may be of any race.

1. What information do the bar graphs provide? Write a brief explanation of the data. Is there anything missing? ....

....

....

....

....

2. What information does the table provide? Write a brief explanation of the data. Is there anything missing? ....

....

....

....

....

3. Compare the bar graphs in Figures 1 and 2 to Table 1. Which visual provides more information? Which provides information in the clearest way? ....

....

....

....

....

4. The author of the article "The Effect of Environmental Air Pollution Triggers on Respiratory Illnesses" will use the bar graphs and the table to support the claim that there are demographic differences in children who suffer from asthma. Write one to three sentences for the article that refer to the bar graphs and help the reader see their usefulness to the paper.

....

....

....

5. Write one to three sentences that refer the reader to the table and help the reader interpret the table. ....

....

....

....

Go to MyEnglishLab to complete a vocabulary exercise and a skill practice and join in collaborative activities.

For more about RELATING VISUALS TO TEXT, see W and OC ENVIRONMENTAL ENGINEERING .

LANGUAGE SKILLS
EXAMINING SENTENCE STRUCTURE AND SUBJECT-VERB AGREEMENT

WHY IT'S USEFUL Subject-verb agreement is using the correct form of the verb for the subject of a sentence. By using correct verb forms, you avoid confusing your reader.

Explanation	Example
The verb or verb phrase agrees with the subject in person (first, second, third) and in number (singular or plural). In English, with the exception of *be,* subject-verb agreement is required only with simple present forms where the choice is base form or base form plus -s. *Subject-verb agreement does not apply to modals, nonfinite verb forms such as the -ing form, or imperatives.* In writing, the key to accuracy and the challenge with subject-verb agreement is knowing what the **subject** is and whether the subject is singular or plural. The subject will always be a noun or noun phrase.	Air pollution **exacerbates** respiratory illnesses. Triggers **initiate** asthma attacks. Air pollution **can exacerbate** respiratory illness Triggers **can initiate** asthma attacks.
Singular, plural, and noncount nouns Common nouns can be count or noncount. Count nouns can be singular or plural. Take special note of irregular singular nouns that end in -s and irregular plural nouns that do not end in -s.	Environmental phenomena **are** being studied by scientists. (Irregular plural form not ending in -s) Mathematics **is** required for anyone entering the field of Engineering. (Irregular singular noun ending in -s)
Noncount nouns, collective nouns (especially in American English), titles, and gerund phrases are singular.	Air pollution **has** contributed to many deaths from respiratory illnesses. (noncount noun) The staff **is** compiling the data. (collective noun) The New York Times **has** an article on air pollution in Asia. (title) Breathing **is** impacted by air pollution. (gerund)
Indefinite pronouns Although they seem to have plural meaning, indefinite pronouns are singular in formal English. (The pronoun *they* is commonly used for a person whose gender is unspecified or unknown in speech, but it is being used more frequently in writing.)	Anybody **is** susceptible to the effects of air pollution. Everybody **benefits** from clean air. Someone **succumbs** to respiratory illness and **is** hospitalized every day. Each **is** a trigger that may cause an attack. The director of research is doing a new study. They **are** going to focus on people over the age of 65.
Relative pronouns When you use a relative pronoun as the subject of a dependent clause, the verb agrees with the antecedent—the noun that appears earlier in the sentence.	People who **have** respiratory illnesses are susceptible to pollutants. People with COPD can use a monitor, which **alerts** them to high levels of ozone. The ability to breathe is one of the things that **are** monitored.

Continued

Explanation	Example
Compound subjects Most subjects with *and* are plural except when the parts form a single unit. Nouns with *each* and *every* are singular.	**plural subject** Aerosols and dust **contribute** to air pollution. **single unit** Anger and anxiety **is** common among those who struggle to breathe. **singular nouns** Every man, woman, or child **is** affected by air pollution.
With *either/or* and *neither/nor*, make the verb agree with whichever subject is nearer. If one subject is singular and the other plural, putting the plural last is best.	Neither asthma nor COPD **is** communicable. Either pollution or dust mites **are** the trigger that caused her asthma attack.
Subjects following verbs The verb agrees with the subject even when it follows the verb. The verb agrees with the subject and not the subject complement.	There **is** a relationship between air pollutants and asthma attacks. A common air pollutant **is** particles in the air. A monitor and meter **are** equipment that measures air pollution.
Subjects separated from verbs The verb agrees with the subject, not words that come between, including phrases like *as well as, in addition to, accompanied by, together with,* and *along with.* It is easy when writing to lose sight of the subject. A good way to determine the subject is to ask the questions, *Who is?* or *What is?*	The samples on the tray **need** to be analyzed. High levels of air pollution **exacerbate** respiratory illnesses. The scientist, along with his research team, **was** on the trip.
Expressions of quantity and measurements Expressions of quantity and measurement can take either a singular or plural verb, depending on whether the subject following *of* is singular or plural. *All of, both of, some of, most of, many of, much of, a lot of, a number of, few/a few of, little/ a little of and none of* (meaning "not one" is singular), *50 percent of, two of, a great deal of, hardly any of, thousands of, one-fourth of, two inches of, three kilos of*	All of the children in the study **have** asthma. All of the air **was** polluted. A few of the triggers **are** avoidable. Little of the pollution **is** from factories due to government controls. Three-fourths of the pollution **comes** from cars. Ten percent of children in that region **were** diagnosed with asthma. Two pounds of particles **were** emitted by the factory each week. A milliliter of that medicine **is** the proper dose for her asthma.
Expressions of time, distance, amount, and percent (money, weight, length) used as the subject usually take a singular verb if the reference is to a single measure or quantity. *Five pounds **is*** *Three days **is*** *A hundred dollars **is*** *20 miles **is***	Four days **is** a long time to wait if you are having trouble breathing. Doctors say that 100 meters **is** too far to walk when a person has COPD. They believe that 10 percent **is** too high a percentage of children with asthma.
Adjectives used as nouns Adjectives used as plural nouns take a plural verb. *The poor, the rich, the sick, the French, etc.*	The poor **are** more susceptible to respiratory illnesses. The English **are** as interested in pollution controls as other Europeans.

EXERCISE 5

Circle the subject(s) of each sentence and decide whether each is singular or plural. Underline all quantifiers and measurement expressions. Write the correct form of each numbered verb in parentheses. Compare your answers with a partner and discuss why this verb form was used.

Asthma .... (1. be) one of the most common chronic illnesses that .... (2. affect) children. It .... (3. be) estimated that seven million children under the age of 18 .... (4. have) asthma. Asthma is .... (5. be) a leading cause of hospitalization among children. Millions of lost school days .... (6. be) associated with asthma as well. The combination of absence and potential emergencies in the classroom .... (7. reduce) student productivity and can negatively affect children's performance in school. There .... (8. be) several factors that .... (9. have) been linked to asthma. A number .... (10. be) environmental. Many studies .... (11. have) linked exposure to air pollution and second-hand cigarette smoke to asthma, but neither of these .... (12. be) a proven cause. Asthma in children .... (13. be) controllable by using medication and avoiding triggers such as indoor and outdoor pollution that .... (14. bring on) an attack. After a steady increase from the 1980s to the mid-1990s, the number of children with asthma .... (15. have) remained steady over the past decade—between eight and ten percent. It is estimated in 2013 that eight percent of children .... (16. have) asthma. More older children .... (17. have) asthma than younger children, but some of the difference .... (18. be) probably due to undiagnosed asthma in younger children. Asthma is most common in children who .... (19. live) in families with incomes below the federal poverty level. The poor often .... (20. live) in areas with higher levels of known pollutants and other environmental triggers.

EXERCISE 6

Edit the paragraph for subject-verb agreement errors. Find the mistake, cross it out, and write the correct form above. There are six errors in the paragraph.

Air pollution is anything introduced into the air by people that have a damaging effect on the environment. There is different kinds of air pollution. Carbon dioxide is a greenhouse gas that is warming the earth. While carbon dioxide is emitted by living organisms, it is considered a pollutant when cars, factories, and other human activities that involve fossil fuel emits it into the air. Sulfur dioxide, a component of smog, is another source of pollution. Sulfur dioxide, like other similar chemicals, cause acid rain. Sulfur dioxide in the atmosphere reflects light. Sulfur dioxide, associated most often with volcanic eruptions, also cool the earth. While volcanoes were once the main source of sulfur dioxide, today the activity of people are. Most countries today are working to reduce the level of these substances put into the air by human activity.

Go to MyEnglishLab to complete skill practices.

APPLY YOUR SKILLS

WHY IT'S USEFUL By applying the skills you have learned in this unit, you can successfully create and use visuals to enhance support for your ideas and edit your work for greater accuracy and visual appeal.

ASSIGNMENT

How does air pollution affect peoples' respiratory health? Prepare a manuscript for publication on the influence of air pollution on respiratory health. Research a case study that focuses on a particular area and how pollution has affected its population. Summarize the aim and results of the study, and create an original visual that illustrates the effects of air pollution on this community. Provide a caption for the visual. Edit your summary and visual.

BEFORE YOU WRITE

A. Before you begin your assignment, discuss these questions with one or more students.

    1. Given the connection of air pollution to respiratory illness, what can we do to decrease the environmental effects of air pollution so that everyone benefits?

    2. Why is decreasing the environmental effects of air pollution of importance to everybody—even those without respiratory illness?

B. As you consider your assignment, complete the tasks below. Then, share your ideas with another student. Get feedback and revise your ideas, if necessary.

    1. Briefly share the case study you chose to research.

        a. Area and how pollution affects the population ....

        b. Aim and results of the study ....

    2. Discuss any visuals that were used in the study.

    3. Brainstorming—List ideas for the visual you will create. Share your ideas with a partner.

C. Review the Unit Skills Summary. As you begin on the writing task on page 122, apply the skills you learned in this unit.

UNIT SKILLS SUMMARY

Use visuals to present information in writing
- Understand the purpose of different types of visuals.
- Locate and create original visuals to support the text.

Edit text and visuals
- Edit the text and visuals of a document for accuracy.
- Edit the design elements of a paper to increase readability.

Relate visuals to text
- Use appropriate visuals to support ideas.
- Refer to visuals effectively in your writing to clarify how the visual supports your message.

Examine sentence structure and subject-verb agreement
- Use the correct verb form for the subject of a sentence to avoid confusion.

THINKING CRITICALLY

Discuss the questions about the case study you have found with another student. Get feedback and revise your ideas if necessary.

1. Is your case study transferable to other areas?

2. Are pollution problems in a specific area of concern to all of us?

3. If you were to conduct a follow-up study in this area, what would the aim of your study be and why?

THINKING VISUALLY

A. Look at the graph from the National Health Interview Survey. Write one or two sentences that refer to the graph and help readers understand the data and its relevance to one of your points.

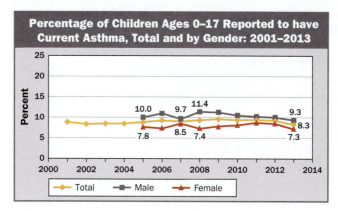

Percentage of Children Ages 0–17 Reported to have Current Asthma, Total and by Gender: 2001–2013

B. Now find (or create) another graph that provides information relevant to your assignment. Write a citation for this source.

THINKING ABOUT LANGUAGE

Read the passage. Underline the noun that is the subject of each verb in parentheses, and circle the verb form that agrees with the subject.

A number of studies [have/has] shown a link between COPD and air pollution.

A study in Denmark found that exposure to air pollution caused by traffic over a long period of time [is/are] linked to an increase in the likelihood of developing COPD. Over 35 years of data [was/were] analyzed. Another study in Australia also found that poor air quality [contribute/contributes] to COPD. That study compared the mortality rates of two towns in Australia that [was/were] burning wood. When one town reduced smoke from burning wood and other organic matter, the number of COPD deaths [was/were] lower. Today, many years of regulation [mean/means] that outdoor ambient air pollution in the United States [is/are] not as great a concern to COPD sufferers. However, pollutants in indoor air [is/are] increasing due to use of aerosol products and the chemicals in many household cleaners. Doctors suggest that people at risk for COPD [avoid/avoids] exposure to these irritants.

WRITE

A. Revisit the assignment and your answers to the questions in Before You Write Part B. Identify a case study that describes the respiratory health effects of air pollution on a particular area that you would like to research.

B. Research this case and locate information and visuals (or data for visuals) that support your position. Create a thesis statement of the aim of the study and an outline of the results for your summary.

....

....

....

C. Summarize the study using your thesis and outline in Part B. Create a visual. Write text that refers to the visual. Then revise and edit as necessary.

> **BEYOND THE ASSIGNMENT**
>
> Write a research paper. Analyze the effects of air pollution on a particular area. Include data, both text and visual, to support your analysis. Use all the skills you learned in this unit.

▶ Go to MyEnglishLab to listen to Professor Clerici-Arias and to complete a self-assessment.

PART
2

Critical
Thinking Skills

Part 2 moves from skill building to application of the skills that require critical thinking. Practice activities tied to specific learning outcomes in each unit require a deeper level of understanding the academic content.

SOCIOLOGY

Fact and Opinion

UNIT PROFILE

Civil disobedience is the refusal to obey governmental demands or commands, especially as a nonviolent and usually collective means of forcing concessions from the government to right wrongs. In this unit, you will be introduced to the topic of civil disobedience; specifically, you will learn about the sit-ins and Freedom Rides which occurred during the American civil rights movement. You will also learn about the Salt March and the March to Selma, led by famous civil rights leaders, Mahatma Ghandi and Martin Luther King Jr.

You will use facts and opinions to construct an analysis in a research paper. Choose an event or moment in a civil rights movement. Examine whether your subject was successful in achieving its goal. Take a position, research facts, and evaluate opinions to support your claims.

OUTCOMES

- Support claims with facts and opinions
- Evaluate others' opinions
- Distinguish fact and opinion and make claims
- Signpost facts and opinions

GETTING STARTED

▶ Go to MyEnglishLab to listen to Professor Greenberg and to complete a self-assessment.

Discuss these questions with a partner or group.

1. Look at the photo of one of the most famous acts of civil disobedience in American history: the 1965 Selma to Montgomery march. Have you ever participated in an act of civil disobedience? If so, describe the event and discuss the outcome. Was it successful?

2. How did groups organize for acts of civil disobedience prior to having the Internet and social media as means to reach out to others? Has the technology made it easier to engage in civil disobedience or not?

3. Do you agree that nonviolent acts of civil disobedience can be as effective as more dramatic, even violent measures? Why or why not?

For more about **SOCIOLOGY,** see **2** **3**. See also R and OC **SOCIOLOGY** **1** **2** **3**.

CRITICAL THINKING SKILL
USING FACTS AND OPINIONS IN RESEARCH WRITING

WHY IT'S USEFUL By using facts and opinions in your research writing, you can make your claims stronger. Including relevant and accurate facts also adds to your readers' understanding of the topic. Opinions that are based on factual evidence and the opinions of experts provide strong support for your ideas.

In academic writing, it is essential to back up your ideas with support that is convincing to your readers. Both facts and opinions are commonly used as support for claims in research papers.

Facts are ideas and pieces of information that are generally accepted as true. Facts are observable, verifiable, and based on evidence. Facts are often presented as statistics and other numerical data that can be seen or proven to be true as long as the methods used to gather the information are sound. Facts can also include testimonies of participants and witnesses. Reports of events from the viewpoint of a participant or eyewitness create vivid and powerful images for the reader. Facts give strong support for your ideas in a research paper, but facts alone are not sufficient to convince a reader of the claims you have made. Facts must be appropriate, fit the context, and help you draw conclusions to fully support claims in research.

Types of Facts	Example
Verifiable data	The majority of acts of civil disobedience of the Civil Rights movement occurred between 1954 and 1968.
Statistics	African Americans made up 21% of the population of the South in 1960.
Testimony	"I remember being grabbed up by my belt and thrown to the floor and dragged out of the store," said Clarence Graham, a Friendship Nine member.

Opinions are ideas that people have about a subject. Opinions can be strong support for claims in academic work, but they must be supported; otherwise, they may not have the power to convince a reader. **Supported opinions** are based on evidence or in-depth study or analysis. Supported opinions are judgments based on factual evidence, but they are not always completely verifiable. The opinions of experts in a given field are supported opinions when the expert is considered to have knowledge gained through in-depth study of a topic. Supported opinions represent a sincere and honest effort to draw a logical or reasonable conclusion from data. Opinions are changeable, depending on how evidence is interpreted, so opinions used alone, just like facts, are not always considered adequate proof in research. You should always demonstrate to your reader that the opinions you use are supported in some way.

Types of Opinions	Example	Explanation
Evidence-based opinion	The sit-ins at lunch counters across the South during the Civil Rights movement caused immediate change, which is why many believe they had the greatest impact.	There is factual evidence about the changes that resulted from the sit-ins to support the opinion that sit-ins had the greatest impact.
Expert opinion	Nick Gier, Professor Emeritus at the University of Idaho, identified several principles of civil disobedience and stated that "the first principle is that you maintain respect for the rule of law even while disobeying the specific law that you perceive as unjust." Using sit-ins and refusing to leave was an act of disobeying a specific law that was unjust in the eyes of the participants of the sit-ins.	An expert who has studied the topic extensively supports the idea that sit-ins were acts that disobeyed a specific unjust law.

Opinions that can be used to **support a claim** in academic writing should not be confused with beliefs. Beliefs are ideas based on faith, morals, and values, whether personal or cultural. Even though beliefs express an opinion, they are not based on facts or evidence. They cannot be proved or disproved or even contested in a logical way. Therefore, while often used in writing to appeal to a reader's emotions, they are generally not considered acceptable support for claims in most academic work.

Types of Beliefs	Example
Based on personal morals	Discrimination is morally wrong.
Based on cultural value	Men and women should be segregated because this is what is done in my culture.
Based on faith	There is a higher power that we all must answer to.

Facts, when accurate and appropriate, and **supported opinions that are evaluated** carefully used together offer valid and credible support for claims made in a research paper.

NOTICING ACTIVITY

Notice the highlighted text in the introduction to a research paper on the use of sit-ins during the American Civil Rights movement. Which color is highlighting facts? Which color is highlighting opinions?

The Civil Rights movement in the US had as one of its primary goals to end racial segregation and discrimination against black Americans. Several acts of civil disobedience of the Civil Rights movement occurred between 1954 and 1968. The most commonly used nonviolent acts of civil disobedience were boycotts, marches, and sit-ins. While people are more likely to recall Rosa Parks' refusal to give up her seat and move to the back of the bus, which led to the Montgomery boycotts in 1955 and the marches such as the March to Selma in 1965, sit-ins may have actually had the greatest impact. In many cases, sit-ins resulted in businesses making rapid changes to policies that discriminated against African Americans. The sit-ins at lunch counters across the South during the Civil Rights movement caused immediate change, so many believe they had the greatest impact.

Go to MyEnglishLab to complete a vocabulary exercise and a skill practice and join in collaborative activities.

SUPPORTING SKILL 1
SUPPORTING CLAIMS WITH FACTS AND OPINIONS

WHY IT'S USEFUL By using both facts and opinions to support your claims, you can write a convincing argument. Providing enough factual data shows your reader that you have carefully researched your topic. Supporting your ideas with well-thought-out and appropriate opinions presents your ideas as reasoned judgments that draw appropriate conclusions.

Facts and supported opinions provide convincing evidence to support claims made in a research paper.

Using Fact	Using Opinion
Present verifiable and observable facts based on evidence that are:	Provide supported opinions that draw from clearly stated evidence or factual data and / or expertise of the person providing the opinion that:
• Accurate • Relevant (address or have a bearing on the controlling idea of your claim) • Appropriate (specific to your topic)	• Draw logical and reasoned conclusions • Are not overly biased • Are not beliefs based solely on personal or cultural faith or morals, which cannot be proved or disproved

A blend of factual data and supported opinion that fit together provide the best support for your claims in a paper. Notice how the facts and opinions below can be improved to better support this claim:

> **Claim:** As nonviolent acts of civil disobedience, sit-ins were highly effective in bringing about immediate change to the policies of businesses that segregated African Americans.

Original Fact	Problem	Improvement
The Greensboro sit-in started when more than 20 students sat at the Woolworth lunch counter.	This fact is not accurate.	The Greensboro sit-in started when four college students sat at the Woolworth lunch counter. (The number of students who sat at the Woolworth counter is now correct.)
The Greensboro students were all men.	While this might be accurate, the gender of the students has no bearing on the intent of the claim, which is to prove that sit-ins were effective in bringing about change.	The Greensboro students dressed neatly, were respectful and sat quietly. (This illustrates how the students participating in the sit-in appeared and behaved which is relevant to the sit-in as an example of an act of nonviolent civil disobedience.)
Sit-ins have been used for other causes.	This fact is not relevant since it does not contribute to supporting the claim about changes to segregation policies.	Sit-ins to protest segregation spread to other cities in North Carolina and then to other states. (Delete the original fact and replace with an appropriate one. The fact that the sit-ins spread to other cities is appropriate as it supports the idea that they were effective.)

Original Opinion	Problem	Improvement
Sit-ins had a major effect on the community.	While this opinion may be a logical and reasoned conclusion, there is nothing in the text to support it.	Panelists at a program, co-sponsored by the NAACP Nashville and the First Amendment Center, focusing on how the news media covered the early civil rights movement in Nashville, agreed that the sit-ins had a major effect on the community. (This is a logical and reasoned conclusion because it is supported by factual data and evidence and agreed upon by a group of experts.)
It was a big news story.	Without information about who said this and to show that this statement is based on factual data and evidence, this opinion may appear overly biased.	"It was a big news story," said First Amendment Center Founder John Seigenthaler, who was a reporter at *The Tennessean* when the sit-ins occurred. [This does not appear overly biased because it is based on the testimony of someone who witnessed the event and is now considered an expert.]
Sit-ins are a great idea and inspire others.	This opinion is a belief, because as stated, it is not provable.	Commenting on the fact that sit-ins spread to other cities in the South, Historian Linda Wynn of the Tennessee Historical Commission said, "The success of Nashville's highly organized movement was both a model and an inspiration to other cities." (This is not a belief because it is based on factual evidence and expressed by a person whose expertise is clearly stated in the text.)

EXERCISE 1

A. Read the excerpt from "Greensboro Sit-Ins" What claim is being made? Underline it. What facts are presented in support of the claim? Highlight the facts. Check your answers with a partner.

As nonviolent acts of civil disobedience, sit-ins—the occupation of an area by a group as a protest to promote change—were highly effective in bringing about immediate revisions to the policies of businesses that segregated African Americans. Many sit-ins occurred in the late '50s and early '60s, primarily in the South. Sit-ins clearly contributed to the overall strategy of using civil disobedience to lead to the passage of the Civil Rights Act of 1964, which ended legal racial segregation in the United States. However, it was the sit-ins' immediate effect in breaking down the barriers at the local level that may have been their greatest contribution.

While not the first sit-in, the sit-in in Greensboro, North Carolina on February 1, 1960, is a good example of an act of civil disobedience that resulted in a policy change in a short period of time. The Greensboro sit-in began with four university students who sat at a Woolworth lunch counter and stayed until closing even though they were refused service and asked to leave by the manager. The Greensboro Four, as they were later called, returned the next day accompanied by more than twenty students and by the fourth day, there were more than 300 students participating, and the sit-in had spread to another store.

Initially, Woolworth, then a national chain of five-and-dime stores, held firm that it would allow individual stores to follow local customs and keep their policies. But in May of 1960, after the Greensboro store had suffered major losses, Woolworth began to serve all customers at its lunch

> **CULTURE NOTE**
> Founded by John Seigenthaler, the **First Amendment Center** is an operating program of the Freedom Forum and is associated with the Newseum and the Diversity Institute.

counters and desegregated its stores. Some individual stores continued to discriminate against customers based on race, though. A portion of the Greensboro sit-in lunch counter is now in the Smithsonian.

Another factor in the effectiveness of the sit-ins was the attention they received. The media covered the sit-ins and raised national awareness of the reality of segregation in the region. The sit-ins resulted in a wave of other similar actions across the South. Within a week of the first sit-in in Greensboro, sit-ins began to occur in other North Carolina cities. Then, the movement spread to other states in the South. In Nashville, Tennessee, students started sit-ins just a few days after the Greensboro students and also achieved desegregation of store lunch counters by May 1960. In many towns, the sit-ins resulted in ending segregation of lunch counters and other public places.

> **CULTURE NOTE**
>
> **F. W. Woolworth Company** *Often referred to as Woolworth's, or Woolworth, the F.W. Woolworth Company was a nation-wide chain of stores in the United States that was very popular in the first half of the 20th century. Woolworth, and other stores like it, are called* **five-and-dime stores***, which means they sold a wide variety of inexpensive household and personal items and often had an area that sold food commonly referred to as a lunch counter.*

> **CULTURE NOTE**
>
> **The Smithsonian Institution** *The Smithsonian Institution established in 1846 is a group of museums and research centers administered by the government of the United States. It is a high honor to be included in the Smithsonian, as exhibits are seen as the ultimate representation of American history and heritage.*

US cities where sit-ins where staged, 1955–1961

Thus, the Greensboro sit-in and those that both preceded and followed it were instrumental in bringing about more immediate change than other acts of civil disobedience used during the Civil Rights movement.

B. Read the practice assignment. Reread the excerpt in Part A and answer the questions to support the claim you underlined in the excerpt.

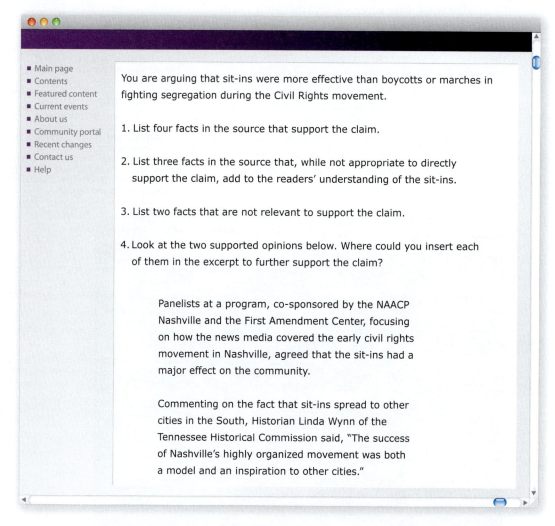

- Main page
- Contents
- Featured content
- Current events
- About us
- Community portal
- Recent changes
- Contact us
- Help

You are arguing that sit-ins were more effective than boycotts or marches in fighting segregation during the Civil Rights movement.

1. List four facts in the source that support the claim.

2. List three facts in the source that, while not appropriate to directly support the claim, add to the readers' understanding of the sit-ins.

3. List two facts that are not relevant to support the claim.

4. Look at the two supported opinions below. Where could you insert each of them in the excerpt to further support the claim?

> Panelists at a program, co-sponsored by the NAACP Nashville and the First Amendment Center, focusing on how the news media covered the early civil rights movement in Nashville, agreed that the sit-ins had a major effect on the community.

> Commenting on the fact that sit-ins spread to other cities in the South, Historian Linda Wynn of the Tennessee Historical Commission said, "The success of Nashville's highly organized movement was both a model and an inspiration to other cities."

C. Discuss your responses in Part B in a small group. Do you agree with the other students' answers? If you were writing this article, what other facts and opinions could you use to support the claim?

Go to MyEnglishLab to complete a vocabulary exercise and a skill practice and join in collaborative activities.

SUPPORTING SKILL 2
EVALUATING OTHERS' OPINIONS

WHY IT'S USEFUL By evaluating the opinions of others to support claims in a research paper, you ensure that you are supporting your ideas with opinions that are valid. You also show the reader how reasoned and well-thought out judgments will help you prove your points.

When using opinion as support in academic work, it is important that the opinions be supported. As stated on page 127, supported opinions are opinions based on factual data, evidence, and / or careful study and analysis, usually by an expert or someone who is knowledgeable about the topic. When opinions draw conclusions, they should be logical and reasoned judgments based on facts and evidence.

When **evaluating opinions to include as support in your paper**, you need to consider several factors:

Who is the person expressing the opinion? Is the person an expert? What is the person's expertise based on?	Opinions provided by experts who are knowledgeable in their field and have studied the topic extensively can effectively support a claim.
Are there others who agree with the opinion?	When opinions are corroborated, that is, held by more than one expert, the opinion's validity is strengthened.
Are there others who disagree? Can their opinions be countered?	When opposing views are addressed, it shows that those ideas have been considered.
When was the opinion expressed?	Opinions expressed at the time of an event may differ from those expressed after time has passed. Consider how time may have altered the views of the person expressing the opinion.
What is the source of the opinion?	As with any source, you need to evaluate its reliability. The place where the opinion is published may be biased, or the opinion may have already been challenged.
What factual data or evidence is mentioned to support the opinion?	Factual data and/or evidence strengthen an opinion.
What are the assumptions on which the opinion is based?	If the assumption underlying a claim is a belief that can't be proved or disproved, then the opinions themselves most likely are not debatable either.
Is the opinion appropriate and relevant to support the claim?	Like facts, the opinions used to support a claim should be specific to the topic of the claim (appropriate) and address the controlling idea of the claim rather than stating generalities about the topic (relevant).
Are conclusions logical and based on evidence?	If the opinions are conclusions that have been drawn about the claim, they must be accompanied by evidence to support them that shows that they are logical and reasonable judgments and conclusions.

> For more on evaluating sources and organizing research, see ECONOMICS, Part 1, 2.

Look at opinions and the explanation of why one is supported and one is not.

Opinion	Evaluation
Claim Early in the civil rights movement, the potential of nonviolent resistance to fight segregation was recognized by its leaders. James Farmer, the founder of the Congress of Racial Equality, CORE, co-organized what was one of the first sit-ins, which took place in Chicago in 1942. He reported in an interview on NPR in 1975 that he believed that the timing was right to adapt Mahatma Gandhi's technique of nonviolent resistance and saw the use of the sit-in as an experiment in applying these techniques to segregation in the United States.	**Supported** • It is expressed by an expert. • It contains factual data and his testimony as a participant. • It expresses a logical and reasonable judgment and conclusion. • It is from a reliable source.
Claim The Civil Rights Act of 1964 should be rescinded. Many Americans believe that because the civil rights movement eliminated segregation in the United States, there is no further need for the protections afforded by the Civil Rights Act of 1964!	**Not supported** • It is not from an expert, and the phrase *many Americans* is too vague. • It makes a conclusion based on an assumption that cannot be proved or disproved. • It has no evidence or factual data to support the conclusion that it draws. • No source is given.

EXERCISE 2

A. Read the passage about the Rock Hill sit-in. What claim is being made? Underline it. Find the two supported opinions expressed in the second paragraph. Highlight them. Check your answers with a partner.

The sit-ins that occurred during the American Civil Rights movement as a form of nonviolent civil disobedience were having an impact and leading to the desegregation of businesses in the South. They were, however, costly to the movement. Many of the students who sat at lunch counters were being arrested, and the cost of bail and fines were factors as the student groups did not have sufficient funds to pay them all. The sit-in at the McCrory's lunch counter in Rock Hill, South Carolina on January 31, 1961, brought an important change through a new strategy called "Jail, No Bail." Through the decision to use a new strategy of accepting jail sentences rather than bailing out, the Rock Hill sit-in most likely contributed to the success of the civil rights movement and may even have saved it.

The "Jail, No Bail" strategy reduced the costs groups were facing as the movement spread and more students joined the sit-in movement. The nine students, referred to later as the Friendship Nine, who were picketing McCrory's to protest segregation policies, were arrested when they sat down at the lunch counter and refused to leave. The next day, the nine students and an organizer were convicted of trespassing and sentenced to 30 days hard labor or a $100.00 fine. Eight students and the organizer chose to do the jail time. In his Pulitzer Prize-winning book about the civil rights movement, *Parting the Waters: America in the King Years 1954–1963,* Taylor Branch expressed his opinion that the students' decision was in response to the problem of limited funds which he said was crippling the movement. Political Science Professor Adolphus Belk Jr. of Winthrop University concurs that the decision of the Friendship Nine rescued the civil rights movement, which was running out of money, by shifting the financial cost to the system. He went so far as to suggest that if the students hadn't been willing to do this, the sit-in movement would have died.

> **CULTURE NOTE**
> *McCrory Stores* or *J.G. McCrory's*
> Like Woolworth, McCrory Stores or J.G. McCrory's was a chain of five-and-dime stores that included lunch counters.

Friendship Nine members stand in front of a historical commemorative marker in Rock Hill, South Carolina, December 2014.

B. Write a brief evaluation of the two opinions you highlighted in Part A. Why are they supported? Consider the questions in the chart on page 131 and give specific information from the excerpt.

....

....

....

....

....

C. Work with a partner. Discuss your evaluations of the opinions in Part B.

Go to MyEnglishLab to complete a vocabulary exercise and a skill practice and join in collaborative activities.

READING-WRITING CONNECTION
DISTINGUISHING FACTS AND OPINIONS AND MAKING CLAIMS

WHY IT'S USEFUL By distinguising fact and opinion, you can more easily detect bias in writing, which is critical for determining how reliable a source's information is. When making claims about a subject, it is important to support your point of view by using a balance of factual evidence and supported opinion from more than one source.

As stated earlier, a **fact** is information that is based on a known truth, whereas an **opinion** is based on a personal belief or judgment. When reading texts, you should analyze whether or not writers are supporting their claims with both facts and supported opinions. If you find little factual support or evidence, it is highly likely that the writer is biased toward a particular view and has based the text's claims largely on personal beliefs as opposed to factual support or expert opinions.

When analyzing a writer's claims, ask these questions:

- Are the claims supported by both facts and opinions?
- Are the opinions supported with evidence?
- Are the opinions mostly positive, negative, or neutral?
- What is the purpose of the text? To argue, inform, entertain, or so on?
- What do you know about the writer?
- Based on this information, do you think the writer's claims are reliable?

The claims you make throughout a paper should support your central thesis. When **making claims**, it is essential that they be debatable. Writers are responsible for proving that their claims are true by supporting them with facts, expert opinion, quotations, and/or statistical data. Remember, claims should not include one's personal beliefs as these are not arguable.

When supporting your claims, it is more effective to refer to more than one expert in the field. Your claims are stronger when you can support them with multiple sources. Also, in addition to having a variety of facts and opinions and sources of evidence, it is essential that the information you use to support your claims is both appropriate and relevant to your argument.

EXERCISE 3

Read the claims. Which claim is more effective? Why?

Claim 1	Claim 2
"Although some acts of nonviolent civil disobedience have brought about positive social change, the risks far outweigh any potential benefits of using this method."	"Acts of nonviolent civil disobedience have been used throughout history to bring about positive social change in various communities around the world."

EXERCISE 4

A. Read the two examples providing evidence in support of this claim. Then answer the questions.

"Although some acts of nonviolent civil disobedience have successfully brought about social change, the risks far outweigh any potential benefits of using this method."

Example A

(1) There are occasions in history when acts of civil disobedience did not produce positive change but instead resulted in the breakdown of a peaceful society. (2) One such event was India's separation from British rule in 1947. (3) Mahatma Gandhi had led many peaceful protests with the aim of India becoming independent, united, and peaceful. (4) However, Gandhi's dream was never achieved because India's separation from Britain was bloody and ended in the partition of India into two distinct countries. (5) This event and many others exemplify Thomas Hobbes and Sophocles' arguments against civil disobedience. (6) Hobbes, a classic philosopher and writer, believed that authoritarian rule protected societies against lawlessness. (7) In *Leviathan*, Hobbes states that in a lawless society there would be "… No arts; no letters; no society; and which is worst of all, continual fear and danger of violent death; and the life of man solitary, poor, nasty, brutish, and short." (8) Like Hobbes, King Creon in Sophocles' play *Antigone* professes that civil disobedience will lead to anarchy and should not be tolerated; "Anarchy—show me a greater crime in all the earth! She, she destroys cities, rips up houses, breaks the ranks of spearmen into headlong rout" (Sophocles, lines 746–757). (9) Both Hobbes and Creon describe a society rife with destruction. (10) This view has become reality on occasion throughout history and should serve as a caution to those who engage in acts of civil disobedience.

Example B

(1) King Creon in the famous Greek play *Antigone*, written by the philosopher, Sophocles, professes that any act of civil disobedience is a threat to the peace and security of society. (2) In this tragic play, the heroine Antigone tries to bury her brother against the king's order. (3) In response to her insolent behavior, the king sentences Antigone to death and explains why any act of civil disobedience will not be tolerated. (4) In a speech, King Creon declares, "Anarchy—show me a greater crime in all the earth! She, she destroys cities, rips up houses, breaks the ranks of spearmen into headlong rout" (Sophocles, lines 746–757). (5) He asserts that civil disobedience will lead to total disorder and result in the destruction of the city. (6) In order to avoid this from becoming reality, he contends that laws must be followed no matter what; "that man the city places in authority, his orders must be obeyed, large and small, right and wrong" (lines 748–751). (7) King Creon describes a society rife with despair and destruction and believes an authoritarian ruler is needed to maintain the peace, regardless of whether or not the leader's decisions benefit society. (8) There are occasions throughout history when acts of civil disobedience did not produce positive change but instead resulted in bloodshed and the breakdown of a peaceful society. (9) Therefore, it would be wise to pay attention to cautionary tales like Sophocles' play *Antigone* in order to avoid the destructive outcomes that are caused by those who engage in acts of civil disobedience.

B. Answer the questions.

1. Circle the facts and underline the opinions in each example. Then compare with a partner and discuss any differences. Are some more difficult to distinguish than others? Why is this? ....

....

2. What types of evidence are used in each example to support the claim? ....

....

3. Identify any evidence that is not appropriate or relevant to the claim. ....

....

4. What are the sources of evidence in each example? Which example has a greater variety of evidence? ....

....

5. Which example is more effective in supporting the claim? Why? ....

....

C. Rewrite the claims to make them stronger.

1. Sophocles' play *Antigone* does not maintain a positive view of civil disobedience. ....

    ....

2. Thomas Hobbes thought it was immoral to break the law. ....

    ....

3. Both Hobbes and Sophocles' King Creon believed that any act of civil disobedience was a threat to the peace and security of society. ....

    ....

EXERCISE 5

A. Read the passage about civil disobedience. Then answer the questions.

Civil Disobedience: An Impetus for Change

1   Civil disobedience acts of the past century brought about dramatic social change and created waves that eventually capsized regimes and governmental policies. Conscientious protest, however, is hardly a subject that brings up amicable opinions, and many believe it to be both a public nuisance and a possible match that could light the fires of anarchy. Civil disobedience as a construct calls for the refusal to obey certain laws based on moral opposition to the law. Typically, civil disobedience follows nonviolent resistance principles, which are to advocate for the repeal of unjust laws while simultaneously submitting to violations of the law, and to respect the rule of law, even in the face of physical attack. A further principle of nonviolent resistance seeks conversion and understanding from the opponent.

2   Famed American writer Henry David Thoreau's classic 19th century essay "Civil Disobedience" first coined the term that prominent nonviolent civil resistance leaders later adopted and followed. Thoreau was an abolitionist[1] and deeply opposed the Mexican-American War. His political convictions led to his refusal to pay a government tax, which resulted in his sentence of a night in jail. Thoreau writes, "Under a government which imprisons any unjustly, the true place for a just man is also a prison." Thoreau's argument that unfair laws can be broken by individuals who have just cause was the underlying basis for modern civil rights leaders Mahatma Gandhi and Martin Luther King Jr.

3   Civil disobedience acts by Gandhi and King succeeded in forcing influential policy change. Two examples of civil disobedience protests stand out among many as successful, both in terms of the ripples of disruption they caused and in their adherence to nonviolent principles.

Gandhi's Salt March

4   In 1930, Mahatma Gandhi led a march to protest British colonialism that catapulted the Indian cause for independence to the world stage. During its colonial rule, the British prohibited Indians from collecting or selling salt so that

Ghandi in 1947, 17 years after he led the Salt March. He continued to fight against social injustice throughout his life.

[1] An *abolitionist* was a person who wanted to end slavery in the United States.

Indians had to purchase heavily taxed, imported British salt. Gandhi and his followers organized a 240-mile march to the sea to produce, transport, and use the country's own salt, thus avoiding the payment of tax to Britain. Tens of thousands of people joined Gandhi in the march, and it sparked similar protests elsewhere in the country.

5   Gandhi's strategy behind the protest was to force the British to change laws that discriminated against Indians and to draw world attention to what he termed a battle of right against might. The British colonial troops arrested and jailed Gandhi, and they attacked thousands of protestors, who adhered to nonviolent principles and did not fight back. Gandhi's strategy captured the attention of the world after the protests prompted outcry from nations abroad and eventually led to pressuring the British to negotiate with Indian leaders. Gandhi's vision of an independent, united, and peaceful India was never fully realized. The final stage of India's separation from Britain was bloody, chaotic, and ended in the partition of the nation into separate countries.

March to Selma

6   Martin Luther King Jr. followed in the footsteps of Gandhi in 1965, when he organized a march from Selma to Montgomery, Alabama, to protest

Women sing freedom songs during March to Selma in 1965.

the US government's denial of voting rights to black people. Though the Constitution gives the right to peaceful assembly, the state of Alabama issued a cease and desist warning to King and his 600 followers. King planned the march, however, knowing they would be arrested and likely beaten. Indeed, state police and deputized civilian groups attacked the protesters, who did not fight back, and many were hospitalized on a day that came to be known as Bloody Sunday.

7   The US government, the state government, and many social institutions protected racial segregation at the time of the civil rights movement. While King believed in following laws that were fair, he argued that a person had a moral responsibility to disobey unjust laws, and his strategy for the march was born out of this moral conviction. King's call to others to uphold ethical values through protesting the law projected the cause for civil rights to the national stage by drawing in millions of followers. The graphic images from the protest sparked outrage in America and worldwide, and made the issue an embarrassment to the government. Within three months, Congress passed the Voting Rights Act.[2]

8   King's tactics were successful, but not all people who advocated for equal rights agreed with his strategy. Separatist leaders like Malcolm X argued that civil disobedience did not go far enough. King dreamed of an integrated society, but Malcolm X disparaged the idea, arguing instead that black people should revolt against the oppressor and use violent means if necessary.

9   Civil disobedience is a controversial method portrayed both as the ideal way to prod a government to change and as a precursor to civil war. The fear of such protests leading to anarchy in society or the anger that some people use as a basis for revolt will always stand as arguments against nonviolent civil disobedience.

---

[2] The *Voting Rights Act of 1965* is legislation that prohibits racial discrimination in voting.

B. Discuss the questions with a partner. Analyze how facts and opinions are used in the text.

1. In one or two sentences, summarize the main idea of the text. Compare with your partner and discuss any differences.

....

....

2. Highlight the opinions in the text. Compare with your partner and discuss any differences.
3. What is the ratio of fact to opinion? Is there a balanced amount of facts and opinions?
4. How are the opinions supported?
5. Are the opinions mostly positive, negative, or neutral? How do you know?
6. What is the purpose of the text and how does this affect the ratio of fact to opinion?
7. Based on this information, do you think this text is a reliable source of information?

C. Write three claims about nonviolent civil disobedience and support them using evidence from the reading. Then find an additional source you could use to support these claims.

D. PEER REVIEW. Exchange your claims with a partner. Respond to the questions to evaluate each other's work. For responses marked No, give feedback in the Notes column to help your partner revise.

	Yes	No	Notes
CLAIM 1			
Is the claim debatable?	☐	☐	
Does the writer use relevant evidence from the reading to support his/her claim?	☐	☐	
Does the writer successfully prove the claim?	☐	☐	
CLAIM 2			
Is the claim debatable?	☐	☐	
Does the writer use relevant evidence from the reading to support his/her claim?	☐	☐	
Does the writer successfully prove the claim?	☐	☐	
CLAIM 3			
Is the claim debatable?	☐	☐	
Does the writer use relevant evidence from the reading to support his/her claim?	☐	☐	
Does the writer successfully prove the claim?	☐	☐	

Go to MyEnglishLab to complete a vocabulary exercise and skill practices.

For more about FACTS AND OPINIONS, see [OC] SOCIOLOGY 2.

LANGUAGE SKILLS
SIGNPOSTING FACTS AND OPINIONS

WHY IT'S USEFUL By signposting facts and opinions in academic writing, you guide your reader, signaling when you are introducing support from another source and revealing your attitude or evaluation of another author's claim. It is important to indicate your position in relation to experts in the field in order to connect your research and views to ongoing research in the field.

In general, **signposting** refers to how a writer uses language to guide a reader through a text. In the context of facts and opinions, use signposting to signal evidence or reveal your position about a claim by using linking words and phrases. It can be helpful to use a phrase, transition word, or reporting verb to signal a fact or opinion, but it is not always necessary. Look at the examples. Are signposts used to signal facts or opinions?

Many of the more well-known acts of civil disobedience of the Civil Rights movement occurred between 1954 and 1968. [No signposts.]

It is a fact that African Americans made up 21 percent of the population of the South in 1960.

The sit-ins at lunch counters across the South during the Civil Rights movement caused immediate change, which is why many **believe** they had the greatest impact.

In my view, using sit-ins and refusing to leave was an act of disobeying a specific law that was unjust in the eyes of the participants of the sit-ins.

Signposting Facts	Signposting Opinions
It is a fact that …	According to X,
The facts show that …	In my opinion,
The results of the study demonstrate …	In my view,
The results indicate …	It is the opinion of X that …
In fact,	The author thinks, states, feels, believes, suggests, argues that …
Indeed,	

When revealing one's position, writers use a variety of techniques to either hedge or boost a claim. **Hedges** are used to reduce the certainty of a claim, whereas **boosters** are used to show that writers have confidence in their claims and those of the sources cited. Modal verbs of certainty, possibility, and ability, adverbs of frequency and certainty, and evaluative adjectives are commonly used to soften and strengthen views in academic writing. Writers can also use multiple hedges and boosters within a sentence to indicate their position.

Hedges	Examples
Modals: *may, might, can, could, should*	This reaction **may** mean that the protest is having a positive impact.
	This reaction **could** mean that the protest is having a positive impact.
Adverbs: *approximately, arguably, generally, hardly ever, in most cases, least, less, perhaps, possibly, probably, relatively, roughly, seldom, sometimes, somewhat, theoretically, typically, unlikely*	It will **probably** be more effective than the last demonstration.
	It was **arguably** the most difficult decision he had to make during the Civil Rights Movement.
	This is **somewhat** surprising, considering the amount of evidence in support of the case.
	Theoretically, this outcome should have heightened their awareness of social inequities.
Adjectives: *ambiguous, difficult, doubtful, less uncertain, unclear, unconfirmed, unreliable, vague*	It is **unclear** whether or not his speech had any impact on the protesters.
	The findings in her article were somewhat **ambiguous**.

Boosters	Examples
Modals: *will, must, can*	Acts of civil disobedience **will** **not** **be** tolerated by the government.
	His actions proved that people **can** make a difference in society.
Adverbs: *certainly, easily, especially, frequently, indeed, in fact, likely, more, most naturally, normally, obviously, of course, often, notably, particularly, significantly*	It was **certainly** more effective than the last demonstration.
	It was **obviously** the most difficult decision he had to make during the Civil Rights Movement.
	This is **particularly** surprising, considering the amount of evidence in support of the case.
	This outcome **significantly** heightened their awareness of social inequities.
Adjectives: *accurate, certain, clear, confident, effective, essential, evident, interesting, noteworthy, obvious, positive, useful, valid*	It is **clear** that his speech unified the community and gave them strength to continue their cause.
	The data she presented was **effective** in supporting her argument.

EXERCISE 6

A. Read the passage. Underline the examples of signposting and identify whether signposts hedge or boost the writer's opinions. Compare with a partner and discuss why the writer made these choices.

   Sit-ins, a form of nonviolent civil disobedience that involves a group of people occupying an area, were a highly effective method for bringing about immediate change to the policies of businesses that segregated African Americans. Many sit-ins occurred in the late '50s and early '60s, primarily in the South. Sit-ins certainly contributed to the overall strategy of civil disobedience that lead to passage of the Civil Rights Act of 1964, which ended legal racial segregation in the United States, but it was their immediate effect in breaking down the barriers at the local level that may have been their greatest contribution.

   While not the first sit-in, the sit-in in Greensboro, North Carolina on February 1, 1960, is a good example of a sit-in that resulted in a policy change in a short period of time. The Greensboro sit-in began with four university students who sat at the Woolworth lunch counter and stayed until closing even though they were refused service and asked to leave by the manager. The Greensboro Four, as they were later called, returned the next day accompanied by more than twenty students and by the fourth day, there were more than 300 students participating, and the sit-in had spread to another store.

   The media covered the sit-ins and raised national awareness of the reality of segregation in the region. In fact, the sit-in in Greensboro resulted in a wave of other sit-ins across the South. Within a week of the first sit-in in Greensboro, sit-ins began to frequently occur in other North Carolina cities. Then, the movement spread to other states in the South.

   While initially, Woolworth, then a national chain of five-and-dime stores, held firm that it would allow individual stores to follow local customs and keep their policies, in May of 1960, after the Greensboro store had suffered major losses, it began to serve all customers at its lunch counter, and Woolworth desegregated its stores, though some individual stores continued to discriminate against customers based on race. A portion of the lunch counter is now in the Smithsonian. Thus, the Greensboro sit-in and those that both preceded and followed it were obviously instrumental in bringing about more immediate change than other acts of civil disobedience used during the civil rights movement.

B. Underline the examples of signposting in "Civil Disobedience: An Impetus for Change" on pages 136–137. Then identify the signposts that hedge or boost the writer's opinions. With a partner, discuss why the writer made these choices.

C. Rewrite the passage below, inserting signposts when possible. Use hedges and boosters appropriately, making sure not to change the writer's position. Compare with a partner and discuss how the signposts affect the writing.

(1) There are occasions throughout history when acts of civil disobedience did not produce positive change but instead resulted in bloodshed and the breakdown of a peaceful society. (2) One such event was India's separation from British rule. (3) Mahatma Gandhi had led peaceful protests with the aim of India becoming independent, united, and peaceful.

(4) However, Gandhi's dream was never achieved because India's separation from Britain was bloody and ended in the separation of India into two distinct countries. (5) This event and many others exemplify Thomas Hobbes and Sophocles' arguments against civil disobedience. (6) Hobbes, a classic philosopher and writer, believed that authoritarian rule protected societies against lawlessness.

EXERCISE 7

A. Rewrite the statements, first using hedges, then using boosters. Compare with a partner.

1. Social institutions protected racial segregation at the time of the civil rights movement.

   Hedge: ....

   Booster: ....

2. The argument Thoreau and Gandhi make for conscientious protest is not agreed upon throughout history.

   Hedge: ....

   Booster: ....

3. While King believed in following fair laws, he argued that people had a moral responsibility to disobey unjust laws.

   Hedge: ....

   Booster: ....

4. The graphic images from the protest sparked outrage and made the issue an embarrassment to the government.

   Hedge: ....

   Booster: ....

5. King's tactics were successful, but not all equal rights advocates agreed with his strategy.

   Hedge: ....

   Booster: ....

6. Malcolm X argued that black people should revolt against oppressors, using violence if necessary.

   Hedge: ....

   Booster: ....

7. Civil disobedience is seen both as an ideal way to incite change and as a precursor to civil war.

   Hedge: ....

   Booster: ....

8. The fear of such protests stands as an argument against nonviolent civil disobedience.

   Hedge: ....

   Booster: ....

B. Revise the claims you wrote in Exercise 4 Part C in response to "Civil Disobedience: An Impetus for Change." Use hedges or boosters to soften or strengthen your claims.

   ....

   ....

   ....

   ....

   ....

   ....

Go to MyEnglishLab to complete skill practices.

APPLY YOUR SKILLS

WHY IT'S USEFUL By applying the skills you have learned in this unit, you can successfully use fact and opinion to show your reader that you have done sound research and can support your claims with credible sources.

ASSIGNMENT

Choose an event or moment in a civil rights movement. Examine whether the event or moment was successful in achieving its goal. Take a position, and then research facts and evaluate opinions to support your claims. Write a thesis statement and an outline of your claims and support.

BEFORE YOU WRITE

A. Before you begin your assignment, discuss the questions with one or more students.

1. What were the goals of the American civil rights movement?

2. What are the advantages of nonviolent civil disobedience to protest unjust laws or policies? What are the disadvantages?

3. What event or moment in a civil rights movement are you interested in? Describe it to your group. Do you think this event or moment was successful in achieving its goal? Why or why not?

B. **As you consider your assignment, complete the tasks below. Then, share your ideas with another student. Get feedback and revise your ideas, if necessary.**

1. List two or three facts about your topic. ....

....

....

....

2. List two or three common opinions about your topic. ....

....

....

....

3. Write a thesis statement. ....

....

C. **Review the Unit Skills Summary. As you begin the writing task on page 145, apply the writing and language skills you learned in this unit.**

UNIT SKILLS SUMMARY

Use signpost fact and opinion to support claims
- Use verifiable facts that are accurate, appropriate, and relevant.
- Use supported opinions based on evidence and factual data.
- Use opinions of knowledgeable experts and from reliable sources.

Evaluate others' opinions
- Evaluate others' opinions to ensure they are valid and reliable, based on appropriate assumptions and draw logical conclusions.

Distinguish fact from opinion and claims
- Look for the ratio of fact to opinion and writer bias.
- Write claims that are debatable.

Fact and opinion
- Use signposting language to guide your reader.
- Reveal your position through boosting and hedging.

THINKING CRITICALLY

As you consider your assignment, discuss the questions with another student. Get feedback and revise your ideas, if necessary.

1. What is your position on civil disobedience as a way to protest unjust laws or policies?
2. If you lived in a community where acts of civil disobedience were not tolerated, what other methods would you use to protest unjust laws or policies?
3. What types of civil disobedience acts do you think are most effective? Why?

A. Look at the timeline describing civil rights demonstrations from the 1950s and '60s. Make a claim about the sit-ins and support it, using three or four facts from the visual.

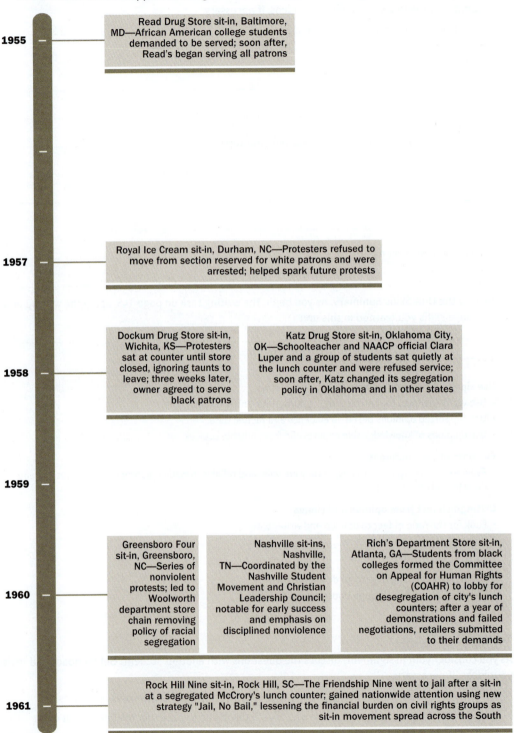

1955 — Read Drug Store sit-in, Baltimore, MD—African American college students demanded to be served; soon after, Read's began serving all patrons

1957 — Royal Ice Cream sit-in, Durham, NC—Protesters refused to move from section reserved for white patrons and were arrested; helped spark future protests

1958 — Dockum Drug Store sit-in, Wichita, KS—Protesters sat at counter until store closed, ignoring taunts to leave; three weeks later, owner agreed to serve black patrons

Katz Drug Store sit-in, Oklahoma City, OK—Schoolteacher and NAACP official Clara Luper and a group of students sat quietly at the lunch counter and were refused service; soon after, Katz changed its segregation policy in Oklahoma and in other states

1959 —

1960 — Greensboro Four sit-in, Greensboro, NC—Series of nonviolent protests; led to Woolworth department store chain removing policy of racial segregation

Nashville sit-ins, Nashville, TN—Coordinated by the Nashville Student Movement and Christian Leadership Council; notable for early success and emphasis on disciplined nonviolence

Rich's Department Store sit-in, Atlanta, GA—Students from black colleges formed the Committee on Appeal for Human Rights (COAHR) to lobby for desegregation of city's lunch counters; after a year of demonstrations and failed negotiations, retailers submitted to their demands

1961 — Rock Hill Nine sit-in, Rock Hill, SC—The Friendship Nine went to jail after a sit-in at a segregated McCrory's lunch counter; gained nationwide attention using new strategy "Jail, No Bail," lessening the financial burden on civil rights groups as sit-in movement spread across the South

....

....

....

....

....

THINKING ABOUT LANGUAGE

Add signposts that signal facts and opinions in the passage. Include hedges or boosters to soften or strengthen the writer's claims. Then compare with a partner and discuss your choices.

The sit-ins used during the American Civil Rights Movement as a form of nonviolent civil disobedience were having a(n) .... impact and leading to the desegregation of businesses in the Southern states. These sit-ins were, however, ... costly to the movement. .... students who sat at lunch counters were being arrested and the cost of bail and fines was .... a factor as the student groups did not have sufficient funds to pay them all. The sit-in at the McCrory lunch counter in Rock Hill, South Carolina on January 31, 1966, brought an important change through a new .... strategy called "Jail, No Bail." Through the .... decision to use a new strategy of accepting jail sentences rather than bailing out, the Rock Hill sit-in .... contributed to the success of the civil rights movement and .... saved it.

WRITE

A. Revisit the writing assignment and your answers to the questions in Before You Write Part B. Identify the moment or event that you would like to research. Determine whether or not you think this event or moment was successful.

B. Research this event and locate factual evidence and expert opinions that can support your position.

C. Develop and narrow your thesis statement.

....

....

D. Create an outline of claims and support. Revise and edit as necessary.

BEYOND THE ASSIGNMENT

Write a research paper analyzing a specific act of civil disobedience. Make claims which you support with facts and opinions. Use all the skills you learned in this unit.

▶ Go to MyEnglishLab to listen to Professor Greenberg and to complete a self-assessment.

Individual choices impact the global economy.

ECONOMICS

Reading Critically for Effective Writing

UNIT PROFILE

In this unit, you will be introduced to the topic of externalities. Externalities are effects on a third party not directly related to a business transaction. Specifically, you will learn about positive and negative externalities and their implications and solutions such as a carbon tax to address environmental externalities.

Write a critical response to an idea in an article you have found that discusses how positive and/or negative externalities of a particular good or service impact society. Read the article critically to ensure that you select an appropriate article, identify evidence in the article to support your idea, and integrate that information into your critical response.

OUTCOMES

- Select sources
- Integrate sources to provide evidence
- Respond to inference
- Write a critical response
- Use direct quotations and reported speech

GETTING STARTED

▶ Go to MyEnglishLab to listen to Professor Clerici-Arias and to complete a self-assessment.

Discuss these questions with a partner or group.

1. The decisions we make affect us directly, but they can also have an impact on society. This is an externality. When you decide to walk or bike instead of drive, what are the possible benefits to you as an individual? What are the benefits to society—the positive externalities? What are the negative externalities? What are other decisions individuals make that impact others? Discuss the externalities of those decisions.

2. Look at the photo of a structure where commercial fishing boats unload their catch. Eating fish is generally seen as a healthy alternative to eating meat and processed foods. Can you name other positive aspects of the rise in commercial fishing? What are some negative aspects?

3. What role do externalities play in economics? Why do you think economists are interested in externalities?

For more about **ECONOMICS**, see ② ③. See also ⌊R⌋ and ⌊OC⌋ **ECONOMICS** ① ② ③.

CRITICAL THINKING SKILL
READING CRITICALLY FOR EFFECTIVE WRITING

WHY IT'S USEFUL Strong writers are strong readers. By critically reading texts, you will be able to identify ideas and information you want to include in your own writing. You will also be able to judge how to most effectively use the ideas and information to support your own ideas for a well-developed paper.

Reading critically means **reading actively**. Critical readers underline and highlight text and annotate—that is, take notes about their reactions in the margins. They skim for information; they read, reread, and question ideas they don't fully understand or agree with. They don't take what they read at face value. Critical readers ask questions, look for implications and connections to other texts and their ideas, and make inferences about the meaning of what they read.

Throughout this unit, you will be developing the skills of **selecting sources** and **integrating ideas from those sources** as evidence in your writing. Reading critically is essential to these skills. Here are guidelines for reading critically:

- Identify important passages.
- Highlight or mark key ideas and information.
- Write questions in margins.
- Annotate or note your reactions to ideas and arguments in margins.
- Link parts of the text to each other, other texts, or your ideas.

Start reading critically with curiosity, note new information, and highlight key phrases. Later, develop a more skeptical attitude and challenge the arguments in the texts. Don't accept everything you read as true, but be open to ideas even if you don't agree with them. Ask questions, look for things inferred that might not be stated explicitly, note similarities and differences to other sources, and consider the implications for your own writing.

Pay attention to the ideas presented. What are the author's main point and key ideas? What evidence is provided to support ideas? Is there new information? Is the information difficult to understand? Are the ideas presented similar to or different from other texts on the topic? Think about how you might use these ideas in your writing as support or as evidence for an argument, for example.

Reading critically also means reading rhetorically. Notice how the text is organized and formatted. You may be able to use that organization in your own writing. Often disciplines follow common patterns, such as the use of headings, bulleting, and numbering. Consider how graphics, tables, charts, and illustrations are used in the source. You may want to use similar visuals in your paper.

NOTICING ACTIVITY

A. Read the first two paragraphs from the article the externalities. Notice the key ideas and graphs and read the annotations in the margins. Discuss the graphic with a partner. Is it helpful? Can you think of other externalities, both positive and negative, in everyday activities? Write them in the margin next to the graphic.

EXTERNALITIES

1   In economics, externalities are effects on a third party not directly related to a business transaction. They can occur as a result of production or consumption and can be positive or negative. Positive externalities are benefits to a third party and negative externalities are costs to a third party.

2   Economists separate both benefits and costs into those that are social—effects on society—and those that are private—effects directly on the producer or consumer. Externalities are benefits and costs to society, the third party. Benefits and costs to the producer or consumer are private and, therefore, not externalities. With positive externalities the benefit to society is greater than the benefit to the producer or consumer. A negative externality occurs when social costs are greater than private costs.

3   Externalities are not exclusive to business and occur in most everyday activities, but it is in business that they are examined most closely. There are many examples of both positive and negative externalities in common human interactions.

externality = effect on 3rd party, positive = benefit and negative = cost

Benefits and costs = both social (to society) and private (to producer and consumer)

Externalities = social only

Can something have both positive and negative externalities? "How are externalities measured?"

B. Read the remaining paragraphs critically. Work with a partner and identify key ideas and information you would highlight or underline. Discuss reactions and questions you might write in the margins.

4   Economists measure externalities the same way they measure everything else: according to people's willingness to pay. Pollution is an example of an externality but only if it is perceived to be a big enough problem that people are willing to pay for cleaner air. If they are, a negative externality exists. If not, there is no externality.

5   The question then becomes who should pay for the negative externality? In an unregulated market, producers don't have to take responsibility for external costs, which are then passed on to society. Thus producers have lower marginal costs than they would otherwise have. Because they don't pay the external costs, the product or service continues to be produced in too great a quantity. This overproduction results in what economists call a market inefficiency since the cost to society outweighs the benefit. This market inefficiency is usually referred to by economists as market failure.

6   Let's look at the example of pollution as a negative externality, where a manufacturing company is pumping pollutants into the air. While the company has to pay for electricity, materials, and so on, it is not paying the cost of the pollution it is causing. Therefore, the people living near the factory are paying for the pollution because it will cause them to have a poorer quality of life, including possible health problems and lower property values. Thus the production of whatever the firm is making has a negative cost to the people surrounding the factory—a cost that the firm doesn't pay.

7   So, who pays? Many believe for the well-being of society, all costs and benefits should be internalized by those making production and buying decisions. This leads to the next question: how can this be accomplished?

● Go to MyEnglishLab to complete a vocabulary exercise and a skill practice and join in collaborative activities.

SUPPORTING SKILL 1
SELECTING SOURCES

WHY IT'S USEFUL By selecting appropriate sources, you will be able to integrate ideas and information into your paper to support your ideas. Critically reading your sources will help you to select ones that will provide the most support for your own ideas.

Integrating information from sources into a research paper is one of the most important skills you can acquire in your academic career. A first step in the process is **selecting sources** that will help you support your ideas. Before you select the sources, you will need to critically read them to ensure they have information that is appropriate for your paper.

As you critically read your sources, keep in mind the requirements for your paper and the limitations—that is, time, length of the paper, and your knowledge or expertise—but don't limit your options. Ask yourself if the source presents possibilities or opportunities you haven't discovered yet. Know the type of source: Is it an opinion column, an article in a magazine or newspaper, or a peer-reviewed article in an academic journal? Is the source reputable? What kind of source is it? Is it a primary or secondary source? If it is a secondary source, it means you are viewing the topic through eyes of other researchers, so consider factors that affected the author's ideas.

For more on evaluating sources, see ECONOMICS Part 1.

You will also need to consider your **purpose** and **audience** when selecting sources.

Purpose	Audience
• Will the information in the source help you accomplish your purpose? • Is the information relevant to your research question and preliminary thesis? • Can you use this information to support the points you want to make? • Does this source offer new information or a new perspective on your topic? • Do the ideas and arguments counter your ideas? • Is the source more useful than other sources?	• Would my reader want to know this? • Would my reader find it interesting? • Would my reader find it convincing? • Would my reader find the evidence credible? • Would my reader learn something from its inclusion in my paper?

Information from sources is used for different things. It can introduce an idea, provide evidence for your ideas, define and / or illustrate concepts, or contrast with your ideas or the ideas of other sources.

Careful selection of information from a source:

- allows you to present strong arguments while maintaining a balanced tone.
- provides evidence for your assertions.
- enhances your credibility if the source is considered an expert in the field.
- defines concepts.
- provides illustrations, tables, charts, and other graphics that help your reader.
- helps you present contrasting ideas.

A good way to select sources is to:

- **Skim** to determine if the source is valuable.
- **Read actively** to understand, question, and evaluate.
- **Read rhetorically** to notice text organization and useful visuals.
- **Reread** passages you've marked as important or things you don't understand.
- **Annotate** the source for ease in finding information for your paper.

EXERCISE 1

A. Read the excerpt for possible selection as a source for an article analyzing a local government intervention.

IMPLICATIONS OF EXTERNALITIES

1   A negative externality of goods or services is usually viewed as a failure of the market because the level of consumption or production is higher than what society requires or wants and costs to society have not been taken into account. Should businesses be left to self-regulate and make the necessary adjustments to compensate for externalities? In many cases, they are. Should governments intervene? Governments can and do intervene. But should they?

2   Bryan Caplan, a professor of economics at George Mason University, posits that externalities are probably the argument for government intervention that economists most respect. A government can intervene by granting a subsidy on a positive externality and taxing a negative one or regulating both money and commerce, which most governments do to a greater or lesser extent.

3   While the concept of externalities is not very controversial in economics, its application is. Proponents of laissez-faire usually argue that the impact of externalities is small and manageable, whereas critics of free markets see externalities as having a large impact.

4   The most accepted examples of activities with large externalities are probably air pollution, violent and property crimes, and national defense. Other externalities, such as the environment and education are more controversial, and there is much debate over whether there really are demonstrable externalities, and if so, how great the impact is. Externalities may also be in conflict with human rights. An example is the needs of refugees fleeing their country or regional security during civil wars or conflicts. Externalities can be used to rationalize prohibitions or bans on substances and control of behaviors. An example is national security versus the right to privacy.

5   Another question raised by economists is whether it is worth trying to correct externalities. From an economic point of view, some externalities are not worth correcting. A common opinion is that many activities have both positive and negative externalities, which means that they roughly cancel each other out. For example, manufacturing goods has the positive externality of increasing employment in the neighboring area but the negative externality of pollution. In this case, is it better to simply do nothing?

6   The answer to how to manage externalities and who should be involved is clearly complex, and there are probably as many answers as economists. Government involvement is a major factor, especially where there is agreement that there are major negative externalities. But, to what extent? Clearly, the impact on society and the welfare of the citizens of a country is something each government considers when making decisions about its economy and whether to regulate or tax its citizens to adjust for externalities.

B. Read the practice assignment. Answer the questions that follow.

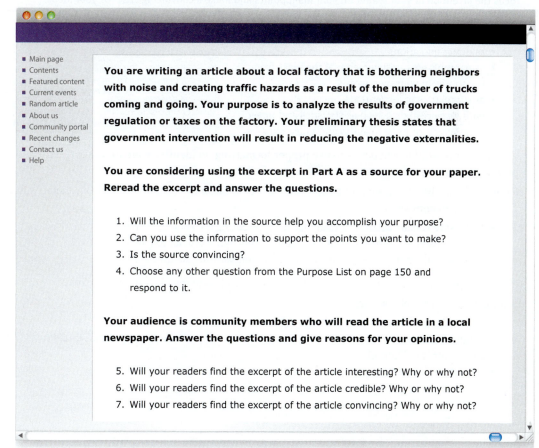

- Main page
- Contents
- Featured content
- Current events
- Random article
- About us
- Community portal
- Recent changes
- Contact us
- Help

You are writing an article about a local factory that is bothering neighbors with noise and creating traffic hazards as a result of the number of trucks coming and going. Your purpose is to analyze the results of government regulation or taxes on the factory. Your preliminary thesis states that government intervention will result in reducing the negative externalities.

You are considering using the excerpt in Part A as a source for your paper. Reread the excerpt and answer the questions.

1. Will the information in the source help you accomplish your purpose?
2. Can you use the information to support the points you want to make?
3. Is the source convincing?
4. Choose any other question from the Purpose List on page 150 and respond to it.

Your audience is community members who will read the article in a local newspaper. Answer the questions and give reasons for your opinions.

5. Will your readers find the excerpt of the article interesting? Why or why not?
6. Will your readers find the excerpt of the article credible? Why or why not?
7. Will your readers find the excerpt of the article convincing? Why or why not?

C. Read the statements. Find an example in the excerpt that illustrates each statement. Underline it in the excerpt and note the paragraph number below.

1. Allows you to present a strong argument while maintaining a balanced tone ....

2. Helps you present contrasting ideas ....

3. Enhances your credibility because the source is considered an expert in the field ....

4. Defines a concept ....

5. Provides evidence for an assertion ....

D. Discuss the excerpt in Part A and your responses to B and C in a small group. Do you agree with other students' answers in B? Do you agree with their choices in C?

⏵ Go to MyEnglishLab to complete a vocabulary exercise and a skill practice and join in collaborative activities.

SUPPORTING SKILL 2
INTEGRATING SOURCES TO PROVIDE EVIDENCE

WHY IT'S USEFUL By integrating appropriate sources to provide evidence, you show that you have researched your topic and are not simply presenting your own unsupported ideas. Evidence helps you focus the attention of your reader on your main points and make a convincing case for your ideas.

You can **integrate sources** into your paper in a variety of ways:

- as direct quotations.
- as paraphrases—restatements of the ideas from the source in your own words.
- as summaries of longer texts.
- with numerical data such as statistics and images.
- with visuals or links to audio and video clips.

> **TIP**
> To avoid plagiarism, sources must be integrated, using correct formatting, and a full citation must be included in a Works Cited or Reference page at the end of the paper. Typically, the style of citation depends on your subject or discipline. Your professor or department is the best source for information on which style to use.

The key to successful integration is to **use proper formatting**, to **identify your source correctly**, and to **provide a context** for the source information you are using.

Paraphrases can be used to support a point you make or to illustrate or add to a point from another source. To integrate paraphrases:

- Make sure you are accurate and are fairly representing the source. (Many errors occur when writers misread a source, so critical reading skills play a crucial role here.)
- Make sure the paraphrase fits the context and tone of your document.

Use **signal phrases** to ensure a good transition from your ideas to the ideas from your source.

Some common signal phrases are:

- According to [author]
- [Author] writes
- In the words of [author]
- As [author] suggests

> For additional reporting verbs, see ECONOMICS Part 1

Cite the source accurately according to the documentation style you are using.

Evidence is information to support a point or assertion in your paper. Evidence is usually taken from source materials and should be integrated into a paper following the guidelines above. Evidence must be:

- sufficient
- appropriate
- accurate
- interpreted fairly
- presented clearly
- convincing

Evidence Can Be	Examples
Opinions of an expert (appeal to authority)	Bryan Caplan, a professor of economics at George Mason University, posits that externalities are probably the argument for the government intervention that economists most respect.
An *if / then* statement (appeal to logic)	If the cost to society is higher than the cost to business, then a negative externality exists.
Empirical (numerical or statistical data)	Ninety percent of economists accept that externalities can result in losses, but they don't agree on how best to solve the problem created by the losses.
Examples that show rather than tell	For example, a local factory has machinery and equipment that is very loud and disturbs the people living in a nearby neighborhood.
Facts	Externalities are not exclusive to business and occur in most human activities.
First-hand accounts of people affected by an issue	A neighbor living close to the factory told me that the noise emitted from the factory was so loud at times that he and his wife could not carry on a normal conversation on their patio.

EXERCISE 2

A. Write the type of evidence that best supports each point or assertion.

opinion of an expert	*if / then* statement	empirical data
example	fact	first-hand account

.... 1. Proof that the noise level is harmful

.... 2. Support for the idea that government should intervene to reduce costs to society

.... 3. The result of an action taken by the factory

.... 4. Statistics on harmful noise levels

.... 5. Opinions of the neighbors who are being affected by the noise and traffic

.... 6. A serious traffic accident due to the heavy traffic near the factory

B. Discuss the evidence in Part A. What is the topic of a paper this evidence would support? With your partner, write a possible thesis statement for the paper. ....

....

C. Discuss each type of evidence using these questions.

1. Are all the types of evidence appropriate?

2. In which types of evidence is accuracy a potential problem?

3. Which types of evidence might be subject to unfair interpretation? How?

4. If presented clearly, would each type of evidence be convincing? Would some evidence be more convincing than others?

5. Taken together, is the evidence sufficient to fully support the controlling idea?

▶ Go to MyEnglishLab to complete a skill practice.

SUPPORTING SKILL 3
RESPONDING TO INFERENCE

WHY IT'S USEFUL By responding to inferences in your sources, you can more accurately and clearly represent ideas in your own writing.

When using sources to integrate ideas into your paper, an important subskill of reading critically is understanding and **responding to inferences**. Writers don't always state their ideas and opinions explicitly, so you need to read carefully and critically to interpret the writer's intended meaning.

Inferences require educated guesses that are based on the **textual evidence** combined with the **experience** and **knowledge** the reader brings. Not surprisingly, then, what you know and understand of a topic beforehand affects how well you can infer meaning.

When you want to integrate information inferred from a source in your own work, it is important that you read critically to first interpret the inferences correctly and then to incorporate the ideas as accurately and clearly as possible to fairly represent the intended meaning. Read this statement:

> Bryan Caplan, a professor of economics at George Mason University, posits that externalities are probably the argument for government intervention that economists most respect.

You can infer from this that economists do not accept all arguments for government intervention. You, however, can't infer that all economists accept externalities as an argument for government intervention. If you wrote in your paper that economists dislike government intervention except in cases of externalities, you would not be accurately representing Professor Caplan's idea.

EXERCISE 3

A. Read the paragraph. What did Ronald Coase infer about the points listed below?

An interesting perspective on externalities and how to manage them came from the ideas of Ronald Coase, a Nobel laureate, who believed in letting externalities solve themselves. All activities have some costs, whether great or small, called transaction costs, which are the costs incurred in a business transaction. He proposed that strong property rights could overcome the problem of externalities using transaction costs rather than arguing whether an activity had externalities or not. Given that a government assigned clear property rights—ownership—and there were negligible transaction costs, he made a strong case that those affected could voluntarily work out reasonably efficient solutions.

1. externalities ....

....

2. property rights ....

....

3. transaction costs ....

....

4. efficient solutions to externalities ....

....

5. government role ....

....

B. Discuss the inferences with a partner. Did you agree?

⬡ Go to MyEnglishLab to complete a skill practice and join in collaborative activities.

READING-WRITING CONNECTION
WRITING A CRITICAL RESPONSE

WHY IT'S USEFUL By expressing your reactions in a critical response paper, you can show your instructors how well you understand the course material and concepts by expressing your personal reactions. Response papers are also a helpful way to explore ideas for a longer research paper.

There are several ways to respond to a text, including analyzing, comparing and contrasting, or explaining the material. The most common response is agreeing or disagreeing. **Writing a critical response** allows students to explore a particular point in a reading more deeply and formulate an argument about it. Unlike a summary, response papers should include your personal opinion, experiences, and ideas in support of your claim. It is important to clearly state your position, summarize the text that it is responding to, and give reasons to support your opinion.

Here are some questions to think about during and after you read a text. These questions will help you identify a specific point in the reading that you will respond to in your paper. As you read the text, practice your critical reading skills by making annotations, identifying where you agree/disagree with the author, or noting where you have questions. After you are finished reading, respond to these questions using your notes.

- What is the text about?
- Who wrote it?
- What is the main idea?
- How do you feel about the ideas in the text? Do you agree or disagree with them?
- Why do you feel this way? What experiences have you had that influence the way you feel?
- Have you read a similar or contradictory article on the same topic? Were the ideas the same?
- Have you seen a lecture, film, or news report on the same topic? Do the ideas support or contradict the text?
- Can you identify with what you have read? Why or why not?
- Which particular point in the reading do you want to explore further in a response paper?
- Why is your critique of this point relevant or important?

Here are some helpful guidelines for developing a response paper.

1. Begin by stating your position about the key idea you are responding to. Critical responses are concise, so you do not need a comprehensive introduction.

2. Be sure to include the writer's full name and the title of the article when introducing the reading.

3. Summarize the specific idea from the reading that you will be discussing. You should only be responding to one idea from the text. Therefore, you should not summarize the entire article.

4. Be sure to paraphrase, using reported speech, or use direct quotations. Be selective about the information you paraphrase or quote; only choose information that is directly relevant to your claim.

5. Support your claim by sharing a personal experience or relating your ideas to another source on the topic.

6. Conclude with a summary of your argument or an answer to a question you explored throughout your response.

7. Review your response and be sure you have clearly stated your position, accurately summarized the author's point, and provided evidence for your claim. Remember, critical responses are brief, so all the evidence you include should directly support your argument.

Because a critical response includes your opinion and experiences, you will use personal expressions throughout your response. This helps your reader identify when you are sharing an experience or opinion, as opposed to summarizing information from a source. Here is a list of common expressions used in critical responses:

From my experience	I agree / disagree with the author's view that …
From my perspective I find that / I have found this to be	I agree / disagree that …, but I … Although I agree that …, I do not support his claim that …
Personally, I find that	While the author states that …, the findings contradict this information.
I can understand that My personal bias against	Though I disagree with …, I completely endorse …
The author's point about … is useful	I support the author's position that …, but I find … more relevant
The author is mistaken because …	

EXERCISE 4

A. Read the critical response to the article, "Profits, Despite What You Hear, Do Not Equal Environmental Pollution."

1   In the article, "Profits, Despite What You Hear, Do Not Equal Environmental Pollution," Fred Smith argues that industry and businesses will self-regulate in order to prevent negative externalities, such as pollution because companies have a financial incentive to turn residuals into a useable product. According to Smith, it can cost businesses a great deal to dispose of the "leftovers" from their production. He contends that because companies aim to maximize their profits, we do not need governments to step in and regulate waste; it is more efficient and effective to let companies self-regulate. In my opinion, Smith's argument is flawed in several respects.

2   First, while this argument holds true for companies that are large and predictable, smaller companies are not incentivized to reduce residuals because the volume it takes to recoup the cost of managing waste isn't realistic for small businesses. For example, small local grocery stores often have to buy their own equipment to compact and bale their packaging waste. The cost for the machinery and the labor to do this often exceeds the value of the recycled product. My cousin, who works for one of the world's largest soft drink companies, sees this routinely in both large and small grocery stores where his waste packaging is put into trash dumpsters as opposed to being recycled.

3   A second example exists in the commercial fishing industry. One crab fishery in the Pacific Northwest was nearly destroyed because even as the crab disappeared, the fishermen kept going

out, scrambling to catch whatever they could. This is because in small business, the factor that often determines one's business practice is the immediacy of cash flow. Many small business people cannot invest in changing their practices, as they often spend nearly everything that is earned. In the crabbing example, the government had to eventually step in. Many fishermen sold their boats to the government for enough money to effectively retire, and the number of crab allowed to be harvested was drastically reduced, forcing other fishermen to change and diversify their businesses. The author may be correct that large companies will self-regulate; however, it is unrealistic to think that all businesses have a viable financial incentive to manage negative externalities in ways consistent with the future health of their own industries and the health of the communities around them.

B Answer the questions.

1. Where does the writer state his or her position? Does the writer agree or disagree with the article?

....

2. Paraphrase the particular point in the article that the writer is responding to. ....

....

3. Where in the response does the writer include the title and author? ....

....

4. How is the response organized? ....

....

5. What evidence or reasons does the writer use to support his or her claim? ....

....

....

6. How does the writer refer back to the source in the response? Does the writer use reported

   speech and/or direct quotations? Circle them. ....

....

....

7. How does the writer conclude the response? ....

....

....

8. Do you think this response paper includes all of the characteristics of a good critical response?

   Why or why not? ....

   ....

   ....

C. Make a list of all the expressions used in the critical response on pages 156–157. Then state the rhetorical purpose of each: *agreeing, disagreeing, both agreeing / disagreeing,* or *introducing an experience / reason.*

   ....

   ....

   ....

   ....

   ....

D. List more expressions (not presented in this unit) that you can use to state your opinion or share a personal experience. When you are finished, compare with a partner and add their expressions to your list.

EXERCISE 5

A. Read the article critically. As you read, highlight the main ideas of each section and mark whether or not you agree or disagree with them.

The Hidden Externalities of Fishing

By Cynthia Flanagan

1   Fish and other forms of seafood are important staples in many world cuisines; for many coastal-dwelling populations, they continue to be the primary source of dietary protein. Today, the worldwide demand for fish, from luxury Bluefin tuna to cheap forage fish, has increased dramatically due to population growth and consumer preference. Technological advancements have made it easier to catch fish at every stage of their life cycle, but such tools have only sped up the rate of overharvesting. Overfishing, in fact, remains rampant; quotas are nearly unenforceable. Well-equipped, high-tech fleets from wealthy countries fish off the shores of underfunded nations that, with limited maritime resources, are unable to enforce legal restrictions.

2   The entire situation is a tragedy of the commons—fishing boats have little incentive to follow environmental regulations when they can instead maximize personal gain. The oceans' resources are effectively nonexcludable, and it is very difficult to keep anyone with a boat from catching as much fish as they are able—especially in international waters. Throughout the world, critical populations of marine life are threatened and dwindling in the face of overfishing. Beyond the obvious price increases that will occur as shortages worsen, this disregard for the welfare of the world's oceans is already having a number of deleterious effects on both people and the earth's ecosystem. Like all externalities, they affect things and people that are not even involved in the "transaction"

of fish harvesting and consumption. Examining these externalities demonstrates why global overfishing is a crisis that requires international cooperation and strict government regulation if we hope to preserve the Earth's oceans for future generations.

Overfishing is a nonsustainable use of the oceans that leads to an overall degradation of the system.

3   Overfishing has many obvious effects on fish populations; multiple species, including many forms of tuna, face either extinction or "commercial extinction." This is largely due to technological advances that allow fishing boats to catch fish not just at geographically convenient locations but at every point of their migration. Bluefin were historically caught only at specific points in their life cycle by fishermen located in a geographical position that made such fishing feasible. Modern fleets follow schools of fish all over the world, constantly depleting populations at all stages of a fish's life cycle. These practices are not limited to high-value fish meant for the dinner table such as tuna and cod—cheaper fish unfit for human consumption can still be valuable as livestock feed and pet food. Depletion of such fish can impact the food supply of other, larger fish, further disrupting the food chain.

4   Modern fishing practices don't simply harm fish populations being sold to consumers—they also negatively impact other species. *Bycatch* is an industry term for fish and animals caught accidentally. Dolphins, sea turtles, and even birds can end up as bycatch. Many animals caught as bycatch die before the nets are even pulled up. A crew's first priority is usually to secure and store

the most profitable fish, so even though most bycatch is thrown back to sea, it is often dead or injured by the time this occurs. Other illegal but widely practiced fishing methods like bottom trawling[1] can destroy large sections of coral reef; the practices remain in widespread use despite environmental damage because large quantities of fish are caught this way.

5   People living in places historically associated with fishing are already feeling the effects of this decreasing global fish population. Subsistence fishing villages that have, for years, lived off the sea are now pulling up empty nets with increasing frequency. Unable to survive the way their ancestors did, these populations are forced to either relocate or find another food source. Even populations that saw fishing primarily as a source of income are forced to explore other options. As the shortages get worse, already illegal fishing operations will only be incentivized to continue their unsustainable practices—shortages lead to price increases, which means that the fishing operations that can still deliver in times of shortage will find fishing to be exceedingly profitable—even when the fish are reproducing too slowly to replenish their numbers. The industry has already ignored obvious problems such as the destruction of coral through bottom trawling, so it is unlikely that anything short of extinction will force boats to voluntarily follow regulations.

6   Worse, as the global population continues to grow, more and more people will wish to purchase fish despite dwindling yields. Since prior regulations have been meekly enforced and largely ignored, it is imperative that various governments work together to better monitor the industry. Companies must no longer be able to turn a blind eye when it comes to the boats and crews they acquire their stock from. Nations must truly cooperate and set aside petty territorialism to enforce a strict, global set of regulations, even in international waters. The world's oceans are in grave danger, and the negative externalities are too dire to ignore. Without immediate and forceful regulation it may soon be too late to make a difference.

---

[1] Bottom trawling is a form of fishing that involves dragging a net along the sea floor.

B. Answer the questions.

1. Which idea(s) in the article are most interesting to you? Do you agree or disagree with them?

....

....

2. Explain why you agree or disagree with the ideas you found most interesting. Share experiences you've had or give reasons that support your position.

....

....

3. Why is your critique of this point relevant or important?

....

....

C. Use the information you highlighted in the reading to complete the outline.

Title of the article and name of the author:

_____

Summary of the main idea of the article:

_____

_____

A paraphrase of the idea you would like to explore in your response:

_____

A quote you would like to incorporate into your response (optional):

_____

Your claim (Do you agree or disagree with the author? Why or why not?):

_____

_____

Evidence to support your claim (Explain, using personal experience and / or other sources):

_____

_____

Conclusion (Summarize your point):

_____

_____

D. Write a 400–500 word critical response of the article, using your outline.

E. <u>PEER REVIEW</u>. Exchange responses with a partner. Respond to the questions to evaluate each other's work. For responses marked No, give feedback in the Notes column to help your partner revise.

	Yes	No	Notes
Does the response include the title and author of the original text?	☐	☐	
Does the response clearly state the writer's position about a key idea from the text?	☐	☐	
Does the response accurately summarize the key idea the writer is responding to?	☐	☐	
Does the response include enough support for the writer's position?	☐	☐	
Does the response include only information that is relevant to the argument?	☐	☐	
Does the response repeat information?	☐	☐	
Is the response well organized?	☐	☐	
Are the paraphrases and / or use of quotations correct?	☐	☐	
Is the response concise?	☐	☐	

▶ Go to MyEnglishLab to complete vocabulary exercises and skill practices.

LANGUAGE SKILLS
USING DIRECT QUOTATIONS AND REPORTED SPEECH

WHY IT'S USEFUL Knowing how to correctly use both direct quotations and reported speech is necessary when integrating ideas from other sources into your writing. By integrating sources properly, you add credibility to your ideas.

There are two standard ways of including information from a source in your writing: **quoting** and **paraphrasing**. If you are using **direct quotations**, you must use the exact words from the source, putting them in quotation marks and presenting them in context. If you are paraphrasing and using **reported speech**, be sure that you are accurately capturing the essence of what the person said but restated in your own words. In either case, it is essential that you cite the source of the comment.

DIRECT QUOTATIONS

Be selective when using quotations. Only choose quotations that help to frame the argument you are making. Start by setting up the quotation—introduce your idea and state who you will quote to support it. Then include the quotation. After the quotation, you must immediately explain why it is relevant to your point. This can be called a *quote sandwich*

Introducing the quote

Quoted speech
[which supports your argument]

Explanation of the quote

Note how the writer frames the quotation in the response at right.

Introducing the quote: Cynthia Flanagan, a well-renowned writer, describes the negative externalities that are a result of unregulated fishing practices. In her article, "The Hidden Externalities of Fishing," she reports that the demand for fish has led to illegal fishing practices that are destroying marine environments. Flanagan asserts that

Quoted speech: "The industry has already ignored obvious problems such as the destruction of coral through bottom trawling, so it is unlikely that anything short of extinction will force boats to voluntarily follow regulations" (2015).

Explanation of the quote: In other words, like me, she believes that strict regulations need to be enforced in order to prevent negative externalities from ruining the world's oceans.

Here are some common ways to introduce a quotation. Note the punctuation in each example.

- [Author] [reporting verb] that "..."
- [Author] [reporting verb], "..."
- According to [the author or the title of text], "..."
- In the article, "...," [Author] argues that "..."
- In [Author's] opinion, "..."
- [Author] disagrees / agrees with this point when she states, "..."

REPORTED SPEECH

Aside from mentioning the source and using the correct reporting verb, it is important to accurately **paraphrase** the information by restating it in your own words when you use reported speech.

For more on reporting verbs, see ECONOMICS Part 1.

Here is a helpful method for paraphrasing:

1. Without looking at the text you have just read, summarize it, using your notes.
2. Use content-specific words from the text that describe concepts within that discipline. However, you should make sure you use synonyms for other words in the text.
3. Alter the structure of the text by changing active to passive voice (or vice versa), moving clauses around in complex sentences, or reducing clauses to phrases.

Note how the writer paraphrases the quotation:

Quote: "Other illegal but widely practiced fishing methods like bottom trawling can destroy large sections of coral reef; the practices remain in widespread use despite environmental damage because they catch large quantities of fish."

Paraphrase: In her article, "The Hidden Externalities of Fishing," Flanagan argues that the profitability of catching large amounts of fish incentivizes illegal fishing practices even though they destroy marine environments.

EXERCISE 6

Read the passage. Underline the reported speech. Then write the parts of the passage next to the correct sections.

Cynthia Flanagan, the author of "The Hidden Externalities of Fishing," contends that technological advancements in the fishing industry have led to overharvesting. She explains that overfishing "is largely due to technological advances that allow fishing boats to catch fish not just at geographically convenient locations but at every point of their migration" (2015). Flanagan's comment supports my point that regulations need to be enforced before further technological advancements are made.

Introducing the quote: ....

....

Quoted speech: ....

....

Explanation of the quote: ....

....

EXERCISE 7

Change the direct quotations to reported speech. Use accurate reporting verbs and be sure to paraphrase. See page Economics Part 1 Language Skills for examples of reporting verbs.

1. "Today, the worldwide demand for fish, from luxury Bluefin tuna to cheap forage fish, has increased dramatically due to population growth and consumer preference."

2. "An externality is really just a form of market failure where individuals not involved in an economic transaction incur some sort of cost from it."

3. "Not all externalities are negative. Positive externalities are things that benefit those not involved in a transaction. For example, living next to a neighbor with honey bees may help your garden flourish."

4. "The entire situation is a tragedy of the commons—fishing boats have little incentive to follow environmental regulations when they can instead maximize personal gain."

5. "The world's oceans are in grave danger, and the negative externalities are too dire to ignore."

EXERCISE 8

Complete the introductions to the quotations from "The Hidden Externalities of Fishing." Use phrases from page 163 to help you. Be sure that the phrase you have chosen works grammatically in the sentence. Compare answers with a partner. There is more than one way to introduce each quote.

1. ...., "The Hidden Externalities of Fishing," .... "examining these externalities demonstrates why global overfishing is a crisis that requires international cooperation and strict government regulation if we hope to preserve the Earth's oceans for future generations."

2. ...., "throughout the world, critical populations of marine life are threatened and dwindling in the face of overfishing."

3. Flanagan .... "Many animals caught as bycatch die before the nets are even pulled up."

4. The author .... us .... "subsistence fishing villages that have, for years, lived off the sea are now pulling up empty nets with increasing frequency."

5. .... Flanagan's ...., "it is imperative that various governments work together to better monitor the industry."

6. .... "without immediate and forceful regulation, it may soon be too late to make a difference."

▶ Go to MyEnglishLab to complete skill practices.

APPLY YOUR SKILLS

WHY IT'S USEFUL By applying the skills you have learned in this unit, you can successfully use critical reading skills to analyze texts, integrate sources to add credibility to your writing, and construct an argument in a critical response paper.

> **ASSIGNMENT**
>
> Write a critical response to an idea in an article you have found that discusses how positive and/ or negative externalities of a particular good or service impact society. Be sure to read the article critically to ensure that you have selected an appropriate article, identify evidence in the article to support your idea, and integrate that information into your critical response.

BEFORE YOU WRITE

A. Before you begin your assignment, discuss these questions with one or more students.

1. What are some externalities that concern you? (Environmental? Educational? Economic? Human Rights?) Explain why they concern you and how you think the externalities will change—or why they won't change—in the near future.

2. Is there an externality that has directly affected you? Explain how it has affected you and whether you think the situation can or will change.

B. As you consider your assignment, complete the tasks below. Then, share your ideas with another student. Get feedback and revise your ideas, if necessary.

1. What externality would you like to research? Why is it interesting to you? ....

....

....

2. Choose one idea that you are thinking of writing a critical response to. Why did you choose this idea?...

....

....

3. What evidence do you think you will find in support of your position? ....

....

....

C. Review the Unit Skills Summary. As you begin on the writing task on page 167, apply the skills you learned in this unit.

THINKING CRITICALLY

As you consider your assignment, discuss the questions with another student. Get feedback and revise your ideas, if necessary.

1. A carbon tax is a tax on businesses and industries that produce carbon dioxide through their operations. The tax is designed to reduce the output of greenhouse gases and carbon dioxide into the atmosphere. So, if an industry is making enough money, they can pay the tax and not work to change their practices. Do you think this tax is an easy way out for some industries?

2. Can you think of a way to apply the principle of a carbon tax to other industries?

3. Do you think governments should attempt to remedy externalities? Why or why not?

THINKING VISUALLY

Look at the graph showing the effect of a negative externality using a supply curve. Answer the questions about the information it conveys.

1. When the social cost is used, is the price higher or lower? Why? ....

....

2. When the private cost is used, why is the quantity produced greater? ....

....

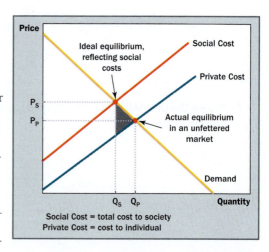

Social Cost = total cost to society
Private Cost = cost to individual

3. The triangle represents the loss. Why is there a loss if social costs are not considered?

....

....

4. Is the graph useful in understanding the social loss in a negative externality? Why or why not?

....

....

THINKING ABOUT LANGUAGE

Paraphrase the passage. Accurately restate information in your own words. Then compare your paraphrase with that of another student.

In the article, "Profits, Despite What You Hear, Do Not Equal Environmental Pollution," Fred Smith argues that industry and businesses will self-regulate in order to prevent negative externalities, such as pollution because companies have a financial incentive to turn residuals (waste) into a useable product. According to Smith, it can cost businesses a great deal to dispose of the leftovers from their production. He contends that because companies aim to maximize their profits, we do not need governments to step in and regulate waste; it is more efficient and effective to let companies self-regulate.

WRITE

A. Revisit the writing assignment and your answers to the questions in Before You Write Part B. Find an article that discusses how positive and / or negative externalities of a particular good or service impact society. Identify the idea that you would like to respond to.

....

....

....

B. Write a summary of the specific idea you have chosen for your critical response.

C. Write a critical response. How can you relate your experience to the information you found? Include direct quotations and reported speech.

BEYOND THE ASSIGNMENT

Write a critical response to the entire article you selected. identify evidence in the article to support your ideas, and integrate that information into your critical response.

▶ Go to MyEnglishLab to listen to Professor Clerici-Arias and to complete a self-assessment.

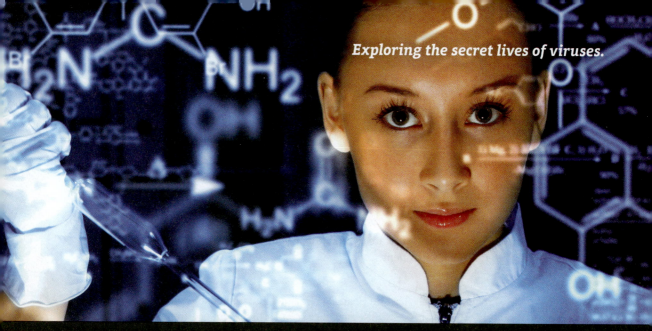
Exploring the secret lives of viruses.

BIOLOGY

Process Writing

UNIT PROFILE

The process for creating a new vaccine and making it available to the public is lengthy and complex. In this unit, you will read and write about how vaccines combat viruses. Specifically, you will learn about how vaccines are made, tested, and monitored. You will also learn about the Zika virus and its probable link to the rise in certain birth defects.

UNIT ASSIGNMENT

Choose a virus and research its characteristics and latest treatment methods, including vaccines used to fight it. **Write a 2–3 page analytical process paper** explaining how the method, drug, or vaccine works. You may also include information about how the treatment was discovered and tested.

OUTCOMES

- Structure a process
- Explain a procedure
- Formulate a hypothesis
- Form conditional clauses

GETTING STARTED

▶ Go to MyEnglishLab to listen to Professor Siegel and to complete a self-assessment.

Discuss these questions with a partner or group.

1. Have you been vaccinated against childhood diseases such as measles or chickenpox? If so, which ones? Do you get a flu shot? Why or why not? Why do people get vaccinated?

2. Why are vaccinations an important world health issue? Why might some people refuse to vaccinate their children?

3. What is the significance to society of verifying an assertion about a viral illness?

For more about **BIOLOGY**, see ① ③. See also R and OC **BIOLOGY** ① ② ③.

CRITICAL THINKING SKILL
PROCESS WRITING

WHY IT'S USEFUL By explaining a process, describing the steps involved, and presenting them in a logical order, you help your reader understand how something is done.

Process writing is an essential mode of writing in many academic disciplines as well as many fields of work such as technology, manufacturing, and business. Process writing typically is instructional or analytical and is sometimes combined with narrative, especially in business writing. In academic settings, process writing is most commonly used in fields like science and engineering when explaining processes and procedures in research and experiments. Process writing is also used in fields like sociology and anthropology to describe, for example, how customs vary in different institutions within a society or in different cultures; in literature to explain the steps in analyzing a literary work; and in economics to describe how a series of actions led to an economic consequence, such as a banking crisis.

Instructional (also called directional) process writing is basically a "how to" in that the reader is being taught how to do a process with the goal of being able to recreate the process. For example, recipes for cooking and instructions for setting up and using devices are common instances of process writing. In academic work, the writer might instruct or direct the reader in how to set up a piece of monitoring equipment, plan a research paper, or use a new computer program.

Analytical (also called informational) process writing provides an explanation and description of how something works, how something happens or happened, or how something is done. The purpose is for the reader to learn about the process and understand it, not recreate it. This is the most common type of process writing in academics. In an analytical process, the writer might explain how a monitoring device gathers data, how a research project is or was conducted, or how a statistical analysis is performed using a particular software program.

In all process writing, clearly explaining the steps or stages in **structuring a process** or **explaining a procedure** with description and examples is necessary. The steps might be as short as the few seconds it takes to turn on a piece of equipment to the extended period of time it takes to monitor an experiment or observe a natural phenomenon over decades.

NOTICING ACTIVITY

Read the two process paragraphs. Notice their similarities and differences.

> Use the scientific method when you conduct empirical research. To conduct an experiment using the scientific method, follow these steps. First, choose what you want to observe and record and pose a research question. Next, identify a hypothesis worth investigating. Third, decide what test or experiment will provide the data you need. Carefully design your experiment. Closely follow accepted procedures for conducting your test or experiment to avoid error during this phase, and be sure the data you gather relates to the hypothesis. Your experiment must be reproducible by others. Then, analyze and interpret your data to see if it supports your conclusion. Account for data that does not support your hypothesis. Finally, report your results and conclusion.

Continued

It is important to understand the scientific method when analyzing empirical research. The scientific method follows these steps. Once the researcher has decided what he or she wants to observe and record, a research question is posed. Then, one or more hypotheses are identified that are deemed worthy of investigating. After that, the type of test or experiment that will best provide the data needed will be chosen, and the testing or experiment will be carefully designed. The researcher conducts the experiment in a controlled manner, taking care to follow established procedures. The test or experiment must be reproducible by others. The final step is an analysis of the data, which the researcher will interpret in order to determine if the data supports the hypothesis. Any data that does not support the hypothesis must be accounted for. After completion of the study, the results and conclusion are shared with others.

1. Which paragraph is instructional? Could you follow the steps and complete the process?

2. Which paragraph is analytical? Is the explanation clear and is there enough detail that you fully understand? Could you explain the process to someone else?

3. How are the two paragraphs similar? How are they different?

A hypothesis is formulated in response to a research question and serves as the basis of an empirical research study. You will learn more about hypotheses later in this unit.

Go to **MyEnglishLab** to complete a skill practice and join in collaborative activities.

SUPPORTING SKILL 1
STRUCTURING A PROCESS

WHY IT'S USEFUL By structuring a process you ensure that your reader can follow the steps or stages and understand the process and its connection to the research or paper it is a part of.

Structuring process writing means **explaining, describing**, and perhaps **exemplifying steps in a process or procedure**. Graphics commonly provide visual support in understanding the process.

In structuring a process, you need to first introduce it and make its purpose clear to the reader. The introduction must attract the reader's attention and convince the reader of the importance of understanding the process. You might state how the process will affect the reader, if applicable.

Just as in other writing, considering the audience is essential. If the reader has little knowledge of the topic the process is describing, more explicit and detailed information, including definitions of terms, may be required, whereas if the audience has strong knowledge of the field, less detailed explanation may suffice.

For more on audience, see Professor Siegel's interview in BIOLOGY Part 3.

The **introduction** to a process paper needs to include a strong central idea in a thesis statement that names the process and indicates its purpose. Typical organization of the introduction to a process is general-to-specific.

For more on general to specific organization, see BIOLOGY Part 1.

An introduction to a paper on how scientists conduct research might include a statement like this:

> Whether you are conducting your own experiments or reading the research of others, it is important to understand the scientific method.

To create a coherent process paper, **arrange the steps or stages in a logical order,** typically chronological, sequential, or enumerative as the steps are listed, named, or labeled, and explained in the order they occur in time. Use transition signals—*first, second, third, last* and adverb clauses with *before, after, once,* or *as soon as* that indicate order and *while, during, over* (+ time) and *between* that indicate duration to achieve cohesion and coherence. Here are some examples:

For more on coherence and cohesion, see BIOLOGY Part 1.

> **Third,** decide what test or experiment will provide the data you need.

> **Once** scientists or researchers have decided what they want to observe and record, a research question is posed.

> Closely follow accepted procedures for conducting your test or experiment to avoid error **during** this phase.

To fully **develop the steps or stages,** the body paragraphs should include a complete explanation with enough detail and description supported by examples or illustrations to help the reader understand the material. Do not include information that is irrelevant to the process and make sure the process has unity.

Look at the illustration supporting the explanation of the scientific method.

For more on using visuals to support writing, see ENGINEERING Part 1.

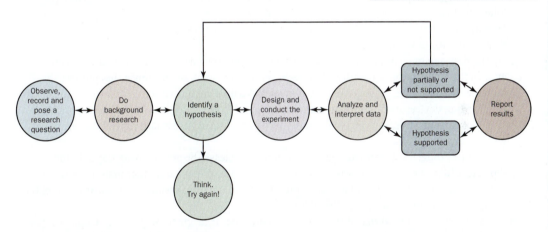

Here are some guidelines on language use for process papers.

Language to structure a process paper			
Instructional		**Analytical**	
• 2nd person—*you* • Imperative	First, [you] **choose** what you want to observe and record, and **pose** a research question.	• 3rd person—*he / she; they* • Passive	Once <u>the scientists</u> have decided what <u>they</u> want to observe and record, a research question **is posed**.
Use verbs that are specific and clearly explain or describe actions performed, including: *identify, pose, create, develop, propose, design, plan,* and *conduct* among others.			

Look back at the two paragraphs in the Critical Thinking Skill, pages 169–170, to find other examples of transition signals, use of person, verbs, and passive voice.

A final part of a process paper is a **conclusion**. The conclusion might summarize the process, discuss results, or place it in a larger context. Here are two examples:

> Carefully following the steps of the scientific method in your experiments will ensure that they are viewed in a positive light and considered useful contributions to the field.

> Understanding the scientific method will help you analyze and judge the contribution of research conducted in the field.

EXERCISE 1

A. Read the essay.

How Vaccines Are Created

1 Vaccines are used to stop contagious diseases from spreading by preventing them in individuals, which in turn protects whole communities. Vaccines have the potential to eradicate diseases, which is why no one has smallpox today. Vaccines work by mimicking bacteria and viruses and stimulating the immune system to defend against them. The creation of a vaccine takes the work of many scientists and medical experts collaborating together, and it usually requires many years of research before the vaccine is ready for use. This is why we are still waiting for a vaccine against the viruses responsible for HIV, Ebola, and Zika.

2 There are different types of vaccines that vary, depending on how they can best stop a particular disease, and new experimental vaccines are always in the works. However, there are required stages, steps, and formal procedures that are followed by all researchers. While the following brief explanation of creating a vaccine seems simple, it represents a very complex, lengthy, and vitally important process in combating the viruses and bacteria that still cause disease and death worldwide.

3 The first step in creating a vaccine against a pathogen, the virus or bacteria that is causing an infectious disease, is to identify an antigen, the specific toxin or substance that induces the immune response. The pathogen is grown in a lab. Viruses are grown in cell cultures, and bacteria are grown in devices using a growth medium. The goal is to yield as much antigen as possible. This step can take several years of laboratory research as scientists seek the specific antigen that will prevent the disease.

4 After the antigen is identified, the second step is to release the antigen from the cells and separate it from the material it was grown in. At this stage, protein and other materials used in growing the virus or bacteria may still be present. Again, scientists want to release as much of the antigen of the virus or bacteria as possible.

5 Once a sufficient quantity of the antigen is collected, it needs to be purified. Depending on the type of vaccine, a live attenuated, an inactivated (killed), or a subunit / conjugate vaccine[1], an appropriate method of further separating the antigen is employed, and ultra-filtration is

---

[1] To create a live attenuated vaccine, a live microbe, weakened so it cannot cause the disease, is grown in a lab. Because this vaccine is the closest to a natural infection, it often elicits life-long immunity. These vaccines are most often created for viruses and have been used against measles, mumps, and chicken pox. The danger of live vaccines is that they might later mutate into a virulent form that will cause disease. They cannot be given to people with weakened immune systems. They also must be refrigerated, so they are harder to store and transport.

To create an inactivated vaccine, scientists first kill the bacteria or virus with chemicals, heat, or radiation. These are more stable vaccines that don't require refrigeration, making them easier to ship and store. They can also be given to people with compromised immune systems, but they require more doses and don't usually provide life-long immunity, requiring booster vaccines to be given later. These were among the earliest vaccines.

To create a subunit / conjugate vaccine, which contains only antigens, a specific protein or carbohydrate that induces an immune response is isolated for use in the vaccine. To create these vaccines, the virus or bacteria is grown in a lab, and chemicals are used to break them apart and gather the antigens. Chances for an adverse reaction are lower because they don't contain all the molecules of the virus or bacteria. Pertussis vaccine is an example of a subunit / conjugate vaccine.

used to achieve the purest form possible to ensure it is safe and reliable. The scientists now have a form of the vaccine that is ready for trials, but it still needs to be put into a formula that can be administered to patients. The fourth step, then, in preparing a useable vaccine is to add an adjuvant that enhances immune response, stabilizers that preserve shelf life, and preservatives that allow safe use of multidose packaging. The final step is to mix the vaccine in large enough quantities to achieve uniformity and meet the demand for the vaccine. The vaccine is then packaged for distribution over a large area, perhaps even worldwide.

B. Answer the questions.

1. How does the introduction attract the reader's attention and convince the reader of the importance of understanding the process? Does the introduction state how the reader is affected by the topic? Is the introduction effective? Can you think of a better way to introduce the topic?

   ....

   ....

   ....

   ....

2. What is the purpose of the paper? ....

   ....

   ....

3. Who is the audience for the paper—someone who is unfamiliar with the topic or an expert? Use examples from the essay to support your opinion. ....

   ....

   ....

4. Write the thesis statement. Underline the process once and the purpose twice.

   ....

   ....

5. How is the paper organized? Circle the transition signals in the body paragraphs.

   ....

   ....

6. List the verbs that are used to explain or describe the process. How often is the passive voice used?

....

....

....

7. Create a reverse outline in the chart by listing each step in three or four words. Hint: Use the verbs you listed in question 6 in the imperative form. Then note the purpose or reason for each step. Is each step in the process fully explained and understandable?

	Step	Purpose or reason
1		
2		
3		
4		
5		

8. Write a one- or two-sentence conclusion for the essay.

....

....

....

C. Discuss your answers, reverse outline, and conclusion with a partner.

EXERCISE 2

A. Read the practice assignment and write a paragraph.

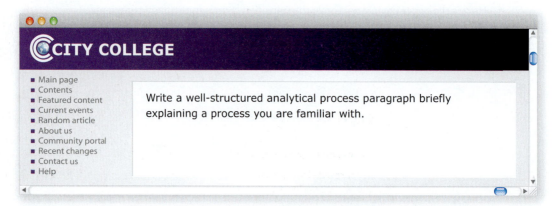

CITY COLLEGE

- Main page
- Contents
- Featured content
- Current events
- Random article
- About us
- Community portal
- Recent changes
- Contact us
- Help

Write a well-structured analytical process paragraph briefly explaining a process you are familiar with.

B. **<u>PEER REVIEW.</u>** Exchange your paragraph with a partner. Respond to the questions to evaluate each other's work. For responses marked No, give feedback in the Notes column to help your partner revise.

	Yes	No	Notes
Does the writer convince you of the importance of the process?	☐	☐	
Is there a clear central idea?	☐	☐	
Is the purpose clearly expressed?	☐	☐	
Are the steps in the process in a sequential or chronological order?	☐	☐	
Are there transition signals to make the paragraph cohesive?	☐	☐	
Are there enough steps?	☐	☐	
Is each step fully explained and understandable for the intended audience?	☐	☐	
Is the paragraph coherent and unified?	☐	☐	
Does the writer conclude effectively?	☐	☐	

Go to MyEnglishLab to complete a vocabulary exercise and a skill practice and join in collaborative activities.

SUPPORTING SKILL 2
EXPLAINING A PROCEDURE

WHY IT'S USEFUL By explaining a procedure, you break down the tasks in a process into clear steps. Written procedures ensure consistency in how something is done.

Procedures are best defined as a series of actions or fixed steps that must be followed in a particular order and certain manner to complete a task and maintain consistent standards and quality. Process and procedure are often hard to distinguish, and the terms are used differently in different fields of study and work. Understanding how process and procedure differ is helpful in developing your skills at writing and explaining procedures.

Procedure	Process
Detailed steps that describe how a process is performed	Bigger picture of what needs to be done
How to do or complete a task	How to accomplish a goal or achieve a desired outcome
Fixed steps that must be followed in order	Methods and relationships between tasks
A course of action with a start and end point	Actions to achieve a purpose
One role	Multiple roles
Instructional	Analytical and instructional
Language use:	Language use:
Medical, i.e., the doctor performed a procedure	Biological, i.e., process of respiration

In all fields of work and study where strict policies or licensing is required, written procedures are essential. Written procedures are usually necessary when the tasks in a process:

- are lengthy.
- are complex.
- need to be done in a consistent manner by many people.
- involve significant change in how something is done.
- have serious consequences if done wrong.
- need to be documented.

Written procedures are precise, factual, short, and to the point. They are easy to read in simple direct language and provide only enough detail to perform the tasks correctly. They are often written as bulleted text, listing the steps in the procedure.

For more on creating bulleted text, see ENGINEERING Part 2.

In academic and other writing, explanations of procedures are provided when it is necessary or helpful for the reader to understand the specific tasks involved in a complex process in greater detail. Procedure explanations are often embedded in process writing, especially in empirical research reports and articles. They are typically found in the methods and materials section.

Well-written explanations of procedures list the steps but also provide enough additional information for the reader to fully understand the actions. As with processes, the audience—how much the reader already knows—will be a factor in deciding what information is appropriate to include and how much detail is needed.

EXERCISE 3

A. Read the explanation of a procedure.

MAKING A SAFE VACCINE

Once researchers have identified the antigen for a particular virus, conducted pre-clinical testing, and are ready to develop and produce a vaccine for use in humans, they must follow a strict procedure.

Investigational New Drug Application

The first step in the approval process is to submit an Investigational New Drug (IND) application to the US Food and Drug Administration (FDA). This application must demonstrate that the vaccine has passed tests for safety and purity, present all clinical data, explain how the drug works, propose a plan for human testing, and describe how it will be manufactured.

Testing and Clinical Trials

Second, when the FDA has approved the IND, the vaccine must be tested in these phases.

- Phase I is typically done on 20 or fewer adult subjects and is a test primarily for safety and to determine the extent of the immune response.
- Phase II has 50 or up to hundreds of subjects and tests for the best dosage, preliminary data on effectiveness, and schedule and method of immunization delivery.
- Phase III has thousands to tens of thousands of volunteers and thoroughly studies the vaccine's safety and efficacy—the ability to protect against the disease and lead to natural immune responses to the pathogen by the body.

Application for Biologics License

If the vaccine has performed well in the testing phase, the final step in the procedure to produce the vaccine is to apply for the Biologics license. The researchers must provide the results of all human testing, including safety, purity, and potency and describe manufacturing and testing methods. In addition, the FDA inspects the manufacturing facility, which must meet government standards for equipment, personnel, packaging, and record keeping.

The vaccine is reviewed by an advisory committee of experts, scientists, physicians, statisticians, and consumer representatives, who vote on whether to recommend FDA approval.

Post-licensing Monitoring

When a vaccine is approved and in use, there are further procedures that must be followed. The FDA continues to monitor the production of the vaccine and has the right to conduct its own tests of the manufacturing process. The FDA and CDC (Centers for Disease Control and Prevention) review the licensed vaccine for anything unusual. Anyone can report adverse reactions through the Vaccine Adverse Event Reporting System. Phase IV testing, optional testing of large numbers of people, is typically done by the manufacturer to see if there are any rare or delayed reactions to the vaccine.

B. Answer the questions.

1. What is the goal or desired outcome of the process? ....

....

....

2. How will the purpose be achieved? ....

....

3. Name the required three steps to produce a vaccine. Begin each step with a verb.

1. ....

2. ....

3. ....

4. Why is a procedure necessary to produce a vaccine? ....

....

....

5. Create a brief outline of the procedure explained in the article. List each step in the procedure and the tasks that must be completed in each step. Begin with the steps in Question 3 and add a fourth step for the procedure after the vaccine is produced.

    I.

    II.

    III.

IV.

6. Does the explanation of the procedure provide enough information? Is it detailed enough?

....

....

C. Compare your responses in Part B with a partner.

D. Explain a procedure. List the steps in a procedure you are familiar with in your field of study and explain it in a brief paragraph. Include why it is necessary in your explanation.

E. **PEER REVIEW.** Exchange your list and paragraph with a partner. Respond to the questions to evaluate each other's work. For responses marked No, give feedback in the Notes column to help your partner revise.

	Yes	No	Notes
Does the writer's procedure meet the necessary criteria for a written procedure?	☐	☐	
Is the writer's list precise and in clear language?	☐	☐	
Are there any unnecessary details in the list?	☐	☐	
Are the steps in the procedure in a logical order?	☐	☐	
Does the paragraph explain the procedure effectively?	☐	☐	
Was appropriate information to explain the actions in the procedure added?	☐	☐	

Go to MyEnglishLab to complete a vocabulary exercise and skill practice and join in collaborative activities.

READING-WRITING CONNECTION
FORMULATING A HYPOTHESIS

WHY IT'S USEFUL By formulating a hypothesis, you will be able to conduct empirical research and advance scientific knowledge.

A **hypothesis** is a statement that proposes an explanation for a phenomenon and can be tested through observation or experimentation. A hypothesis is formulated in response to a research question and serves as the basis of an empirical research study, which is a common type of writing in the physical and social sciences. *Empirical* refers to research that is based on experimentation or observation as opposed to theories or beliefs.

Before conducting a study, researchers begin with a tentative hypothesis that often includes a prediction of the results. After testing the hypothesis and interpreting the data, a determination is made about whether the results support, partially support, or fail to support the original hypothesis. In some cases, the data can lead to the formulation of a new hypothesis altogether. This investigative process is part of the scientific method described earlier in the Critical Thinking Skill.

Before formulating a hypothesis, you must first develop your research question. Carrying out a literature review can help narrow your research question and determine what research has already been done on the topic so that you do not repeat an earlier study. Discussion and conclusion sections of research articles are especially helpful as they often indicate areas needing further investigation. This can help you generate or confirm an unanswered research question.

Here is an example of a research question that seeks to examine the effects that antibacterial hand sanitizer has on the immune system: *How does the use of antibacterial hand sanitizer affect the immune system?* Once you have identified your research question, you can begin formulating a hypothesis.

Characteristics of an Effective Hypothesis

- Hypotheses are often written in the form of an ***if* / *then* statement**. The *if* part of the sentence shows the relationship between the variables that you will test. The *then* part of the clause includes a prediction of your intended results.

  If antibacterial hand sanitizer weakens the immune system by killing good bacteria the body needs to keep disease-causing bacteria away, then decreasing the amount of antibacterial hand sanitizer used will result in lowering the number of illnesses caused by a weakened immune system.

- Your hypothesis should include **dependent** and **independent variables**. The dependent variable is the phenomenon that is impacted by the independent variable. It is critical that your hypothesis only include one independent variable. This will enable you to determine the cause of any observed effects. There can be more than one dependent variable, depending on how many effects you decide to measure in your study.

  Independent variable: antibacterial hand sanitizer [cause]
  Dependent variable: weakened immune system [effect]

- Your hypothesis should include **directional predictions** that state how the independent variable affects the dependent variable(s).

  Decreasing antibacterial hand sanitizer used → Lowers number of illnesses

- Your hypothesis should be **specific**. When relevant, specify the population, material, or object you are investigating. For example, in our hypothesis, we specified that illnesses would decrease if less hand sanitizer were used. If the intent of our research were to study the effects of hand sanitizer on the immune system over time, the hypothesis could be specified further:

  If early exposure to germs creates a stronger immune system as we age, then decreasing the amount of antibacterial hand sanitizer used by children will result in lowering the number of illnesses people have when they are older.

- Make sure your hypothesis is **testable**. It must be possible to measure the relationship between the independent and dependent variables through experimentation or observation. Not all *if / then* statements are hypotheses: *If I graduate with a high GPA, then I will get a good job.* This is an example of a prediction, not a testable hypothesis. To change a prediction to a hypothesis, introduce measureable variables in the *if* clause:

   If graduating with a high GPA is an important hiring criterion for top law firms, then there will be a higher number of lawyers who graduated with a 3.8 or above employed by top law firms than those who graduated with a GPA below a 3.8.

EXERCISE 4

A. Analyze the statements and determine whether or not they include the characteristics of an effective hypothesis. If elements are missing, rewrite the hypothesis to be more effective.

1. If fleas need humidity of 50 percent or higher to live, then setting a dehumidifier to less than 50 percent will eliminate fleas from a home. ....

   ....

   ....

2. If sharing a border causes countries' political systems to be similar, then countries that share borders with democratic nations will be more likely to follow a democratic system.

   ....

   ....

3. If a person smokes cigarettes, then they will be at a higher risk for lung cancer than people who do not smoke. ....

   ....

   ....

4. There will be fewer cases of the flu in areas where people are vaccinated.

   ....

   ....

5. If caffeine stimulates women more than men, then women who have caffeine will have a greater increase in heart rate than men. ....

   ....

   ....

6. Car emissions cause global warming; therefore, reducing the amount that people drive cars will lower the temperature of the earth. ....

   ....

   ....

7. If the immune system is healthy, then reducing stress will strengthen the immune system.

   ....

   ....

8. If repeated use of antibiotics causes antibiotics to become less effective in eliminating bacteria, then mortality rates will increase for patients who have used antibiotics repeatedly to treat bacterial infections. ....

....

....

9. If eating foods high in saturated fat is related to high cholesterol, then people who eat pizza every day will have higher cholesterol than people who do not eat pizza every day.

....

....

....

10. If the more formal education people receive increases the probability that they will become self-employed, then schooling will be important.

....

....

....

B. Compare your revised hypotheses with a partner and discuss what was missing from the original statements. Determine whether your partner's hypotheses are now effective.

EXERCISE 5

A. Read the essay.

The Zika Virus: A Pandemic Threat

1   Viruses that cause infectious illnesses can vary greatly depending on their genetic material and the cytopathic[1] damage they inflict during their replication process. The Zika virus, part of the family of single-stranded RNA viruses known as flaviviridae, emerged as a pandemic threat in 2015. Zika is closely related to other flaviviruses, including yellow fever, dengue, and West Nile, and it resembles these illnesses in its shape, in its transmission through a mosquito, and in some of its symptoms. Generally, only about one in five people infected with the virus manifests symptoms, which are mild and include fever and rash. Zika was first identified in 1947, so it is an established virus, but evidence suggests it may have mutated, or that the population groups exposed to the particular strain found in the 2015 and early 2016 outbreak may not possess

Until there is a vaccine, prevention or reduction of transmission of the Zika virus is dependent on successful mosquito control.

immunity to it. The outbreak has overlapped with an increased incidence of unusual autoimmune and neurological problems, including Guillain-Barré syndrome, a temporary paralysis, and

---

[1] **Cytopathic** refers to a change in the function or form of a cell, leading to its death.

[2] A **congenital anomaly** is a birth defect.

microcephaly, a congenital anomaly[2] in which babies are born with an abnormally small head and brain. While both conditions are concerning, we will limit the scope of this discussion to focusing on the connection between microcephaly and the Zika virus. No such link has been proven, but strong evidence points to a causative relationship between the virus and the condition, including recent tests in which epidemiologists have found the virus in fetal brain tissue.

2   While other infectious viruses like rubella can cause microcephaly, no other viruses in the flavivirus genus are known to cause such complications. More than 4,000 microcephaly cases were reported by the Brazilian Health Ministry between fall of 2015 and early 2016. This surge of cases far exceeds the usual number, which typically falls below 200 total cases per year. In addition, the US Centers for Disease Control (CDC) reported in February 2016 that the Zika virus was found in the brain tissue of two infants who had microcephaly and died shortly after being born. The Zika virus was also present in the brain tissue of two fetuses that were miscarried in the first trimester[3] of pregnancy. The four mothers in the studies had classic symptoms of Zika during their first trimester, according to the health report.[4] Other studies have revealed similar results, including a case in which a complete genome sequence of the Zika virus was discovered in the brain tissue sample of a microcephalic fetus.[5] These cases suggest that the virus may pass through intrauterine[6] transmission. Knowledge of the precise way the virus may affect the brain of the developing fetus is murky, though it appears that Zika, if it is indeed the causative factor for microcephaly, does not necessarily follow the same pattern as other microcephaly-causing viruses. It is

also not clear if complications in fetal development arise from the virus itself or from an immune response in the mother's body.

3   While these early studies are examining the pathogenesis[7] of the virus and establishing evidence for a direct link between Zika and microcephaly, a causal relationship cannot be stated with certainty until scientists use a variety of case-control studies. To understand whether the virus has teratogenic effects[8] and could cause microcephaly, the CDC along with international counterparts is carrying out a study in Brazil to examine a large case group of babies born with microcephaly and an equal-sized control group of babies born without congenital abnormalities. The research will examine environmental and health factors that may have influenced the situation in Brazil, and it will form a clearer picture of how many cases may have resulted from Zika.

4   Several factors may have influenced the incidence of microcephaly. The condition is measured differently by different organizations and doctors, and fluctuating criteria may have influenced the number of babies diagnosed. In addition, microcephaly can occur as a result of many environmental and genetic factors. It can be inherited through chromosomal abnormalities, it can be caused by maternal use of alcohol, or it can be brought upon by other bacteria or viruses. These determiners, which are not related to the Zika virus, may have influenced the occurrence of microcephaly and must be ruled out before researchers can say with certainty that Zika was the primary factor that caused the condition. Finally, regional awareness of the possibility of increased prevalence of microcephaly may have led to more reporting than usual or even over-reporting. Of course, it is also possible that the

---

[3] A **trimester** is a period of three months.

[4] Roosecelis Brasil Martines et al., "Notes from the Field: Evidence of Zika Virus Infection in Brain and Placental Tissues from Two Congenitally Infected Newborns and Two Fetal Losses—Brazil, 2015." *Morbidity and Mortality Weekly Report (MMWR)* (February 19, 2016): 65(6): 159–60. http://www.cdc.gov/mmwr/volumes/65/wr/mm6506e1.htm.

[5] Jernej Mlakar et al., "Zika Virus Associated with Microcephaly." *The New England Journal of Medicine.* (February 10, 2016): http://www.nejm.org/doi/full/10.1056/nejmoa1600651

[6] **Intrauterine** refers to an occurrence that takes places within the uterus.

[7] **Pathogenesis** refers to the development of a disease.

[8] **Teratogenic effects** are the consequences from a harmful substance on a developing fetus.

officials are sounding the alarm. The CDC in February 2016 declared a Level 1 alert, which it only deploys during serious pandemics, such as the H1N1 flu outbreak and the Ebola outbreak. The World Health Organization has issued numerous warnings about the virus, saying that it is linked to microcephaly, and that it is likely to spread into additional countries. Political and health leaders in many nations have begun pushing for researchers to develop a cure. While there are vaccines in use for other flaviviruses, including yellow fever, Japanese encephalitis, and tick-borne encephalitis, the making of a vaccine for dengue proved far more challenging for medical officials, taking decades to develop. Though scientists did eventually create a dengue vaccine, which began to be used in 2015, it is not yet widely in use. Optimistically, however, vaccine technology has advanced greatly in recent years, and the global call to arms over Zika will push a vaccine to the forefront of scientific research. Amid the uncertain causative link between microcephaly and the virus, and despite the unclear pathogenesis of the virus, there is one absolute certainty: Zika has captured the world's attention, and major medical efforts—as well as global funding—are being directed at stopping the illness.

Babies with microcephaly can have a range of health problems, including seizures, developmental delays, intellectual disability, movement and balance problems, difficulty swallowing, hearing loss, and vision problems.

incidence of microcephaly could be underreported in Brazil and other locations. These are a few of the many factors that epidemiologists must consider in the ongoing studies, and undertaking such studies while an outbreak is ongoing is challenging because the number of cases are constantly changing.

5   In the absence of scientific proof but armed with a robust circumstantial connection, health

B. Answer the questions.

1. In what ways is Zika similar to the dengue virus? ....

....

2. What evidence has been found that links the Zika virus to microcephaly? ....

....

3. Aside from the Zika virus, what may be another cause for microcephaly? ....

....

....

4. What factors may have contributed to the rise in microcephaly cases? ....

....

....

5. How is the CDC testing whether microcephaly is caused by the Zika virus? ....

....

....

C. Use your responses from Part B to generate three hypotheses about the Zika virus. Be sure that each of your hypotheses includes the characteristics of an effective hypothesis.

1. ....

....

2. ....

....

3. ....

....

D. **PEER REVIEW.** Exchange your hypotheses with a partner. Respond to the questions to evaluate each other's work. For responses marked No, give feedback in the Notes column to help your partner revise.

	Yes	No	Notes
HYPOTHESIS 1 Is it written in the form of an *if/then* statement?	☐	☐	
Does it include independent and dependent variables in the *if*-clause?	☐	☐	
Does it include a directional prediction in the *then*-clause?	☐	☐	
Does it include specific information?	☐	☐	
Is it testable?	☐	☐	
HYPOTHESIS 2 Is it written in the form of an *if/then* statement?	☐	☐	
Does it include independent and dependent variables in the *if*-clause?	☐	☐	
Does it include a directional prediction in the *then*-clause?	☐	☐	
Does it include specific information?	☐	☐	
Is it testable?	☐	☐	
HYPOTHESIS 3 Is it written in the form of an *if/then* statement?	☐	☐	
Does it include independent and dependent variables in the *if*-clause?	☐	☐	
Does it include a directional prediction in the *then*-clause?	☐	☐	
Does it include specific information?	☐	☐	
Is it testable?	☐	☐	

Go to **MyEnglishLab** to do a vocabulary exercise and a skill practice and join in collaborative activities.

LANGUAGE SKILLS
FORMING CONDITIONAL CLAUSES

WHY IT'S USEFUL By using conditional clauses appropriately, you will be able to express causal relationships, make predictions about future possibilities, and describe general truths and facts.

Conditional sentences describe situations that can take place if certain conditions are met. The condition is included in the subordinating *if*-clause, and the resulting situation or outcome is included in the main clause. Conditional clauses may begin with *if, when, unless,* or *even if*. In academic writing, conditional clauses are often used to explain a situation that would make a claim or hypothesis valid, to express a cause and effect relationship, to explain why a situation is not possible, to make a prediction about a future possibility, or to concede that a limitation exists with an argument but is still true.

REAL CONDITIONALS

· Describe **general truths, facts, or repeated situations and habits** using the present tense. · Use the present tense in both the conditional and main clause. · Use *even if* to describe a condition that does not matter.	If a vaccine **exists**, the disease **cannot spread**. People **recover** from illnesses **when** their immune system **is** strong. **Even if** the results **are** inconclusive, they still **provide** important information.
· Predict a **possible future situation** and the likely results. Are used to formulate **scientific hypotheses**. · Use the present tense in the conditional clause and the future tense (with or without a modal) in the main clause. · Use *unless* to describe a negative condition.	Diseases **will not spread** as rapidly **if** vaccines **are administered** throughout the world. If the Zika virus **causes** microcephaly, then no traces of the virus **will be found** in babies born without microcephaly. **Unless** a vaccine is found, more people will suffer.

UNREAL CONDITIONALS

· Describe a situation that is **currently unreal or untrue** and **imagine the result** if it were true. · Use the past tense in the conditional clause and a modal (*would, could* or *might,* depending on the level of certainty) plus the base form of a verb in the main clause.	If there **were** a vaccine for the Zika virus, there **might be** fewer cases of microcephaly in Brazil. More pregnant women **would visit** Brazil **if** the Zika virus **were not** a concern. If the researcher's claim **were** true, there **would be** fewer cases of the condition.
· Describe an **unreal or untrue situation from the past** and **imagine the result** if it had been true. · Use the past perfect tense in the conditional clause and a modal (*would, could, might*) plus have / has, followed by the past participle of a verb in the main clause.	If they **had included** one independent variable in their experiment instead of two, their data **would** likely **have yielded** more useful results. The doctors **would have been** able to save more people if there **had been** a vaccine.

Here are some tips for understanding and using conditionals.

- Use a comma after the conditional clause if it comes before the main clause.
- Use *were* not *was* for singular subjects in the unreal conditional clause (e.g., If he *were*, not if he *was*). Although *was* is acceptable when speaking, it should not be used in academic writing.
- The subject of both the conditional and main clauses must agree (e.g., *People* recover from illnesses when *their* immune system is strong.).
- Use the correct modal (e.g., real conditionals: *will, can, may;* unreal conditionals: *would, could, might*).

> **TIP**
> ....
> *Modals are used to show different levels of certainty:*
> *Most certain:* will / would
> *Less certain:* can / could
> *Least certain:* may / might

EXERCISE 6

A. Identify what each real conditional sentence is describing: a general truth, fact, repeated situation / habit, prediction, or hypothesis. Some may be used more than once.

1. The outcome will be disastrous if a vaccine is not found soon. ....

2. Diseases spread quickly when drinking water is contaminated. ....

3. If I am presenting research in front of a large group, I usually feel nervous. ....

4. Even if student papers have errors, teachers appreciate the effort. ....

5. If asthma is related to air pollution, then reducing air pollution in large cities will lower the incidence of asthma cases. ....

6. Unless a new study is conducted, a link between the Zika virus and microcephaly may never be found. ....

7. Symptoms can be managed if patients take their medication routinely. ....

8. Optional testing is typically done if there are concerns by the manufacturer. ....

B. Write five real conditional sentences about viruses and vaccines. Compare your sentences with a partner.

1. (General truth) ....

....

2. (Habit) ....

....

3. (Cause) ....

....

4. (Prediction) ....

....

5. (Scientific fact) ....

....

EXERCISE 7

A. Determine whether the unreal conditionals are written correctly or incorrectly. Rewrite the incorrect sentences. More than one answer is sometimes possible.

1. If she had arrived earlier, the outcome would have been different.

   ....

2. If the number of cases was to rise, the situation can result in a global pandemic.

   ....

3. If the FDA would have approved the vaccine the country wouldn't have had such devastation.

   ....

4. I wouldn't give up if I was you. ....

   ....

5. He wouldn't have been so tired if he hadn't stayed up so late. ....

   ....

6. If this were a global threat, people would be more concerned. ....

   ....

7. If the vaccine performs well in the testing phase, we could have applied for the Biologics license.

   ....

8. Vaccines could reach more people if immunization programs were more effective.

   ....

9. If scientists created vaccines that were easier to administer, diseases wouldn't spread so quickly.

   ....

10. Thousands of people could have been treated, if more funding were available.

    ....

Go to MyEnglishLab to complete skill practices.

APPLY YOUR SKILLS

WHY IT'S USEFUL By explaining a process or procedure clearly, you will help readers understand how something is done. By formulating an effective hypothesis you will communicate the basis for an investigation as well as the intended results.

ASSIGNMENT

Choose a virus and research its characteristics and latest treatment methods, including vaccines used to fight it. Write a 2–3 page analytical process paper explaining how the method, drug, or vaccine works to combat the virus. Your paper may also include information about how the treatment was discovered and tested.

BEFORE YOU WRITE

A. Before you begin your assignment, discuss these questions with one or more students.

1. How are the most serious viruses transmitted?

2. What are common ways to treat a virus?

3. Have you heard of any alternative treatments for viruses?

B. As you consider your assignment, list the steps involved in explaining the method to combat the virus you researched and the purpose or reason(s) for each step. List each step in 3–4 words, beginning with a verb (e.g., *Purify* the antigen). Make sure that each step is clear and understandable.

Virus		
	Step	**Purpose or reason(s)**
1		
2		
3		
4		
5		

C. Review the Unit Skills Summary. As you begin on the writing task on page 191, apply the skills you learned in this unit.

UNIT SKILLS SUMMARY

Structure a process
- Introduce the process and its purpose.
- Organize the steps sequentially or chronologically.
- Explain, describe, exemplify, and illustrate the steps of the process.

Explain a procedure
- List the tasks and steps in the procedure.
- Provide additional information and detail to explain the procedure.

Formulate a hypothesis
- Understand the process of formulating a hypothesis.
- Understand the components of an effective hypothesis.

Form conditional clauses
- Use real and unreal conditional clauses appropriately.

THINKING CRITICALLY

As you consider your assignment, discuss the questions with another student. Get feedback and revise your ideas, if necessary.

1. Why is it so difficult to develop vaccines and to make them available to the public? How much should governments get involved in testing, pricing, and distributing vaccines?

2. Have you heard about any health crises that are not getting as much attention as viruses like Zika? Why do you think some issues get more attention than others?

3. How could vaccines be designed differently so that they are more manageable for people living in remote areas to receive?

THINKING VISUALLY

Look at the flowchart illustrating how women are tested for the Zika virus. Analyze this process. Then create a similar flowchart that explains the treatment process for the virus you chose to research.

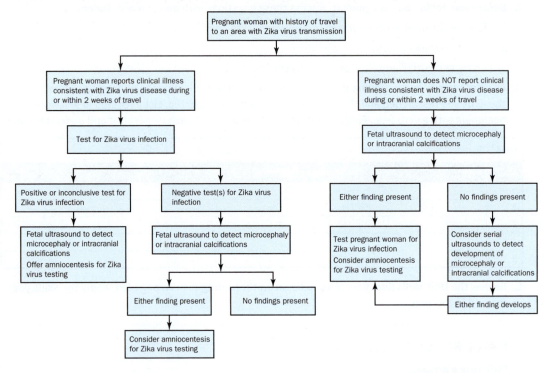

THINKING ABOUT LANGUAGE

Read the paragraphs. Generate five conditional sentences that describe the conditions that must be met in order for a vaccine to be approved.

APPLICATION FOR BIOLOGICS LICENSE

If the vaccine has performed well in the testing phase, the final step in the procedure to produce the vaccine is to apply for the Biologics license. The researchers must provide the results of all human testing, including safety, purity, and potency and describe manufacturing and testing methods. In addition, the FDA inspects the manufacturing facility, which must meet government standards for equipment, personnel, packaging, and record keeping.

The vaccine is reviewed by an advisory committee of experts, scientists, physicians, statisticians, and consumer representatives, who vote on whether to recommend FDA approval.

POST-LICENSING MONITORING

When a vaccine is approved and in use, there are further procedures that must be followed. The FDA continues to monitor the production of the vaccine and has the right to conduct its own tests of the manufacturing process. The FDA and CDC (Centers for Disease Control and Prevention) review the licensed vaccine for anything unusual, and anyone can report adverse reactions through the Vaccine Adverse Event Reporting System. Phase IV testing, optional testing of large numbers of people, is typically done by the manufacturer to see if there are any rare or delayed reactions to the vaccine.

1. ....

....

2. ....

....

3. ....

....

4. ....

....

5. ....

....

WRITE

A. Revisit the assignment and the table in Before You Write Part B. Determine if there is any information that needs to be added to the steps in the treatment method.

B. Describe how the method or vaccine was discovered and tested.

C. Write about the virus and chronologically describe the process for treating it.

> **BEYOND THE ASSIGNMENT**
>
> Expand your unit assignment into a full research paper about the virus. Use all the skills you've learned to write a research paper.

▶ Go to MyEnglishLab to listen to Professor Siegel and to complete a self-assessment.

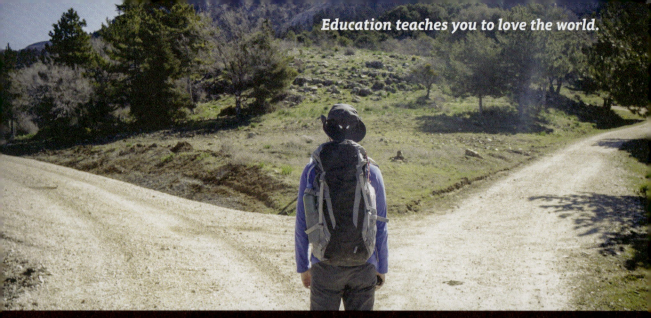

Education teaches you to love the world.

Descriptive Writing

UNIT PROFILE

In this unit, you will read and write about how thoughts and feelings contribute to learning. Specifically, you will learn about how some famous poets and novelists, such as Henry David Thoreau, Mark Twain, Carl Sandburg, and D. H. Lawrence used descriptive writing to shape people's understanding of the world.

UNIT ASSIGNMENT

Write a descriptive essay about an interaction with something you read, heard, or saw that changed your understanding of or knowledge about a concept or an idea. This could be a poem, a short story, a novel, the lyrics to a piece of music, a play or a movie. It could be something you heard from a person who had an impact on your learning. Use expressive writing techniques, including figurative language, sensory details, and descriptive grammar to enrich your writing.

OUTCOMES

- Explore figurative language
- Appeal to the senses
- Analyze descriptive writing
- Use grammar to vary description

GETTING STARTED

▶ Go to MyEnglishLab to listen to Professor Harrison and to complete a self-assessment.

Discuss these questions with a partner or group.

1. What is the difference between thoughts and feelings? Are your decisions influenced more by your thoughts or by your feelings? Do they depend on what the decision is? Give examples.

2. Do you think emotions influence how people learn new concepts, both in and outside of school? Does having emotions about something help or hinder how well you retain knowledge about it? Why?

3. In what ways is "showing" more effective than telling in expressing your ideas? How can you show your ideas rather than tell them?

For more about **HUMANITIES,** see 1 3. See also [R] and [OC] **HUMANITIES** 1 2 3.

CRITICAL THINKING SKILL
DESCRIPTIVE WRITING

WHY IT'S USEFUL By writing descriptively, you create mental images for the reader, establish the context, and develop a mood that evokes an emotional response from readers. The more descriptive your writing is, the better your reader will understand it.

An effective description gives readers a better sense of a subject. Descriptive writing adds to the believability of an experience, enhances understanding of a difficult concept, and even transports a reader into another world. While most people associate descriptive writing with evoking an emotional response in readers and bringing characters to life, it is also essential to use descriptive writing when illustrating a process or procedure in a science paper, comparing and contrasting geometrical shapes in a mathematics class, and describing evidence in support of a claim in a persuasive essay. Descriptive writing may include:

Sensory description	Uses the five senses (sight, sound, touch, smell, and taste) to help the reader feel what is being described.
Evaluative description	Uses evidence to support a claim.
Comparative description	Compares and contrasts two or more things with each other.
Spatial-relational description	Uses an object's location in relation to other objects to give readers a mental map or image.

American poet, essayist, and philosopher Henry David Thoreau details his experiences and observations of natural phenomena in his 1854 book *Walden; or, Life in the Woods.* Note in this excerpt how Thoreau uses language to describe his observation of a thawing sandbank:

^{1}Few phenomena gave me more delight than to observe the forms which thawing sand and clay assume in flowing down the sides of a deep cut on the railroad through which I passed on my way to the village … The material was sand of every degree of fineness and of various rich colors. ^{5}When the frost comes out in the spring … the sand begins to flow down the slopes like lava, sometimes bursting out through the snow and overflowing it where no sand was to be seen before. Innumerable little streams overlap and interlace one with another, exhibiting a sort of hybrid product, which obeys half way the laws of currents, and half way that of ^{10}vegetation. As it flows it takes the forms of sappy leaves or vines, making heaps of pulpy sprays a foot or more in depth, and resembling, as you look down on them, the laciniated lobed and imbricated thalluses of some lichens; or you are reminded of coral, of leopards' paws or birds' feet, of brains or lungs or bowels, and excrements of all kinds. It is a truly grotesque vegetation … ^{15}The whole cut impressed me as if it were a cave with its stalactites laid open to the light.

Laciniated lobed and imbricated thalluses of lichens: Jagged or fringed vegetation of fungi and algae that overlap like tiles.

1. What does Thoreau compare the sand to in lines 5–7? What are the leaves and vines compared to in lines 11–13?

2. Before reading this, how might you have described a thawing sandbank? How does his description enrich your understanding of the thawing sandbank?

Throughout Thoreau's works, he used **figurative language**, including metaphor, simile, personification, and symbolism to express the essence of natural phenomena. For example, in the excerpt he uses metaphor to compare the vegetation on the sandbank to the walls inside of a cave. This perfect metaphor paints an image in readers' minds that enables them to have a richer understanding of the vegetation than they would have had there not been a description of it. **Appealing to the senses** by using sensory detail is another effective way to give readers a deeper understanding of a phenomenon. Thoreau's description of the sandbank appeals to the sense of sight through the use of imagery. Having this rich sensory description draws the reader into the experience.

NOTICING ACTIVITY

Descriptive writing is appropriate in a wide range of rhetorical contexts and academic disciplines. Look at these writing situations and determine the rhetorical purpose for each (to entertain, to express, to inform, or to persuade). When you are finished, discuss with a partner the kinds of descriptions you would use in these writing tasks (sensorial, evaluative, comparative, and / or spatial-relational).

Discipline	Descriptive Writing Task	Rhetorical Purpose
Geography	As a cultural geographer, you will observe a neighborhood in your area and take detailed field notes describing peoples' routines and actions.	
Creative Writing	Write a short story from the point of view of a ten-year-old girl. Describe her life and inner thoughts and feelings. Be sure your story has a good arc with rising and falling action.	
Environmental Science	Write a letter to a public official about an environmental issue. Describe how the issue is negatively impacting the environment and argue why the government needs to address it.	
Business Marketing	In thinking about how to market a new product that would appeal to your generation, identify and describe a defining event for your generation and explore why it had the impact it did.	

Go to MyEnglishLab to complete a vocabulary exercise and a skill practice and join in collaborative activities.

SUPPORTING SKILL 1
EXPLORING FIGURATIVE LANGUAGE

WHY IT'S USEFUL By using figurative language, you create mental images that help the reader better visualize the events or concepts described in the text.

Figurative language uses words or expressions that do not have a literal meaning. These figurative words and expressions are referred to as **figures of speech**. When you use literal language, you state information expressing its basic meaning. In contrast, with figurative language, you express ideas using comparisons or exaggerations to imply meanings that are more complex than what can be expressed using literal language. For example, the implied meaning of the figurative expression *foot of the mountain* means the base of the mountain. Taken literally, the phrase would mean that the mountain has an actual foot.

Figurative language is very common in expressive writing but is also used in persuasive and informational texts. There are many types of figures of speech used in figurative language. These are some of the most common:

Imagery—Imagery is the use of descriptive language to provide a clear mental image of whatever is being described. In these examples, adjectives are used to appeal to our senses of sight and smell.

> The twinkling stars sparkled in the clear, night sky.
> When I stepped into my Grandma's house, I was greeted by the sweet cinnamon
> smell of apple pie just out of the oven.

Simile—A simile is a comparison made between two unlike things using the linking words *like* or *as*. Similes create vivid, memorable descriptions. What two things are being compared in these examples?

> Her wind-swept hair fell across her shoulders like ripples in a dark and mysterious pool.
>
> The icicles hanging from the bow of the ship were as sharp as knives.

Metaphor—A metaphor also compares two unlike things. However, no linking word is used, so it can be more difficult to recognize what is being compared. Metaphor is the most frequently used figure of speech and is prevalent in everyday conversations as well as in different types of texts.

When using metaphors, it is important that your comparison makes sense and is original. Avoid using clichés, which are popular expressions that are overused and do not reflect original thought (e.g., *to walk a mile in my shoes, tip of the iceberg, think outside the box*, etc.). Here are examples of successful metaphors. Can you identify what is being compared?

> Her hair was a sea of golden wheat.
> The dog's love covered his family with warmth.
> The raindrops on the tin roof were cymbal strikes on his eardrums.

Personification—With personification, human characteristics are given to something that is not human.

> The deadly cold chill of night crept into every nook and cranny of the dilapidated house.

Hyperbole—Hyperbole is the use of exaggeration to add emphasis or to express a strong emotion. Hyperbole is often used humorously. American author and humorist Mark Twain, included this example of hyperbole in *Old Times on the Mississippi*:

> "I was helpless. I did not know what in the world to do. I was quaking from head to
> foot, and could have hung my hat on my eyes, they stuck out so far."

Symbolism—Symbolism occurs when a person, place, object, or situation has a deeper, more abstract meaning. Symbols can be difficult to detect and depend on the context, so readers need to read closely and critically to identify symbolism. In this example from Shakespeare's play, *As you Like It*, a *stage* is a symbol for the world and *players* symbolize human beings. These lines are symbolic of how people play different roles throughout their lives.

> All the world's a stage,
> And all the men and women merely players;
> they have their exits and their entrances;
> And one man in his time plays many parts …

EXERCISE 1

A. Read the poem, "Chicago," by Carl Sandburg, first published in 1914.

CHICAGO

1 Hog Butcher for the World,
2 Tool Maker, Stacker of Wheat,
3 Player with Railroads and the Nation's Freight Handler;
4 Stormy, husky, brawling,
5 City of the Big Shoulders:
6 They tell me you are wicked and I believe them, for I
7 have seen your painted women under the gas lamps
8 luring the farm boys.
9 And they tell me you are crooked and I answer: Yes, it
10 is true I have seen the gunman kill and go free to
11 kill again.
12 And they tell me you are brutal and my reply is: On the
13 faces of women and children I have seen the mark
14 of wanton hunger.
15 And having answered so I turn once more to those who
16 sneer at this my city, and I give them back the sneer
17 and say to them:
18 Come and show me another city with lifted head singing
19 so proud to be alive and coarse and strong and cunning.
20 Flinging magnetic curses amid the toil of piling job on
21 job, here is a tall bold slugger set vivid against the
22 little soft cities;
23 Fierce as a dog with tongue lapping for action, cunning
24 as a savage pitted against the wilderness,
25 Bareheaded,
26 Shoveling,

27 Wrecking,

28 Planning,

29 Building, breaking, rebuilding,

30 Under the smoke, dust all over his mouth, laughing with

31 white teeth,

32 Under the terrible burden of destiny laughing as a young

33 man laughs,

34 Laughing even as an ignorant fighter laughs who has

35 never lost a battle,

36 Bragging and laughing that under his wrist is the pulse,

37 and under his ribs the heart of the people,

38 Laughing!

39 Laughing the stormy, husky, brawling laughter of

40 Youth, half-naked, sweating, proud to be Hog

41 Butcher, Tool Maker, Stacker of Wheat, Player with

42 Railroads and Freight Handler to the Nation.

B. Answer the questions.

1. Underline the figures of speech and note in the margin whether it is an example of imagery, simile, metaphor, personification, hyperbole, or symbolism.

2. What does Sandburg compare the city to in these lines?

   Fierce as a dog with tongue lapping for action, cunning as a savage pitted against the wilderness

   ....

3. How does Sandburg feel about the city of Chicago? Give an example from the poem to support your answer. ....

   ....

   ....

4. Why do you think Sandburg decides to personify the city? ....

   ....

5. Which example of figurative language in the poem do you think is most effective? Why?

   ....

   ....

   ....

A. Read the practice assignment. Then read a paragraph from a student's descriptive essay for this assignment. Identify the figures of speech used in the description.

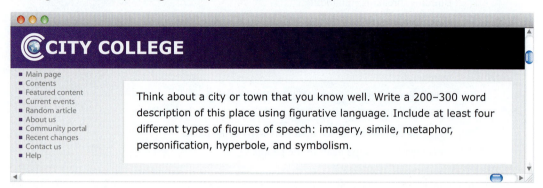

CITY COLLEGE

- Main page
- Contents
- Featured content
- Current events
- Random article
- About us
- Community portal
- Recent changes
- Contact us
- Help

Think about a city or town that you know well. Write a 200–300 word description of this place using figurative language. Include at least four different types of figures of speech: imagery, simile, metaphor, personification, hyperbole, and symbolism.

Every time my husband and I travel, we are glad to get home. As the plane enters the final leg of the journey, the snow-capped peak of Mt. Rainer signals the impending landing like a lighthouse to tired fishermen. Seattle, our home, is now a quick but rough ride right around the corner. The city stands tall and glittery from Highway 99 with the salt water of Elliot Bay shimmering in the lights of the giant buildings and towering Ferris wheel. This city is technology. Streaking headlights stream past like pulses of fiber optic light. Seattle, home of some of the largest tech companies in the world, is known for producing some of the most impressive airplanes ever developed and for being an international hub for shipping and trade. These industries have kept Seattle one of the most desirable places to live in the United States. Combined with a strong economy and a progressive atmosphere, the city offers a quality of life many people envy. This culture shows itself in public policy that values community and environmental health, evidenced by our abundant public green spaces and neighborhood organizations.

B. Write your own 200–300 word description about a place you know well using figurative language. Include at least four different types of figures of speech: imagery, simile, metaphor, personification, hyperbole, and symbolism.

C. <u>PEER REVIEW</u>. **Exchange your description with a partner. Respond to the questions about your partner's description. Give feedback to help your partner revise if needed.**

1. Underline the figures of speech and identify whether each is an example of imagery, simile, metaphor, personification, hyperbole, or symbolism.

2. What does the writer compare the city to? ....

....

3. How does the writer feel about the city? Give an example from the description to support your

answer. ....

....

....

4. Which example of figurative language do you think is most effective? Why? ....

....

....

....

5. Are there any figures of speech that are not effective? If so, give suggestions for how your

partner could revise them. ....

....

....

....

....

Go to **MyEnglishLab** to complete a vocabulary exercise and a skill practice and join in collaborative activities.

SUPPORTING SKILL 2
APPEALING TO THE SENSES

WHY IT'S USEFUL By appealing to your readers' senses using sensory detail, you will create a deeper connection to the images and experiences you are describing.

Descriptive sensory details appeal to our five senses. Sight, sound, touch, smell, and taste are the primary ways that we learn about the world and acquire knowledge. Therefore, including rich, sensory detail engages readers and evokes an emotional response from them.

When describing an experience, event, person, or object, it may be tempting to *tell* your readers how they should feel. However, it has more impact when you *show* readers, using sensory details and figurative language so that they can feel as if they are having a firsthand experience. This also allows readers to make their own interpretation of the experience based on the mood you convey in your description.

Compare two descriptions of the same event. The first paragraph tells us about the experience, whereas the second example uses sensory detail to show us what the writer experienced.

> When I entered the funeral home for my mother's memorial service, it was filled with flowers and my mother's old friends. I was extremely nervous about giving the eulogy. I wasn't sure if I would be able to make it through without crying. I felt totally alone up at the podium and wished that my mom was there to comfort and reassure me. As I began to speak, I felt my mother's presence and somehow knew that she would always be with me.

> As I entered the dimly lit room, a noxious cloud of lilies assaulted my senses, making me feel disoriented. Faces that I hadn't seen since I was a teenager, mournfully mouthed the words, "I'm so sorry," as they slowly passed my chair. My heart hammered in my chest with every step I took toward the podium. I waded through the muted song from the organ intermingled with whispering voices. My mom lay peacefully still beside me. Her strong warm hands that had given me a reassuring squeeze before dance performances, graduation ceremonies, and the birth of my daughter now lay unnaturally still at her sides. I swallowed back the acidic saliva that came rushing into my mouth as I stared at the room full of faces from my childhood. I scraped my knees against the back of the splintery podium to distract myself from my grief and fear. This would be the most important speech of my life, and the first I would deliver without my mother's support. In that moment, my hands trembling, a familiar calm started to wash over me. I looked down at my mother and smiled knowingly.

In the first example, the paragraph describes a woman's feelings before she gives the eulogy at her mother's funeral. Without the inclusion of sensory detail, the writing is vague and does not reveal enough about the woman's experience. In contrast, the description in the second example shows how using all five senses can work together to strengthen a text.

EXERCISE 3

Identify the sensory adjectives, nouns, and phrases the writer uses in the second example and write them under the correct sense. Then discuss how each detail added to the story. Can you find examples of figurative language in the paragraph as well?

Sight	Sound	Touch	Smell	Taste

Here are some tips for incorporating sensory details into your writing:

- Before you begin writing, create a sensory chart and recount as many details about the person, place, experience, or object that you can.
- Think about the mood you would like to evoke in your readers. Do you want them to feel sad, angry, joyful, reflective, etc.?
- Consider the purpose of the text. Are you writing a description to persuade, inform, express, or entertain?
- Consider your audience. Are your readers a group of geologists who will expect detailed descriptions of a field site? Or is your audience a group of close friends and family who are already familiar with your life?
- Review your initial draft to determine where you could include more sensory detail or figurative language to show instead of tell the reader about your experience.
- Avoid including too much sensory detail in a sentence. For example, this sentence is overloaded with detail, making it overwhelming for the reader.

    The overgrown, gnarly, misshaped hedge distracted the well-dressed young couple from seeing the positive attributes of the newly remodeled craftsman home in the expensive popular neighborhood.

EXERCISE 4

A. Read the paragraph. It describes an experience, but does not include enough sensory detail. Then complete the sensory chart imagining the sights, sounds, touches, smells, and tastes the writer may have experienced during this event.

In January of 1986, I was nine years old, and the American space shuttle Challenger was scheduled to launch in a few days. My teacher announced that we would watch it during class. On the morning of the launch, my teacher wheeled in the television set so that we could watch the lift-off during lunch. My teacher was in such a great mood, and all of my classmates seemed happy, too. At 11:39 A.M., the Challenger lifted off in a plume of smoke. A little more than a minute after take-off, it looked like there was an explosion in the sky. My teacher gasped, and the class became very quiet. The broadcasters then announced that the shuttle appeared to have broken up. My teacher started to cry, and I heard some of my classmates crying, too. I felt sick to my stomach.

Sight	Sound	Touch	Smell	Taste

B. Using the sensory chart, rewrite the paragraph in your own words, adding sensory details and figurative language. Be sure to show instead of tell the reader about the event.

C. PEER REVIEW. Exchange your paragraph with a partner. Respond to the questions to evaluate each other's work. Give feedback to help your partner revise if needed.

1. What senses does the paragraph appeal to? ....

....

2. Do all of the sensory details work together to enrich your understanding of the experience? Which sensory detail do you think is the most effective? Why? ....

....

....

3. What mood does the paragraph evoke? Which words or phrases in the paragraph help to convey this mood? ....

....

....

4. What types of figurative language does the writer use? ....

....

....

5. Are there any places where the writer could add more sensory detail or figurative language?

....

....

6. Are there any sensory details or figures of speech that are not effective? If yes, provide suggestions for how your partner could revise. ....

....

....

Go to MyEnglishLab to complete a vocabulary exercise and a skill practice.

READING-WRITING CONNECTION
ANALYZING DESCRIPTIVE WRITING

WHY IT'S USEFUL By analyzing descriptive writing, you will have a deeper understanding of the effect mental images and figurative and sensory language have on comprehension and recall, and you will be able to use various forms of description effectively in your own writing.

In analyzing descriptive writing, as in other types of writing, consider the **rhetorical context** of the text and the **purpose** the description serves in that text.

In *Life on the Mississippi*, Mark Twain successfully weaves description into his account of the Mississippi River, his narrative of life on the river. Twain uses descriptive techniques to express his thoughts and feelings as he tells his story, informs his reader about the river, and persuades that reader of the challenges of piloting a steamboat on the Mississippi.

In expressive writing such as a **narrative**, description helps involve the reader in the story. In telling his story of learning to be a riverboat pilot, Twain, following a dialog about a particular feature of the river with the captain who is teaching him to navigate the Mississippi River, introduces a metaphor of the river as a book. In addition to helping the reader understand piloting on the river, Twain controls the timing of the experience, using the description as a pause in the dialog to give the reader time to connect with and comprehend the river.

> "Now don't you see the difference? It wasn't anything but a wind reef. The wind does that."
>
> "So I see. But it is exactly like a bluff reef. How am I ever going to tell them apart?"
>
> "I can't tell you. It is an instinct. By and by you will just naturally know one from the other, but you never will be able to explain why or how you know them apart."
>
> It turned out to be true. The face of the water, in time, became a wonderful book—a book that was a dead language to the uneducated passenger, but which told its mind to me without reserve, delivering its most cherished secrets as clearly as if it uttered them with a voice.

CULTURE NOTE
Reefs are sand bars—piles or hills of sand in a river, often hidden below the surface of the water. Bluff reef is a term for actual sand bars that pose a threat to riverboats that can hit them. Wind reefs are ripples in the water that appear to be from sand bars but aren't. It was important for a riverboat pilot to be able to tell the types of reefs apart.

In **persuasive** writing, description can inspire or persuade the reader. Twain persuades us of the importance and complexity of learning about the river through his vivid description of the river as a book, and by personifying the river and giving it a "voice."

> And it was not a book to be read once and thrown aside, for it had a new story to tell every day. Throughout the long twelve hundred miles there was never a page that was void of interest, never one that you could leave unread without loss, never one that you would want to skip, thinking you could find higher enjoyment in some other thing. There never was so wonderful a book written by man; never one whose interest was so absorbing, so unflagging, so sparklingly renewed with every re-perusal.

When **informing**, description provides the detail and can move a reader to have feelings about the topic. Twain continues his metaphor to inform us about the difference between the pilot and a passenger. The description of what the pilot sees and what the passenger sees are blended into the text without interrupting the story.

> The passenger who could not read it was charmed with a peculiar sort of faint dimple on its surface (on the rare occasions when he did not overlook it altogether); but to the pilot that was an italicized passage; indeed, it was more than that, it was a legend of the largest capitals,

with a string of shouting exclamation points at the end of it; for it meant that a wreck or a rock was buried there that could tear the life out of the strongest vessel that ever floated. It is the faintest and simplest expression the water ever makes, and the most hideous to a pilot's eye. In truth, the passenger who could not read this book saw nothing but all manner of pretty pictures in it, painted by the sun and shaded by the clouds, whereas to the trained eye these were not pictures at all, but the grimmest and most dead-earnest of reading-matter.

Mark Twain doesn't tell us that a pilot sees the river differently than a passenger. He shows us in vivid language that appeals to emotion—"hideous to the pilot's eye" rather than telling us the pilot sees danger where the passenger sees "all manner of pretty pictures painted by the sun."

To **analyze descriptive text**, begin with your overall impression of it. Consider the purpose of the writer and the point the writer is making. Answer these questions to help you write a comprehensive analysis.

- What point is the writer making?
- What type of description is it? Sensory? Evaluative? Spatial? Comparative?
- How is the description blended into the text? Does it affect how you perceive the experience? By enhancing it? Or interrupting it?
- Does the description seem more thought based or feeling based?
- What emotions does the description evoke? What is the mood of the text?
- Is the description accurate? Dynamic?
- Has the writer created a picture for you? Is it vivid? (Can you picture what is being described in your head?) Does it evoke a feeling of being there? Does it show, not tell?
- What figurative language has the writer used: simile, metaphor, personification, hyperbole, imagery, or symbolism?
- What senses has the writer asked you to use? Sight, sound, smell, touch, and taste?
- Is the description clear, fresh, and interesting? Did the writer avoid clichéd language?

EXERCISE 5

A. Read the excerpt from *Life on the Mississippi* and the analysis that follows.

Now when I had mastered the language of this water and had come to know every trifling feature that bordered the great river as familiarly as I knew the letters of the alphabet, I had made a valuable acquisition.

But I had lost something, too. I had lost something which could never be restored to me while I lived. All the grace, the beauty, the poetry had gone out of the majestic river! I still keep in mind a certain wonderful sunset which I witnessed when steamboating was new to me. A broad expanse of the river was turned to blood; in the middle distance the red hue brightened into gold, through which a solitary log came floating, black and conspicuous; in one place a long, slanting mark lay sparkling upon the water; in another the surface was broken by boiling, tumbling rings, that were as many-tinted as an opal; where the ruddy flush was faintest, was a smooth spot that was covered with graceful circles and radiating lines, ever so delicately traced.

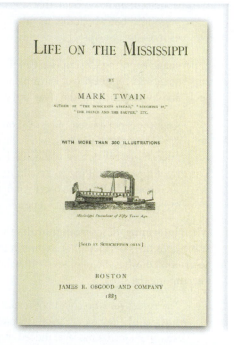

LIFE ON THE MISSISSIPPI

BY

MARK TWAIN

AUTHOR OF "THE INNOCENTS ABROAD," "ROUGHING IT," "THE PRINCE AND THE PAUPER," ETC.

WITH MORE THAN 300 ILLUSTRATIONS

Mississippi Steamboat of Fifty Years Ago.

[SOLD BY SUBSCRIPTION ONLY]

BOSTON
JAMES R. OSGOOD AND COMPANY
1883

There were graceful curves, reflected images, woody heights, soft distances; and over the whole scene, far and near, the dissolving lights drifted steadily, enriching it, every passing moment, with new marvels of coloring.

I stood like one bewitched. I drank it in, in a speechless rapture. The world was new to me, and I had never seen anything like this at home.

But as I have said, a day came when I began to cease from noting the glories and the charms which the moon and the sun and the twilight wrought upon the river's face; another day came when I ceased altogether to note them.

Then, if that sunset scene had been repeated, I should have looked upon it without rapture, and should have commented upon it, inwardly, in this fashion: "This sun means that we are going to have wind to-morrow; that floating log means that the river is rising, small thanks to it; that slanting mark on the water refers to a bluff reef which is going to kill somebody's steamboat one of these nights, if it keeps on stretching out like that; those tumbling "boils" show a dissolving bar and a changing channel there; the lines and circles in the slick water over yonder are a warning that that troublesome place is shoaling up dangerously …

No, the romance and the beauty were all gone from the river. All the value any feature of it had for me now was the amount of usefulness it could furnish toward compassing the safe piloting of a steamboat.

Analysis of *Life on the Mississippi* excerpt

Mark Twain blends his thoughts on what knowing the river as a pilot has meant in terms of what he has lost as well as gained. He uses a comparative description to do this. The overall mood of the excerpt feels nostalgic. While Twain wants to inform the reader about the knowledge required to successfully navigate the Mississippi River as a steamboat pilot, he wants to share its beauty with the reader as well. He paints the pretty picture that the passenger sees that is lost to those who truly know the river, not by telling us the sunset is beautiful, but by showing us. He creates a vivid image, a picture that the reader can see through the use of adjectives that paint the picture—*red hue brightened into gold*, embedded description—*slanting mark lay sparkling upon the water*, and participial adjectives that make the description dynamic—*boiling, tumbling rings, radiating lines and dissolving lights*. He uses figurative language as well: the simile *as many tinted as an opal* and the metaphors of the sun turning the river to blood and river's surface as a face. He evokes our sense of taste in addition to sight by saying he *drank it in*. Through the use of imagery and concrete active description, Twain allows his readers to feel like they are on the river witnessing the sunset. This description is more feeling based. With this pretty picture in the reader's mind, Twain returns us to his narrative about learning about the river and describes what the riverboat pilot he has become sees in the same scene—the dangers to the steamboat of what those sights mean: wind, a rising river, and dangerous changing bluff bars. This part is more thought based. By threading together a sequence of images in each part and contrasting them, Twain has drawn a more complete picture of life on the Mississippi for his readers and on what is lost as well as gained through knowledge and experience.

B. Answer the questions.

1. Why does Twain use the metaphor of a book to describe learning about piloting on the river? Give examples of his comparison of the river and a book. ....

....

....

2. Twain personifies the Mississippi River. Find the examples of this in the passages. Why might he do this? ....

....

....

3. What senses does he use in describing the river? Are there any missing that might have been helpful? Give examples. ....

....

....

4. Has Twain been effective in describing the river as seen by a passenger or someone who isn't familiar with the river? As seen by a steamboat pilot who knows the river? ....

....

....

5. Analyze the comparison of sunset on the river as seen when Twain was first on the river with how he saw the same sunset on the river once he knew it as a steamboat pilot. Give examples of specific points on which the two descriptions differ. ....

....

....

6. Do you agree with the analysis that Twain has been successful in evoking emotions in the reader? In painting a clear picture of life on the river for the reader? ....

....

....

C. Compare your answers with a partner. Did you agree? Did you find the same examples in your analysis in Question 5? Discuss any differences in your opinions.

Go to MyEnglishLab to complete a vocabulary exercise and a skill practice.

EXERCISE 6

A. Read the essay.

Learning a New Dance . . . and a New Worldview

1   The classical Indian dance Bharatanatyam looks nothing like the feather-light ballet of my childhood. The movement in Indian dance is dramatic, with stomping feet and ringing bells, and the dancers communicate religious stories to the audience—a concept mostly absent in Western classical dance. I studied Bharathanatyam in India for four months when I was a nineteen-year-old exchange student, and as I immersed myself in the foreign art, I came to know myself in new and surprising ways. Learning a foreign dance gave me an understanding of the dance, but more than that, it forced me to see a blueprint of myself, framed with traditions and beliefs I had never recognized prior to leaving my native land.

Ballet

2   As a ballet dancer, I learned to strive for perfection in a defined number of carefully controlled movements. What I was not aware of until I began to study Indian dance is the directness inherent in ballet instruction. The foot positions in ballet—only five—are clear through observation. The directness goes beyond the positions and into the instruction as well. My ballet teachers had always shown me routines with clear, specific directions for improving particular moves. I expected this straightforwardness, and it was not until I began learning Indian dance that I recognized it as more than just a characteristic of ballet, but also of my culture.

3   I would argue that international travelers are not blank slates. Aristotle's theory of *tabula rasa* argues that only experiences impart knowledge and understanding. The idea of self-authorship through personal choice won me over in my college days, and I believed then—as I no longer do today—that I would simply absorb instruction in dance like a dry sponge.

4   My expectations were just under the surface as I began my study, and they interfered in my learning. I assumed my Indian teacher would focus on teaching us to perfect individual postures, but that was not the goal. Ballet, rigid and disciplined, holds graceful performance as the ultimate goal. Indian dance, on the other hand, is more fluid in its purpose, and my teacher told us that communicating the story to the audience is just as important as the execution of the dance moves. While I was focusing on perfecting the moves, my teacher expected students to infer what she wanted us to know, based on a more indirect approach to teaching. Because I was used to a straightforward approach, we both became frustrated, and I believe it hindered my ability to learn, at least initially.

5   My teacher's studio, a semi-enclosed outdoor room attached to her family's sun-baked brick house, had no barre, no dance mirror, and no sugary Tchaikovsky. A rooster, instead, crowed near the awning. The teacher's drum pounded out the rhythm, and my bare feet slapped the cement in response. With each stomp or hand gesture, with each pose of Shiva the cosmic dancer, I felt the heavy weights of my own history and cultural background. My feet, purple, bruised things, protested loudly, and each day I fell asleep to aching shoulder muscles. My dance practice had always been goal oriented, focusing on the end product much more than the process. I had

Continued

Bharatanatyam

never recognized this as a cultural value until my teacher kept telling me to slow down, to enjoy the story the dance was telling, rather than concentrate on the movements.

> **CULTURE NOTE**
> *Pyotr Ilyich Tchaikovsky was a Russian composer who is most well-known today for the music of* The Nutcracker, *a classical ballet performed frequently during the Christmas season.*

6   In every American university's Philosophy 101, students wile away a chapter in Plato's cave. Captives in the cave are chained to the rock, lost in darkness. When the puppet master casts a shadow, the lost souls believe what they see is real. What else have they known? Like the philosophers called away from the shadows and faced with reality, students who live in another country face a world unlike anything they have

known. Perhaps enlightenment, however, comes less from learning about other cultures and more from self-reflection on how one's cultural values shape perceptions and experiences. In my dance instruction, I expected direct communication and focus on learning specific postures. Instead, I had to learn story and ritual behind the dance. I was no blank slate—my cultural values played a significant role in my expectations.

> **CULTURE NOTE**
> *Plato's cave is an allegory (also called an analogy, myth, metaphor, or parable) used by the Greek philosopher Plato in his work,* The Republic, *to compare the effect of education or lack of it on our nature.*

7   Dancing daily to my teacher's drumbeat, I adjusted somewhat to the new postures. My feet regained their regular hue. I did not always bend into the automatic plié of ballet. Like dancers trained to certain moves, we can never truly remove ourselves from our ties to our culture. There are strengths in this recognition. Through education, travel, and other experiences, we arrive at self-knowledge, and armed with awareness of our inherent biases and expectations, we possess a more enlightened understanding of others. Understanding is a type of acceptance, and acceptance includes a love of the self and of the world.

8   When I returned to the United States, I performed Bharatanatyam at my university at an international student event. I relinquished some of my need to perform with precision and instead played with the dance, delighting in the movement and the story it told. It was in this moment that I realized that I was no longer bound to approach dance—and my larger life—from a single worldview. I could choose between approaches as I jumped wildly into any unknown.

B. Answer the questions.

1. What point is the writer making? Give examples from the essay of descriptive language she used to support this idea. ....

....

2. What type of description is it?

....

....

3. What is the writer's mood as she describes her efforts to learn the dance? What emotions does the description of the Bharatanatyam dance evoke in you?

....

....

4. What language in the essay helps you picture the Bharatanatyam dance in your mind? Is there enough description to help you see the dance happening? Does the comparison with Western dance help you understand the Indian dance?

....

....

5. What figurative language has the writer used? Find examples of each:

a simile ....

a metaphor ....

personification ....

imagery ....

a symbol ....

6. What senses has the writer engaged in the reader? Find examples of sensory language.

....

....

7. Is the description of the dance blended into the text successfully to support the point the author is making? ....

....

8. How does the metaphor of Plato's cave add support to the writer's controlling idea? Is it effective? ....

....

C. Write a one-paragraph analysis of the description used in the essay based on your answers in Part B.

D. Share your responses in Part B and paragraph in Part C with a partner. Compare the similarities and differences in your ideas.

Go to MyEnglishLab to complete a vocabulary exercise and join in collaborative activities.

LANGUAGE SKILLS
USING GRAMMAR TO VARY DESCRIPTION

WHY IT'S USEFUL By using vivid language your descriptions engage and draw in the reader. Carefully chosen adjectives, use of strong nouns and verbs, and varied sentence structure helps you paint a picture in your writing.

The grammatical choices a writer makes mean the difference between vivid descriptions that enhance and support the rhetorical purpose and writing that is vague and fails to create memorable images that invite the reader into the text. Descriptive words and phrases should be specific, concrete, and sensory rich, evoking physical reactions and creating detailed images for the reader.

USING ADJECTIVES TO DESCRIBE
Most writers first think of adjectives when deciding how to incorporate description in writing. Well-chosen adjectives convey values and judgments, restrict or narrow down meaning, and make an image more precise. Avoid using too many adjectives. Choose only the most powerful adjectives and delete unnecessary ones. Always avoid clichéd figures of speech.

Adjectives that paint a picture	
Use adjectives that paint a picture for the reader. Adjectives that create an opinion, such as *beautiful, happy,* or *nervous,* rather than a visual image can be used as the controlling idea but should be avoided in the description as they do not engage the reader's visual imagination.	Her costume, a flash of rainbow colors and sparkle, swirled around her as she danced. vs. Her costume was beautiful.
Adjectives out of order	
To avoid long strings of adjectives and to create a strong image, one or more adjectives can follow rather than precede the noun.	Large bull moose, red-eyed and angry, charged … Careful movements, controlled and precise
Participial adjectives	
Use participial adjectives, especially the present participle, to evoke action. present participle = verb + *ing* past participle = verb + *ed*	stomping feet; clapping hands framed with traditions and beliefs

USING POWERFUL NOUNS AND ACTION VERBS

Strong, active, concrete words—nouns and verbs, which are specific and more accurately fit an action or paint a scene—can be more powerful than a string of adjectives or adverbs.

Absolutes	
Use two-word combinations of noun + present participle to create a scene.	**hands shaking, feet stomping,** she danced **claws digging,** the cat climbed frantically up the tree
Appositives	
Use a noun or noun phrase that adds a second image to a preceding noun. In fiction this creates an illusion of reality. In nonfiction it implies a foundation of research.	the dancer, **a whirling swirl of color,** flew by the raptor, **a white shadow,** soared overhead the results, **well founded data,** proved convincing
Action verbs	
Use action verbs to replace the feeling of still images with that of motion pictures. Replace the *be* verb with concrete verbs and nouns. Verbs are more powerful than adverbs.	The dancer **flew** by. vs. The dancer went by. The river **stretched out in front of us as smooth as the surface of a mirror.** vs. The river was calm. She **strolled** past her ex-boyfriend's house without a care. vs. She walked casually past her ex-boyfriend's house without a care.

VARYING SENTENCE ORDER

Using varied sentence structure—both long and short, simple, and complex sentences—allows the writer to create more interesting text. Avoid using the same clipped routine subject/verb pattern repeatedly. It can be monotonous and cause even vivid description to lose its appeal.

Adjective clauses and phrases	
Use Adjective clauses and phrases to create a smooth flow in description.	The dancer spun around the room. She was wearing bright colorful clothing. The dancer, (who was) wearing bright colorful clothing, spun around the room.
Embedded elements	
Embed descriptive elements to break a monotonous tone.	The sun sank behind the trees. It was a fiery glowing globe. The sun, a fiery glowing globe, sank behind the trees.
Combined sentences	
Combine sentences to avoid overuse of the subject-verb structure.	The hall was empty. She ran toward the classroom. She entered right after the bell rang. Racing down an empty hall, she skidded into the classroom, breathless, just as the bell clanged above her.
Parallel structure	
Parallel structure creates a music-like quality and develops a rhythm. Use identical grammatical structures to add rhythm and balance to images—clauses, participial phrases, prepositional phrases, and infinitives. Thread sequence of images to create a complete picture.	… there was **never a page** that was void of interest, **never one** that you could leave unread without loss, **never one** that you would want to skip … **Under the smoke,** dust all over his mouth, **laughing** with white teeth, **Under the terrible burden of destiny, laughing** as a young man laughs

EXERCISE 7

Rewrite each sentence to exemplify the grammar in parentheses. Then write an example of your own using the grammar. Your examples could describe the same or a different topic.

1. (adjectives that paint a picture) The river was beautiful as the sun rose. ....
   ....

2. (shift adjectives out of order) What he said caused a strong red-hot angry emotion in her.
   ....
   ....

3. (participial adjectives) He wrote ideas that shocked his readers and made them think.
   ....
   ....

4. (absolute) While she shouted, she gestured wildly with her hands. ....
   ....

5. (appositive) The thought came and went. The thought was fleeting and ill-formed.
   ....
   ....

6. (action verbs) He told us his opinion. ....
   ....

EXERCISE 8

Read the paragraph describing a recent occurrence in space that has astronomers excited. Rewrite it by varying the sentence style and using adjective clauses or phrases, embedded information, combined sentences, and parallel structure to create a more interesting text.

Einstein was right. There is now proof that gravitational waves exist. The proof is dramatic. The signal received by the Laser Interferometer Gravitational-Wave Observatory (LIGO) matches what Einstein predicted. It matches predictions of gravitational waves. The waves are ripples produced by large black holes. They are whirling deep in space. The ripples are the rumblings from a cataclysmic collision of two black holes. The ripples are produced in the final moments before black holes merge. They are swirling together at a great speed when they merge. Black holes are ultra-strong gravitational fields left behind by gigantic stars. Black holes can't be seen with ordinary telescopes. Black holes have been inferred by looking at stars and gas swirling around them. The gravitation wave signal came from the holes as they collided. It is proof that the black holes exist. The ripple washed past earth on September 14, 2015. The ripple was heard as a chirping sound lasting less than a second. As one scientist put it, before they had only eyes. They will have ears now. They were deaf in the past. They can listen to the universe going forward. The universe will speak to them. Scientists are excited about gravitational waves. The wave will tell them more about Einstein's theory of relativity. The waves will tell them more about the universe. The waves will tell them more about the warping of time and space in the universe. Our universe is an extraordinary place.

Go to MyEnglishLab to complete skill practices.

APPLY YOUR SKILLS

WHY IT'S USEFUL By applying the skills you have learned in this unit, you will use figurative language, sensory detail, and vivid language to engage your readers and create a deeper understanding of the experiences or concepts you are describing.

ASSIGNMENT

Write a descriptive essay about an interaction with something you read, heard, or saw that changed your understanding or knowledge about a concept or idea. This could be a poem, a short story, a novel, or play. It could be the lyrics to a piece of music, a play, or a movie you saw. It could be something you heard from a person—a teacher, musician, or an actor who had an impact on your learning. Be sure to use expressive writing techniques and include figurative language, sensory details, and descriptive grammar to enrich your writing.

BEFORE YOU WRITE

A. **Before you begin your assignment, discuss these questions with one or more students.**

1. Do you think knowledge is best acquired through direct experience or from a text?

2. How do you define the concept of thought? Does it depend on the knowledge you have acquired? Can you have thought without feeling?

3. Which do you remember better, abstract ideas or mental images?

B. **As you consider your assignment, complete the sensory chart. Include adjectives, nouns, and phrases that describe the interaction that changed your understanding about a concept or idea.**

Sight	Sound	Touch	Smell	Taste

C. Review the Unit Skills Summary. As you begin the writing task on page 215, apply the skills you learned in this unit.

UNIT SKILLS SUMMARY

Explore figurative language
- Explore figurative language and examine its effect on writing.
- Use different figures of speech appropriately.

Appeal to the senses
- Understand the difference between showing versus telling.
- Use sensory details and figurative language to evoke an emotional response from readers.

Analyze descriptive writing
- Consider rhetorical context, purpose, and the point the writer is making.
- Analyze the type and effect of descriptions and use of figurative and sensory language.

Use grammar to vary description
- Use adjectives (to paint a picture, out of order, and participial), absolutes, appositives, and action verbs in descriptive text.
- Vary sentence order (adjective clauses and phrases, embedded text, combined sentences, and parallel structure—to avoid monotonous text.

THINKING CRITICALLY

As you consider your assignment, discuss the questions with another student. Get feedback and revise your ideas, if necessary.

1. Why was this interaction you will write about a learning moment for you? Did you realize it as a learning moment at the time or only later after reflecting on it?
2. Did you choose your interaction based more on thoughts or feelings? Why did you choose this experience?
3. What did you gain from this experience? What did you lose from it?

THINKING VISUALLY

A. Write a brief description of the picture and analyze its effectiveness in helping the reader understand Mark Twain's description of navigating the Mississippi.

B. Find a picture or photograph that fits the interaction you are writing about. Write a brief description of the picture and explain why you chose it.

VIEW OF THE CITY OF ST. LOUIS, MISSOURI.

THINKING ABOUT LANGUAGE

Rewrite the paragraph to make it a more vivid description. Use adjectives, concrete nouns, and active verbs and vary the sentence structure.

A black hole is a place in space where gravity pulls a lot. Even light can not get out. The gravity is so strong because matter has been squeezed into a small space. This can happen when a star is dying. Scientists think the smallest black holes are small. They are the size of one atom. These black holes are very tiny but have the mass of a large mountain. Scientists think the smallest black holes formed when the universe began. Another kind of black hole is called stellar. Its mass is great. It's mass can be 20 times more than the mass of the sun. There may be many, many stellar mass black holes in Earth's galaxy. Earth's galaxy is called the Milky Way. Stellar black holes are made when the center of a very big star falls in upon itself, or collapses. When this happens, it causes a supernova. A supernova is an exploding star. The star breaks apart. The largest black holes are called supermassive. These black holes have masses. The masses are more than 1 million suns together. Scientists have found proof about galaxies. Every large galaxy contains a supermassive black hole at its center. Scientists think supermassive black holes were made at the same time as the galaxy they are in.

WRITE

A. Revisit the writing assignment and the descriptions you included in the Sensory Chart in Before You Write Part B.

B. Identify the dominant impression or mood you wish to convey. ....
....
....

C. Think about how you would like to organize your essay. Be sure to include examples of figurative language and sensory detail in your description.

BEYOND THE ASSIGNMENT

Find a work of fiction—a short story, a novel, a poem, or another genre of fiction—that has made an impression on you by appealing to your emotions and includes figurative language. Write an essay that analyzes the writer's purpose and how this writer uses literary devices to accomplish that purpose. Analyze what effect these techniques have on the writing. Examine why you think the writer used these literary techniques and how successful the use of the techniques was. Use examples from the work to support your analysis.

▶ Go to MyEnglishLab to listen to Professor Harrison and to complete a self-assessment.

Sound design creates a healthier world.

ENVIRONMENTAL ENGINEERING

Research Writing

UNIT PROFILE

Changes from normal temperatures can contribute to a wide range of atmospheric issues, including trapping high amounts of air pollution in urban areas. In this unit, you will read and write about topics related to temperature inversion and its serious effects on air quality. Specifically, you will learn about the Great Smog event in London in 1952, associations of inversions and emergency department visits for asthma in Salt Lake City, Utah, and methods for collecting and analyzing data.

You will locate a research paper that examines the influence of temperature inversions on air quality. You will then **create text for a research poster** that presents the aim and results of this study. Your text should include all components of a research poster.

OUTCOMES

- Analyze the parts of a research proposal
- Develop an abstract
- Create a research poster
- Examine the influence of function on form

GETTING STARTED

▶ Go to MyEnglishLab to listen to Professor Hildemann and to complete a self-assessment.

Discuss these questions with a partner or in a group.

1. Look at the photo of the Great Smog event in London in 1952. Many cities around the world like Beijing, Los Angeles, and Delhi have issues with air quality today. What factors do you think contribute to air pollution in these areas?

2. How does climate change impact air quality? Do you think global summits on climate change help to mitigate environmental problems like air pollution?

3. Unfortunately, the news often brings stories of environmental diasters on many levels. Can you think of an example of a critical environmental problem we have not seen yet, but that we may see in the future, due to man-made, climate, or technological changes?

For more about **ENVIRONMENTAL ENGINEERING**, see ② ③. See also R and OC **ENVIRONMENTAL ENGINEERING** ① ② ③.

CRITICAL THINKING SKILL

RESEARCH WRITING

WHY IT'S USEFUL Research writing is an integral part of higher education studies and is also required in different forms in many professional careers. For this reason, it is important to become proficient in the various types of research writing that you will encounter as both a student and a professional.

Scientific papers, dissertations, master's theses, argumentative and analytical papers, and review articles are a few of the most common types of **research writing**. Graduate studies always include research writing, but increasingly, undergraduate studies require it as well.

In many cases, the first step in research writing is **developing a research proposal**. All research proposals should specify what you plan to research, how you will carry out the study, and how you will analyze the results. After a proposal is accepted, the type of writing is determined by the purpose of the research (to inform, to explore, to analyze, or to argue) and is influenced by the discipline or field in which you study or work. The approach to the research depends on the writer's goals:

- With **primary research**, you collect your own data in the field, carry out laboratory experiments, conduct observations, issue questionnaires or surveys, or conduct interviews. Primary research is especially useful when investigating a local issue that has not been studied before or writing about a specific person or group.
- With **secondary research**, you analyze and synthesize published works from academic journals, books, magazines, or websites. Secondary research is the most common approach to research and is usually integrated into a paper that includes primary research.

NOTICING ACTIVITY

Look at the aims of five research projects. What do you think is the rhetorical purpose of each paper (to inform, explore, analyze, or argue)? What methods (primary and / or secondary research) could a writer use to answer the research question?

RESEARCH PROJECTS		
Aim	Research Question	Rhetorical Purpose and Research Methods
to present original field or laboratory data to solve a problem	*What are the effects of winter temperature inversions on air quality in the Denver area?*	
to position oneself within a conversation about a topic	*How does Wallace's study on the spatial impacts of temperature inversions on Lake Ontario offer a limited view of the causes of air pollution when compared to Spendley's similar study in New Hampshire?*	
to present various sides of a controversy	*What are the arguments for and against regulating air pollution?*	
to take a stance on a controversy	*Will environmental regulations negatively impact employment?*	
to report an expert opinion about a problem	*What causes have been identified for the increase in temperature inversions?*	

Temperature inversions *occur when the temperature becomes warmer instead of colder as the altitude increases. This can cause the warm air to trap the cooler air underneath it.*

Regardless of the type of research paper, it is important to establish that your research is original and that you are familiar with the literature on the topic. Research writing is competitive, so it is essential to show that you are knowledgeable about other scholarship on the topic and are contributing new information to the field. This will add relevance to your research and garner interest from your readers.

The common structure of a research paper follows the **IMRD format: Introduction, Method, Results, and Discussion.** In addition to these sections, a title and an abstract are included at the beginning of a research paper, and references and appendices appear at the end. **Developing a good abstract** is a critical step because it provides a concise but comprehensive summary of your work.

You will see that some papers combine the Results and Discussion sections, which can make it easier to present the results and discuss their importance alongside each other. In some fields and journals, there is sometimes a Conclusions section that is separate from the Discussion. Because there can be variation in the structure of a research paper, it is important to follow the guidelines of your department or publication. Look at the specific purpose of each section of a research paper.

Section	Purpose
Abstract	Provides a summary of the paper in 200 words or less.
	Includes the problem, hypothesis or goal of the study, major findings, and significance of the study.
	Needs to capture the reader's interest.
Introduction	Explains the rationale for the study.
	States the problem being researched.
	Indicates the importance of the problem.
	Includes the writer's thesis or hypothesis.
	Includes a literature review of other studies related to the topic.
Methods	Describes how the study was conducted.
	Includes the procedures, participants, and materials used.
Results	Presents the research findings or results.
	Uses graphics to present data.
	Includes commentary summarizing data.
	Shows composite results. Does not include raw data.
Discussion (with Conclusions)	Provides an interpretation of the data in response to the paper's research question and in support of the thesis or hypothesis.
	Indicates significance of the findings.
	Provides an explanation of how the results relate to data from other sources.
	May include limitations of the study and suggestions for further research.
References	Provides a bibliography of the sources cited in the paper.
Appendices	Includes any additional materials used to conduct the study, such as questionnaires, surveys, and interview questions.

Go to MyEnglishLab to complete a skill practice and join in collaborative activities.

SUPPORTING SKILL 1

WRITING RESEARCH PROPOSALS

WHY IT'S USEFUL A proposal is a formal request for support of research and is required for any research that is sponsored and needs approval by a person or committee. The research proposal serves as an agreement between the writer and the research committee. By writing an effective research proposal, you will improve the chances that your research will be approved.

Research proposals can be required by an academic department before embarking on a dissertation, master's thesis, or undergraduate research. Funding agencies, such as the National Science Foundation, also require proposals to determine whether or not to fund a project and provide program solicitations or announcements including detailed guidelines for submission. There are three main types of proposals:

Solicited proposals are sent by an agency or organization in the form of an RFP or Request for Proposals.

> RFPs include specific guidelines for the content and formatting of the proposal. For academic research proposals, universities usually have a designated office or staff member who provides students with guidance on parts of proposal writing, such as creating a realistic budget and timeline.

Unsolicited proposals are sent to an agency or organization that has not sent out solicitations but may be interested in the proposed research study and may be willing to fund it.

Pre-proposals are brief (1–2 pages) and provide a summary of the solicitor's study.

> Pre-proposals can be sent to faculty who may be interested in serving on a research committee or a sponsoring agency that may be interested in funding a study. The person or agency that received the pre-proposal will contact the solicitor if there is interest in a full proposal.

GENERAL CRITERIA FOR PROPOSALS

It is important to follow the guidelines you receive when writing the proposal; however, these criteria are usually considered standard. Proposals:

- Are generally 5–10 pages in length and should not be longer than 15 pages.
- Need to be concise and show you understand the topic well; in addition, your thesis or hypothesis must make sense.
- State the intellectual merit of the research, explaining how it will impact the field, university, or others who could benefit from the study.
- Include the cost of carrying out the research and the estimated time it will take.
- State what research has already been done in this area and describe how your research will fill a gap in knowledge.
- Explain how the research relates to the interests of the soliciting agency or organization.
- Present why you, rather than someone else, are best equipped to carry out the project.

Outline of a Proposal

Although there can be variations in the information included in a proposal depending on the type and scope of the research as well as the sponsoring agency, organization, or department, this outline presents the most common components of a research proposal.

Introduction

- Begin with a statement that describes your proposed research. Establish the topic and use language that would be clear for someone who is unfamiliar with the subject.
- Identify the specific problem or issue your research will investigate.
- State the significance of the study by showing why it is important to the field. Indicate the impact that this study could have and convince the faculty member or sponsor why your research should be reviewed and/or funded.

Background

- Include a literature review of other studies to show existing research about the issue or problem you are investigating.
- Present the gaps in knowledge that these studies do not address to show why your study is needed to provide new information.

Methodology

- Provide an overview of your research approach by describing the methods and logic behind your plan.
- Describe what data you will collect and how.
- Describe the site where the research will be conducted and the instruments you will use to answer your research question.
- Indicate how the methods you use are appropriate for attaining your research objective.
- Provide a detailed timeline for completing the work.

Results

- List the potential outcomes you can reasonably expect to find and note how each addresses your research question.
- Connect the potential outcomes to theory and your research question. Remind the reader of the significance of the study.

Bibliography

- List all sources that have informed your study. Some departments require you to include only the sources that you have cited, whereas others expect you to include all sources that are relevant to the research. Check with the department or sponsor for their guidelines.

Budget

- Review the RFP for information about the budget criteria.
- Be clear about how the budget will be used and be realistic about the amount you are requesting.
- Indicate whether or not there are other funding sources and state how costsharing will be divided.

EXERCISE 1

A. Find a research proposal online or through your department and use the questions to analyze it. Compare findings about your proposal with a partner who has analyzed a different proposal.

1. What type of research is it (scientific paper, dissertation, master's thesis, argumentative paper, etc.)?

....

2. Which agency or committee will review the proposal? ....

....

3. Does the proposal follow the outline described here? If not, how are the organization and

content different? ....

....

4. What are the similarities and differences between your analysis and your partner's? Why do

you think these similarities and differences exist? ....

....

....

....

B. Find a research paper in your field of interest. Imagine that you are the author of this paper and are preparing to write the research proposal. Complete an outline for the research proposal. You should paraphrase information, and you do not need to use complete sentences.

Introduction

Topic _____

Problem / Issue _____

Significance of study _____

Background

Already known _____

Gaps in knowledge _____

Methodology

Type of data _____

Instrument(s) used _____

Why appropriate _____

Results

Outcomes _____

Connection to research question _____

C. Find guidelines for writing a research proposal online or through your department and use the questions to analyze them. Compare findings with a partner.

1. What type of research are the guidelines for (scientific paper, dissertation, master's thesis, argumentative paper, etc.)? ....

....

....

....

2. What department, agency, or organization are the guidelines from? ....

....

....

....

3. Do the guidelines follow the information described here? What new information do they include? ....

....

....

....

....

4. What are the similarities and differences between your guidelines and your partner's?

....

....

....

....

Go to **MyEnglishLab** to complete a skill practice.

SUPPORTING SKILL 2
DEVELOPING AN ABSTRACT

WHY IT'S USEFUL By including an abstract, you help readers determine whether or not the work is relevant to their interests and is worth reading.

Abstracts provide a brief summary of a research study and are included at the beginning of a journal article, dissertation, master's thesis, or proposal. The content of an abstract varies across disciplines. For example, some disciplines, especially the sciences, tend to be results-driven because their focus is on the outcomes of the research and the significance of the outcomes. In other areas, such as the humanities, the abstract may include a summary of the introduction and conclusion and leave out the method and results altogether. Here are the two most common types of abstracts:

Descriptive abstracts are approximately 100–120 words and provide an outline of the research without including evaluation of it. This type of abstract usually excludes results or conclusions from the study and instead focuses on the purpose and methods of the research.

Informative abstracts are at least 250 words and vary in length depending on the discipline. This type of abstract goes beyond a description because it also includes the main arguments of the study and presents the key findings and conclusions. This is the most common type of abstract.

Although abstracts can vary across disciplines, consider these elements before writing any abstract:

- the subject area and why it's important
- key words or phrases that help to define the topic
- the problem or issue being researched
- the thesis or hypothesis of the paper
- the methods used for investigating the problem
- the main findings or results from the research
- implications for further research or how the study fills a gap in knowledge

Here are some useful tips for writing an abstract:

1. Check with your department or publication to determine whether the abstract should be descriptive or informative.
2. Highlight key terms and ideas in each section of your paper.
3. Using the highlighted information, summarize each section of the paper in one sentence.
4. Put the summarized sentences together in one cohesive paragraph.
5. Ensure that you include the elements of an effective abstract and follow the department's or publication's guidelines.

NONSTRUCTURED AND STRUCTURED ABSTRACTS

Read the abstracts on page 224. Notice the information the writers include and how it is organized. The first piece is an example of a **non-structured abstract,** which usually consists of one cohesive paragraph. The second example is of a **structured abstract,** which is divided into sections: background, aim, method, results, and conclusions. Structured abstracts are more commonly seen in scientific or medical journals.

The effect of a temperature inversion-triggered smog event on the mortality rate in London in 1952

The winter of 1952 in London produced a smog event that became one of the most grievous public health disasters in history. The event, known as the Great Smog, was precipitated by a temperature inversion that led to a toxic brew of respirable pollutants in the ground-level air, causing the premature mortality of approximately 12,000 individuals during and in the aftermath of the smog. While the pervasiveness of air pollution in London has been observed for centuries, this particular inversion and the air quality of the time led to the most acute case of pollution-related deaths on record for the city. Daily mean air pollution indexes revealed a spike in both smoke and sulfur dioxide, resulting in hazardous particle pollutants that affected lung tissue and greatly exacerbated respiratory illnesses. Deaths more than doubled among residents at the height of the smog event and continued to remain higher than normal for months afterward. The health crisis led directly to the formation of environmental legislation that resulted in pollution-mitigating efforts like building taller chimneys and converting coal heaters to gas, oil, or other smog-reducing heating systems.

The effect of a temperature inversion-triggered smog event on the mortality rate in London in 1952

Background: An intense temperature inversion acts as a cap on trapped lower air and can create heavy smog. Temperature inversions intensify particle pollution and hazardous gases.

Aim: Meteorological conditions in the winter of 1952 in London produced a severe smog event that lasted for five days. This paper will examine the ways in which the smog affected the mortality rate.

Method: Smoke and sulfur dioxide were measured at ten locations in London, and the National Gallery of London measured an approximate level of coarse particle pollution over a five-day period.

Results: The air pollution event caused the premature mortality of approximately 12,000 individuals during and in the aftermath of the smog. Deaths more than doubled among residents at the height of the smog event and continued to remain higher than normal for months afterward.

Conclusion: The temperature inversion dramatically affected the mortality rate of the people in London in 1952. The health crisis resulted in the formation of environmental legislation that mandated pollution-mitigating efforts like building taller chimneys and converting coal heaters to gas, oil, or other smog-reducing heating systems.

EXERCISE 2

A. Analyze the example abstracts on page 224 and answer the questions. Discuss your answers with a partner.

1. Are the abstracts descriptive or informative? How do you know? ....
   ....
   ....

2. Compare and contrast the information included in both abstracts. Is there anything included
   in one but not the other? ....
   ....
   ....
   ....

3. What cohesive devices (transition words, synonyms, pronoun referents, and sentence patterns)
   are used in the nonstructured abstract? ....
   ....
   ....
   ....

4. Do both abstracts include all of the elements of an abstract? ....
   ....
   ....

5. Are both abstracts effective? What information could be added to make them stronger?
   ....
   ....
   ....

B. Read the practice assignment and write an informative abstract.

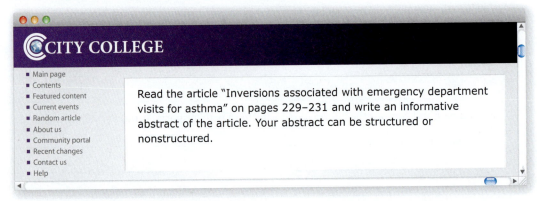

C. <u>PEER REVIEW</u>. Exchange abstracts with a partner. Respond to the questions to evaluate each other's work. For responses marked No, give feedback in the Notes column to help your partner revise.

	Yes	No	Notes
Does the abstract meet the criteria for an informative abstract?	☐	☐	
Does the abstract reveal the main focus of the article?	☐	☐	
Does the writer include all of the elements of an effective abstract?	☐	☐	
Does the abstract accurately represent the information from the article?	☐	☐	
Does the writer use cohesive devices effectively?	☐	☐	
Is the abstract easy to understand?			
Does the writer capture the reader's interest?	☐	☐	

Go to MyEnglishLab to complete a vocabulary exercise and a skill practice.

READING-WRITING CONNECTION
CREATING A RESEARCH POSTER

WHY IT'S USEFUL Research posters are used both in academic and many professional settings to present a summary of research and information to others. By understanding how research posters are designed and organized, you will be able to critically read research posters and present your own ideas in a visual format.

A **research poster** is a tool to communicate ideas, information, and findings quickly and easily in a clear, concise way, using carefully organized and worded text and understandable visuals. An effective research poster attracts and directs the reader's attention to key findings. It can be a visual display of any or all stages of the research process from the research question to the results.

> **TIP**
> Research posters are most commonly used in classrooms, in workshops, and at professional conferences to present research findings, collaborate with peers, and receive feedback.

A good research poster includes these elements:

- **Title**—a compelling short title that quickly conveys the topic and main point
- **Introduction**—brief background information with a clear concise statement of your objective or goals with regard to the problem(s) you are attempting to solve or issue(s) you are investigating
- **Methods** (data collection and statistical analyses)—brief description and summary of samples and measures used, manipulations, comparisons, correlations, and significant differences
- **Visual aids** (labeled with appropriate text to identify and explain them)
- **Summary of results**—findings or outcomes of research expressed qualitatively and / or quantitatively (research in progress can report preliminary results)
- **Discussion of findings / conclusion**—broader implications of your research and findings, including limitations, unanswered questions, and future directions to explore
- **References**—sources used in the research
- **Acknowledgements**—name(s) of the affiliate institution and those who helped you
- **Author(s) and contact information**

Creating text for a research poster

Because the space on a poster is limited, you can't present a complete research paper. Use only the most important ideas and organize them efficiently and succinctly. Your poster should focus on one key idea, and your thesis statement can be a guide to the key idea. A good way to start is to write a 100-word summary of the purpose and main ideas of your research. While design is important to attract attention, the text is where your message is conveyed and is essential to a good research poster. When writing your text:

> **TIP**
> A research poster does not usually have an abstract as the poster itself is a shortened form of the paper.

> **TIP**
> A research poster is similar to a research proposal and an abstract in that they are short and concise and must attract the reader's attention quickly. A research proposal, an abstract, or a full research paper are good starting points when planning a poster.

- List the key information and organize and group central ideas and concepts.
- Keep text clear, short, and simple (for example, avoid unnecessary adjectives).
- Create small blocks of supporting text.
- Use bulleted points rather than full paragraphs.
- Limit the number of words (300–800 total).
- Avoid abbreviations and jargon (terminology of a field of study, known only to a specific group).
- Emphasize key words with boldface (but avoid underlining). Be careful not to overuse bold text, or it will lose its effect.
- Label all visuals, which include figures (graphs, illustrations, flow charts, and photographs) and tables. All visuals should be easily understood without requiring the reader to find information in the poster text.

> For more information on using and labeling visuals, see ENGINEERING Part 1.

Designing a research poster

A good research poster is visually appealing and benefits from the visuals that show rather than tell the story. It should be interesting to a diverse audience and easy for everyone to understand in a very short time.

Your research poster should be easy to read because:

1. It is organized and presents ideas in a logical progression or order.
   - Reads from left to right and top to bottom.
   - Uses headings, numbers and / or arrows to direct the reader where to look next.
   - Has main sections labeled well (with headlines, larger fonts, bolding).
   - Puts the most important information first or central (conclusion in top left corner).
   - Makes the takeaway message bigger and more central so readers will notice it.
2. It is designed with a consistent and clean layout.
   - Is not cluttered and includes sufficient white space.
   - Has clearly divided sections.
   - Uses a carefully chosen color scheme for text and background.
   - Avoids overuse of boxes or borders.
   - Has aligned text in small blocks evenly spaced.
   - Uses readable text fonts and uses no more than two fonts.
   - Uses limited means to differentiate text (bullets, bold, or italics).
   - Uses simple data displays and more than one type of visual.

> **TIP**
> Here is more information on using color:
> - Use light colors for background and dark colors for text.
> - Limit number of colors, avoiding bright or clashing colors.
> - Color code to enhance comprehension.
> - Avoid patterns or complex images that detract in the background.

> **TIP**
> Here is more information on readable text fonts:
> - Sans serif fonts are preferred.
> - Sentence case is easier to read [This is an example of sentence case.] Limit use of all-capital letters.
> - Use a font size large enough for reading quickly from 5-6 feet away.
> - Use 16 pt. minimum, 30–60 pt. for headings and 72 pt. for title.

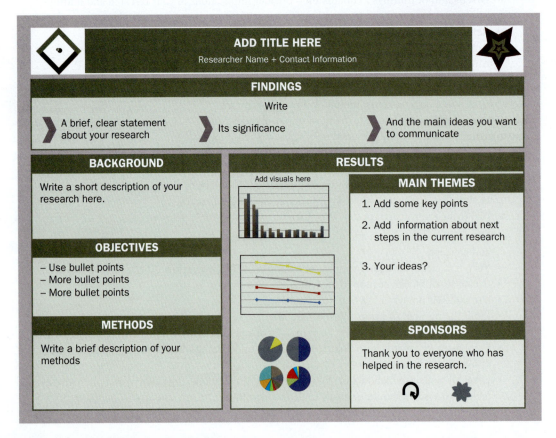

EXERCISE 3

A. Read the research article about temperature inversions in Salt Lake County.

Inversions Associated with Emergency Department Visits for Asthma

INTRODUCTION

1 Winter temperature inversions are layers of air that trap air pollution, resulting in higher concentrations of pollutants and particulate matter. Weather patterns and topographical geography in Salt Lake County, Utah contribute to winter temperature inversions in which a stable layer of cool air is trapped under a layer of warmer air, as shown in Figures 1 and 2. Data show inversions occurred on 57 percent of winter days from 1994–2008 (Bailey, et al., 2011, in Beard, et al.). Air pollution often exceeds National Ambient Air Quality Standards (NAAQS), exposing over 1 million people to the effects of air pollution on respiratory health. The objective of the study was to assess associations between winter temperature inversions and emergency department visits (ED) for asthma in Salt Lake County, Utah, with inversions as an independent risk factor.

METHODS

Data

2 Electronic records of ED visits for asthma and data on inversions, weather, and air pollutants for Salt Lake County, Utah were obtained for the winter months of December through February, from 2003–2004 through 2007–2008 to describe inversions in terms of weather and pollutant concentrations, to estimate associations between ED visits for asthma and the occurrence of inversions and prolonged inversions, and to determine whether

Poor air quality as a result of inversion and calm winds

① Winter sun provides less warmth to the Earth's surface.

② Layer of warm air, like a lid, keeps cooler air below.

③ Air pollution from cars and wood burning is trapped in the stable cooler air.

④ Surrounding mountains can worsen the effects of air pollution.

Figure 1 Winter temperature inversion

Figure 2 Air pollution is a serious problem in many cities.

Continued

TABLE 1 Daily ED visits for asthma and weather inversions for Salt Lake County, December through February, 2003 / 2004–2007 / 2008.

Variable	Total	Inversion No	Inversion Yes	Inversion Day 1–3	Inversion Day 4–6	Inversion Day 7–12	Inversion Day >12
Days [# and %]	452	294 (65%)	158 (35%)	105 (23%)	36 (8%)	11 (2%)	6 (1%)
ED visits for asthma [# and %]	3,425	2,192 (64%)	1,234 (36%)	774 (23%)	319 (9%)	75 (2%)	66 (2%)
Person days[6] [# and %]	14,898	9,681 (65%)	5,217 (35%)	3.385 (23%)	1,221 (8%)	380 (3%)	231 (2%)
Daily # ED visits for asthma [mean ± SD]	8.11 ± 3.40	7.94 ± 3.32	8.41 ± 3.52	7.98 ± 3.45	9.29 ± 3.26	7.58 ± 3.78	11.42 ± 2.76

[6] A person day is either a case day—visit to the ED or a control day—the same day of the week in the other weeks of the month with no ED visit. Person days are a way to account for both case and control days in order to do a statistical analysis based on days with inversions and days with no inversion.

associations between inversions and ED visits for asthma changed when adjusted for concentrations of individual pollutants during inversions, as shown in Table 1.

3 Emergency department data for visits for asthma were obtained from the Office of Health Care Statistics for all 10 Salt Lake County hospitals for the study period. There were 3,425 ED visits with asthma as a primary diagnosis identified. ED records included age, sex, race, classification of diseases, date of admission, and residential ZIP code. All residents living in Salt Lake County were included in the study.

4 The study used data from the release of weather balloons by the National Weather Service office in Salt Lake City. Analysis of this data is a primary way that the presence and strength of inversions is identified. For this study, the bottom of the inversion had to be below the crest of the surrounding mountains to ensure the inversion was low enough to trap pollutants near the ground. Inversions were considered only if they were present at both 4:00 A.M. and 4:00 P.M. Temperatures (maximum and mean), dew point, and humidity were recorded for each day.

5 Data on six air pollutants was obtained from the US EPA Air Data (2012): Carbon monoxide (CO, 4 monitors), nitrogen dioxide (NO_2, 2 monitors), ozone (O_3, 1 monitor), sulfur dioxide (SO_2, 3 monitors), and particulate matter ($PM_{2.5}$, 7 monitors and PM_{10}, 4 monitors). Monitors were located where pollution levels were thought to be highest. Daily one-hour maximum concentrations of pollutants and 24-hour mean concentrations for particulates were used.

STATISTICAL ANALYSIS

6 The study used a time-stratified case-crossover design[1] that uses cases as their own control. When a resident went to the ED for asthma during the study period, it was called a case day. The same day in the remaining weeks in the month were control days. The analysis included 3,425 case days and 11,473 control days. Logistic regression models[2] were used to estimate odds ratios[3] (ORs) and 95 percent confidence intervals[4] (CIs) for the association between inversions and ED visits for asthma.

7 A lag structure of 0–3 days (the day of the ED visit for asthma and the 3 days before for both case and controlling days) was used. Distributed lag models[5] were used to estimate

---

[1] The time-stratified case-crossover design is widely used in environmental epidemiology to analyze the short-term effects of environmental risk factors, such as air pollution or temperature, on human health. It compares the exposure level in the day when the health event occurs (case day) with the levels in control days chosen with alternative selection methods.

[2] Logistic regression measures the relationship between the dependent variable and one or more independent variables by estimating probabilities.

[3] Odds ratio (OR) is a way of qualifying how strongly the presence or absence of x (ED visits for asthma) is associated with the presence or absence of y (inversions) taking the odds of x when y exists and dividing it by the odds of x when y does not exist to see if the presence of y does increase the odds of x happening.

[4] 95 percent confidence intervals is a statistical analysis term stating that 95 percent of all samples taken from a global population will fall within the given 95 percent interval determined from a small sample.

[5] A distributed lag model is a dynamic model in which the effect of x on y occurs over time rather than all at once.

lag-specific and overall effects of inversions relative to noninversions on ED visits for asthma. Models were adjusted for dew point and mean temperature. Separate models were used of each pollutant.

RESULTS

- A mean of 8.11 ED visits for asthma occurred each day during the study period.
- More ED visits for asthma occurred on inversion days—8.41—than noninversion days—7.94.
- The mean number of ED visits also increased by day of inversion and was higher after 12 inversion days—11.42—compared with the first 3 days—7.98. (Standard deviations ranged from + 2.76–3.52.)
- 54 percent of ED visits were by females.
- 25 percent ages 0–4, 20 percent 5–17, 24 percent 18–34, 21 percent 35–54, and 10 percent >54. Inversions occurred on 158 days (35%) during the study period which equated to 5,217 person-days during inversions and 9,681 during non-inversions of ED visits for asthma by residents.
- Ozone (O_3) concentrations were significantly lower on inversion days than noninversion days.
- Other pollutant concentrations were significantly higher.
- Inversion days were colder and more humid than noninversion days.

8 Based on the data, the Odds Ratio (OR) for ED visits for asthma relative to the presence of inversions 0–3 days before the visit compared to no inversions was 1.14, meaning that ED visits for asthma were associated with inversions occurring during the lag period (0–3 days prior). For each additional day of inversion in the lag period, the OR was 1.03, which indicated that the odds of people going to the ED for asthma increased with the number of inversions. When concentrations of individual pollutants were examined separately to see if they altered the association, only particulate matter did.

DISCUSSION

9 The occurrence of multiple, prolonged winter inversions is a unique characteristic of Salt Lake County that made it possible to estimate effects of inversions on rates of ED visits for asthma. The adjusted odds of ED visits for asthma and pollutant concentrations were higher during inversions than noninversions. The association was stronger as the number of inversion days increased during the lag period. While air pollutant concentrations changed during inversions, the odds ratio changed little when individual pollutants were included in the model, with the exception of PM_{10} when temperatures were above median levels.

10 A limitation of the study was the inability to measure individual-level exposure to inversions or pollutants. People with asthma may have remained indoors or self-medicated rather than visiting the ED. ED visits may have also been misclassified, especially on inversion days, if clinicians knew of the association between inversions and air pollution.

11 Increased concentrations of air pollutants during inversions could be at least partly responsible for associations between inversions and ED visits for asthma observed in the study. Further research needs to be done to determine if increased pollutant concentrations are the underlying cause of the associations.

CONCLUSION

12 The study results provided evidence that winter temperature inversions are associated with increased rates of emergency department visits for asthma.

B. Answer the questions.

1. What is the stated objective of the research study? ....

....

....

2. Where was the study conducted, and why was this place chosen? ....

....

....

3. What three sets of data did the researchers use to do the study? ....

....

....

4. What were their results? Summarize in one-two sentences. ....

....

....

5. What was the conclusion of the study? ....

....

....

6. What did the researchers say in the discussion to justify this conclusion? ....

....

....

7. What limitations did the researchers mention?

....

....

8. What is the key idea of the research article?

....

....

C. Write a 100-word summary of the important ideas in the research paper in preparation for writing the text for a research poster.

D. Compare your summary in Part C with a partner.

EXERCISE 4

A. Look at part of a research poster presenting the information from the article above. Answer the questions.

1. What types of ideas are included in the research poster?

2. How is the language in the research poster different from the language in the research article?

3. How does the format of the research poster differ from the format of the article?

4. Does the poster text contain enough information to understand the study's objective and methods (data and statistical analysis)? Why or why not?

WINTER TEMPERATURE INVERSIONS AND ED VISITS FOR ASTHMA

OBJECTIVE
Assess associations between winter temperature inversions and emergency department visits for asthma in Salt Lake County, Utah.

INTRODUCTION
Winter Temperature Inversions: Stable layer of cool air trapped under a layer of warmer air

Salt Lake County: Inversions occurred 57% of winter days 1994–2008 trapping air pollution exceeding health standards

Poor air quality as a result of inversion and calm winds

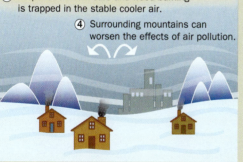

① Winter sun provides less warmth to the Earth's surface.

② Layer of warm air, like a lid, keeps cooler air below.

③ Air pollution from cars and wood burning is trapped in the stable cooler air.

④ Surrounding mountains can worsen the effects of air pollution.

METHODS
Location: Salt Lake County, Utah
Dates: December–February 2003/2004–2007/2008
Data
- ED visits for asthma
  10 hospitals
  3,425 ED visits
  All Salt Lake County residents
- Inversions identified
  Bottom below crest of surrounding mountains
  Present at 4:00 am and 4:00 pm
- Weather
  Temperature (mean and medium)
  Dew point and humidity
- Air pollutants
  Carbon monoxide (CO)—4 monitors
  Nitrogen dioxide (NO_2)—2 monitors
  Ozone (O_3)—1 monitor
  Sulfur dioxide (SO_2)—3 monitors
  Particulate matter ($PM_{2.5}$)—7 monitors
  Particulate matter (PM_{10})—4 monitors

STATISTICAL ANALYSIS
- Time stratified crossover design—ED visits for asthma
  3,425 case days—ED visits with asthma diagnosis
  11,472 control days—same day in remaining weeks in month
  Total: 14,898 person days
- Logistic regression model to determine odds ratio to measure relationship of ED visits for asthma and inversions
- Separate models used for each of 6 pollutants
- Models adjusted for dew point and mean temperature
- Distributed lag models used to evaluate the effect of inversions on ED visits for asthma over time

B. Work with a partner. Discuss and compare your answers in Part A.

C. Read the Results, Discussion, and Conclusion sections from the research article in Exercise 3. Rewrite them as clear, concise blocks of text to complete the research poster in Part A.

Go to MyEnglishLab to complete a vocabulary exercise and a skill practice and join in collaborative activities.

LANGUAGE SKILLS
RELATING FORM TO FUNCTION

WHY IT'S USEFUL By using appropriate forms to convey your message based on the function of the text, you can present your ideas clearly to your reader.

VERB FORMS IN ACADEMIC WRITING

Writers are constantly faced with choices not only about which ideas to include, but also about how to best express those ideas. Just as purpose and audience are considered in developing ideas, they should be considered in grammar choices. **Function** is the use of grammar to create discourse for different purposes in different situations. **Academic writing** is a specialized register that requires the **use of particular forms to fit the function.**

The **simple present** form is used for the function of reporting current trends or general aspects and **simple past** is used when reporting methods completed in the past.

Winter temperature inversions **are** layers of air that **trap** air pollution resulting in higher concentrations of pollutants and particulate matter. [general aspect]

The study **used** data from the release of weather balloons by the National Weather Service office in Salt Lake City. [methods completed in the past]

Analysis of this data **is** a primary way that the presence and strength of inversions is identified. [current trend]

Passive voice is used frequently in research writing to report methods and procedures.

Monitors **were located** where pollution levels were thought to be highest.

Models **were adjusted** for dew point and mean temperature.

EXERCISE 5

Underline and label examples of simple present used for general aspect, simple past used for reporting methods completed in the past, and passive voice for procedures

The effect of a temperature inversion-triggered smog event on the mortality rate in London in 1952

Background: An intense temperature inversion acts as a cap on trapped lower air and can create heavy smog. Temperature inversions intensify particle pollution and hazardous gases.

Aim: Meteorological conditions in the winter of 1952 in London produced a severe smog event that lasted for five days. This paper will examine the ways in which the smog affected the mortality rate.

Method: Smoke and sulfur dioxide were measured at ten locations in London, and the National Gallery of London measured an approximate level of coarse particle pollution over a five-day period.

Results: The air pollution event caused the premature mortality of approximately 12,000 individuals during and in the aftermath of the smog. Deaths more than doubled among residents at the height of the smog event and continued to remain higher than normal for months afterward.

Conclusion: The temperature inversion dramatically affected the mortality rate of the people in London in 1952. The health crisis resulted in the formation of environmental legislation that mandated pollution-mitigating efforts like building taller chimneys and converting coal heaters to gas, oil, or other smog-reducing heating systems.

BULLETED TEXT IN RESEARCH POSTERS

Research posters are designed to be visual so the function of the text is to convey information to a reader quickly. The reader is likely to be skimming the text rather than reading carefully. In fact, writing text for a research poster is challenging as you are taking complex research text and rewriting it in ways that make it shorter and more concise without losing the meaning. **Bulleted text** is one way to convey information quickly and is effective if used carefully and correctly.

Bulleted text can take more than one form. It can be short, concise sentences, or it can be reduced to phrases. Whichever you choose, make all the bullet points consistent, using parallel structure—the same form. Do not mix sentences and phrases. They should all be complete sentences, all noun phrases, all verb phrases, and so on, and they should be about equal in length. It is always a good idea to check on the style used in your discipline and to notice how bullets are used in texts in your field.

To punctuate bullet points:

- Use a period after each bullet point that is a sentence.
- Use a period after a bullet point that completes the introductory stem.
- Use no punctuation after bullets that are not sentences and do not complete a stem.
- Use no punctuation after bullets that complete a stem if they are a list of nouns or short noun phrases.
- Use all capital letters to begin the bullet points or all small letters; do not use a mix.

To create bulleted text from research text:

- Underline or highlight key words and phrases.
- Decide whether you will start with a sentence or an introductory stem. An introductory stem is a clause, and typically each bulleted item completes the stem, making it a sentence.
- Create your list of bullet points, using the same form for each point.
- Punctuate carefully. Use a colon after the sentence or introductory stem that precedes your list.

EXERCISE 6

A. **Read the introduction to the research article on the Great Smog of 1952 and the bulleted text in Part B below. Highlight or underline key words and phrases in the text in both Parts A and B.**

> To fully grasp the level of accumulated pollution in London during the Great Smog, temperature inversions must first be understood. Atmospheric temperatures are typically warmer at the Earth's surface and cooler as air rises, but this temperature-altitude relationship can switch, in what is referred to as a temperature inversion. Surface temperature inversions occur with some regularity during winter months when nights are longer and the frigid ground cools the surface air at a quicker pace than the air at higher altitudes. Warmer air thus accumulates above the colder air, and if there is little to no horizontal air movement, combined with a high atmospheric pressure system over the area, the inversion can linger for several days and act as a lid on the underlying tropospheric air. In an urban area, inversions that coincide with a day's-long stable air dynamic that fails to disperse and mix air results in unsafe concentrations of trapped particle pollution.

B. **Read the bulleted text. Then answer the questions.**

Temperature inversions occur when there is a switch from the typical pattern of warm layers of air beneath cooler air.

Temperature inversions often occur during winter months when:

- Nights are longer.
- Ground is cooler.
- Weaker sun.
- Warm air accumulates over cool air, acting as a lid.
- Cool air is trapped.

If there is little to no horizontal air movement:

- Inversions can linger for several days.
- Stable air fails to disperse and mix air.
- Pollutant concentrations increase to unsafe levels.
- Affects people with respiratory illnesses.

1. Do the bullet points follow an independent clause or an introductory stem?

....

2. Are the bullet points sentences or phrases?

....

3. Are the items in each list parallel in structure? Correct any item that is not.

....

C. Rewrite the bulleted point in Part B as noun phrases.

Temperature inversions often occur during winter months. This is due to:

• Longer nights

• ....

• ....

• Accumulated warm air acting as a lid

• ....

EXERCISE 7

Rewrite the passages from the article as bulleted text.

1. In London on December 5, 1952, substantially cool temperatures, long nights, and calm winds led to a thick layer of smog that lasted for five days. Misty, cold fog combined with particles of sulfur dioxide emitted from coal hearths, tar pollution, and other gaseous particles to form hazardous sulfuric acid.

2. Medical research shows that exposure to air pollution causes acute health problems, particularly in the elderly and those whose respiratory systems are already compromised. After breathing in a pollution cloud for five days, London residents began dying from pollution-related illnesses, including pneumonia, bronchitis, tuberculosis, and heart failure at unprecedented rates. Those with respiratory diseases like asthma and chronic obstructive pulmonary disease were hospitalized.

Go to MyEnglishLab to complete a vocabulary exercise and a skill practice.

APPLY YOUR SKILLS

WHY IT'S USEFUL By applying the skills you have learned in this unit, you can familiarize yourself with the parts of a research paper, a proposal, and a research poster in order to successfully write a research paper and present it in a visual format.

ASSIGNMENT

What effects do temperature inversions have on air quality? With a partner, locate a research paper that examines the influence of temperature inversions on air quality. Then create text for a research poster that presents the aim and results of this study. Your text should include all of the components of a research poster.

BEFORE YOU WRITE

A. Before you begin your assignment, discuss these questions with one or more students.

   1. What are temperature inversions?

   2. When and where do temperature inversions usually occur?

   3. What are the sources of the pollutants that are trapped by inversions?

B. As you consider your assignment, complete the tasks below. Then, share your ideas with another student. Get feedback and revise your ideas, if necessary.

   1. With your partner, write a 100-word summary of the research paper you chose. If your research paper has an abstract, this is a good starting point. Include the objective and key ideas for a research poster.

   2. Share your summary with another pair of students.

C. Review the Unit Skills Summary. As you begin on the writing task on page 240, apply the skills you learned in this unit.

UNIT SKILLS SUMMARY

Analyze parts of a research proposal
- Understand the purpose and criteria for writing a research proposal.
- Locate and analyze the structure and content of a research proposal from your field.

Develop an abstract
- Understand the purpose and content of an abstract.
- Use strategies to create an effective abstract.

Create a research poster
- Understand how to design and organize ideas in a visual format.
- Distill key information and present in a clear and direct manner.

Examine the influence of function on form
- Use appropriate forms to convey your message based on the function of a text.
- Convey information concisely and effectively with bulleted text.

THINKING CRITICALLY

As you consider your assignment, discuss the questions with another student. Get feedback and revise your ideas, if necessary.

1. What is the connection between the increase in temperature inversions worldwide and climate change?

2. What can be done to mitigate the effects of air pollution in areas that experience temperature inversions?

3. Whose responsibility is it to combat air pollution? How does politics affect environmental issues? How do environmental issues affect politics?

THINKING VISUALLY

A. Look at the table from the research article, "Inversions Associated with Emergency Department Visits for Asthma." Write three or more sentences about the data in the table. Is any data missing that would be helpful in understanding the results of the study? What is another graphic way to present the data in the table?

TABLE 1 Daily ED visits for asthma and weather inversions for Salt Lake County, December through February, 2003 / 2004–2007 / 2008.

Variable	Total	Inversion No	Inversion Yes	Inversion Day 1–3	Inversion Day 4–6	Inversion Day 7–12	Inversion Day >12
Days [# and %]	452	294 (65%)	158 (35%)	105 (23%)	36 (8%)	11 (2%)	6 (1%)
ED visits for asthma [# and %]	3,425	2,192 (64%)	1,234 (36%)	774 (23%)	319 (9%)	75 (2%)	66 (2%)
Person days [# and %]	14,898	9,681 (65%)	5,217 (35%)	3.385 (23%)	1,221 (8%)	380 (3%)	231 (2%)
Daily # ED visits for asthma [mean ± SD]	8.11 ± 3.40	7.94 ± 3.32	8.41 ± 3.52	7.98 ± 3.45	9.29 ± 3.26	7.58 ± 3.78	11.42 ± 2.76

....

....

....

....

B. Now find (or create) another table or other graphic that provides information relevant to your assignment. Write a label or caption that explains it. Include a citation for this source below.

....

....

....

THINKING ABOUT LANGUAGE

Create bulleted text for a section of the research article you are using for your writing assignment. Consider the function of research poster text to present ideas in a clear, concise way, and choose a section that will benefit from being presented as a bulleted list.

Use an independent clause or an introductory stem and a list of points. Use parallel structure (the same form) for all the points. Punctuate carefully.

WRITE

A. Revisit the writing assignment and the answers to the questions in Before You Write Part B.

B. Create text for a research poster that presents the aim and results of the research paper you found. Your text should have all the components of a research poster and include concise and clear language.

C. Write a brief description of a visual to include in a research poster based on your article and in support of the text you wrote.

BEYOND THE ASSIGNMENT

Design and create a research poster using the text you wrote from a research paper on temperature inversions and their effects on air quality. Be sure to present ideas in a logical progression and design your poster with a consistent and clean layout. Use all the skills you learned in this unit.

▶ Go to MyEnglishLab to listen to Professor Hildemann and to complete a self-assessment.

PART 3

Extended Writing

Part 3 presents authentic content written by university professors. Academically rigorous application and assessment activities allow for a synthesis of the skills developed in Parts 1 and 2.

NO MORE BIRMINGHAMS

Struggle influences social change.

SOCIOLOGY

Writing as a Sociologist

UNIT PROFILE

In this unit, you will watch a video interview with Professor Jonathan Greenberg who will describe in detail his process for writing a research paper. Have you ever wondered how your professor, or an expert in the field of sociology, develops a paper from draft to final product? This is your opportunity to find out more about the process.

EXTENDED WRITING

BEFORE YOU WRITE

Think about these questions before watching the interview with Professor Greenberg. Discuss them with another student.

1. How do you think sociologists get their ideas for research or writing? How do you get your own ideas?

2. What do you think might be the most difficult part of writing a sociology paper?

3. Do you think there is a specific process for writing a sociology paper? Give an example.

4. What are appropriate sources of evidence in a sociology paper?

THE INTERVIEW

▶ Go to MyEnglishLab to watch the interview with Professor Jonathan Greenberg. Then answer the questions in Check What You've Learned.

CHECK WHAT YOU'VE LEARNED

Answer the questions based on the interview with Professor Greenberg.

1. What does Professor Greenberg say about getting ideas?

   a. He has problems getting ideas.
   b. He gets his ideas mostly from news.
   c. He has many ideas, and the problem is sorting them out.
   d. He rarely uses books for research because there is better information online.

2. After a certain theme comes up, what does Professor Greenberg do?

   a. He reads and comes up with a set of books in order to have a defined project.
   b. He temporarily puts aside other things and reads.
   c. He finds books in his own house and the library.
   d. He starts to write immediately.

3. Why does Professor Greenberg start the writing process by reading a lot and taking notes?

   a. to sort out his ideas
   b. to collect and take more notes
   c. to start piecing together his paper
   d. to avoid writing

4. How does he feel about the writing process?

   a. He thinks the writing process is painful when you don't know exactly what you are going to write.
   b. He thinks it is painful but pleasurable and likes the exploration, uncertainty, and surprise of writing.
   c. He thinks it is surprising because he doesn't know what he is going to say.
   d. He thinks it is surprising that it takes such a long time.

5. What is Professor Greenberg's drafting and editing process?

   a. He writes a draft and then edits it himself.
   b. He writes a draft, and a colleague edits it.
   c. He writes a draft, and an editorial assistant edits it.
   d. He edits his draft as he writes it.

6. What else does he say about editing his papers?

   a. He enjoys all parts of the editing process.
   b. He often has colleagues read and edit his papers.
   c. He is typically prepared to meet his deadlines.
   d. He knows he has to do multiple edits of his drafts.

7. What important advice does Professor Greenberg give about finding and using the right sources?

   a. Because it takes time to find sources, students need to use Wikipedia and other Internet sources to find evidence to support their arguments.
   b. Even though it takes time, students should find and use only primary sources as persuasion to back up the arguments they make.
   c. Students need to take the time to find sources that are authoritative and persuasive other than Wikipedia or other Internet sources, although they can be a starting point.
   d. The best sources are usually the most obvious ones, so students don't need to take too much time finding sources.

8. What is Professor Greenberg's advice about using an interdisciplinary approach?

    a. He suggests that students focus on a particular methodology in a particular discipline because an interdisciplinary approach isn't useful.

    b. He suggests that students seek a wide range of sources from a variety of disciplines to deepen and strengthen their writing.

    c. He believes that students must take an interdisciplinary approach because it is essential.

    d. He says that using an interdisciplinary approach is very time consuming, so it should be done only when absolutely necessary.

9. What does Professor Greenberg advise about motivation?

    a. Students need personal motivation because it's not easy to write research papers.

    b. Writing research papers is boring, so students need to be motivated to complete the process.

    c. Students need to find a research question based on their own personal interests in order to sustain their motivation.

    d. Students will find that they are more motivated at the beginning of the process than they are at the end.

10. What is the best summary of Professor Greenberg's writing process?

    a. He reads the newspaper, listens to the news, and comes up with a topic. He writes a paper through multiple drafts. He thinks it's good to use sources from many disciplines.

    b. He reads a lot and takes notes, develops a theme, and writes papers through multiple drafts. He thinks taking the time to find appropriate sources from many disciplines, including primary sources, is essential in providing authoritative evidence for arguments.

    c. He reads, takes notes, and writes a draft. Then he edits the paper. He thinks the process is boring and takes time but is necessary. He uses primary sources to provide evidence in support of arguments.

    d. He researches all of his ideas, develops a theme, and then writes multiple drafts. He uses one source from each discipline to provide evidence in support of his arguments.

THINKING CRITICALLY

Consider these situations in light of what you have heard in the interview. By yourself or with a partner, apply what you know about the writing process to answer the questions about each situation.

Situation 1 Recently, women in the United States have been advocating for equal pay for equal work. A group of women working in a large company hired a sociologist to gather research and write a position paper for the group to present to the management of the company. What is one claim the sociologist would need to include in the paper, and how might this claim be supported? What would be some useful sources to support this claim?

Situation 2 A sociologist has been asked to write a paper on the top two or three social problems facing society today. What problems might be the focus of such a paper? Define the audience and purpose for the paper. What might be the most useful sources for the paper? How might an interdisciplinary approach be effective in finding sources for this paper?

Go to MyEnglishLab to complete a critical thinking activity.

THINKING ABOUT LANGUAGE

EXPLORING VERB TENSES IN ACADEMIC WRITING

A. Complete each sentence using the correct verb tense—simple present, simple past, or present perfect.

1. Dr. King (ask) .... Wyatt Walker to draw up a plan for a campaign of nonviolent action to force desegregation in Birmingham.

2. The challenges were extremely tough, and the odds might (go) .... against them.

3. Birmingham (shape) .... the course of America's "second revolution," the black freedom struggle.

4. The 1963 Birmingham campaign (maintain) .... a very meaningful place in history today.

5. The "children's crusade" of May 1963 (prove) .... that students' actions can greatly influence necessary social change.

6. Thus the nonviolent Birmingham campaign (generate) .... a historic chain reaction of social and political transformation in the United States.

7. The campaign still powerfully (demonstrate) .... the strategic and moral foundations of King's leadership.

8. There (be) .... other iconic sites in the history of the African American civil rights struggle in subsequent years.

B. Read the paragraph and underline three verbs in the passive voice.

How was this labor secured? A substantial portion of the workforce was filled by the effective re-enslavement of former slaves and their descendants in a vast convict lease system across an archipelago of prison camps, cemetery pits, and extremely hazardous mines, toxic smelters, and furnaces that surrounded the Birmingham region. Compliance with the brutal convict lease system was secured by state agencies throughout the South, seeking to derive large sources of income from black prisoners seized for crimes including vagrancy and unemployment by local corporations eager to purchase servile workers without power to resist coercion.

SIGNPOSTING FACTS AND OPINIONS

Underline the examples of signposting and identify whether the signposts hedge or boost the writer's opinions.

1. Birmingham was "the Magic City," its white citizens proud of its urbanization, economic growth, and progressive business culture and its black middle class and elite wary of actions that might be seen as provocations that could carry a high price.

2. Indeed, the success of the 1963 Birmingham Campaign was caused in large measure by the national and international media attention the campaign generated to racially targeted police brutality under Bull Connor's command.

3. Even more dramatically, pressure from the Birmingham crisis forced President John F. Kennedy to finally confront the white power structure in the Jim Crow South.

4. "Jim Crow" was enforced by local police forces, state troops, and, perhaps most importantly, terrorist violence by extrajudicial organizations and militias such as the Ku Klux Klan.

5. In a follow-up White House meeting with African Americans, Kennedy stated clearly: "But for Birmingham, we would not be here today."

6. One leader in the civil rights movement said, "Birmingham is probably the most thoroughly segregated city in the United States."

7. Taylor Branch wrote, "That meant they must be prepared to put upwards of a thousand people in jail at one time, maybe more."

READ

Go to MyEnglishLab to read "The 1963 Birmingham Campaign: Turning Point in the American Civil Rights Movement" for more practice reading an extended text and using your reading skills. Then do the assignment below.

ASSIGNMENT

Write a research paper on a particular act of nonviolent civil disobedience in the US Civil Rights movement and its impact on the movement. Provide historical background, including facts and opinions about the injustice that led to the act, information on the participants, details about the act, and what resulted from the act.

Be sure to conduct research, collaborate, and share ideas, and evaluate and organize your research.

RESEARCH

A. List words or phrases you already know about the topic and at least two or three questions you have about the topic. Narrow the topic appropriately to one you have a personal interest in.

....

....

....

....

....

....

....

B. Discuss your questions with another student. Then write a few thoughts about the one question you think is most interesting and that you will be able to research. Write a preliminary thesis statement.

....

....

....

....

....

....

....

C. Look for appropriate sources, starting with an online search. Read the keywords and the hits from your search. Which are most likely to provide reliable and relevant information? Rank the hits from most relevant (1) to least relevant (5) Compare and discuss your rankings with a partner.

....

....

....

....

....

D. Conduct your research, including searching for appropriate primary and secondary sources. Critically evaluate your sources for appropriate evidence.

WRITE

A. Choose an article that you've found in your research and want to use in your paper. Reread the article and take notes in the margin. Write an annotated bibliography for the article.

TIP
Choose a topic you have personal interest in to help you sustain your motivation.

B. Using a graphic organizer and your notes, create a detailed outline of your paper.

TIP
Narrowing your topic to one that is manageable and addresses an important issue is critical.

C. Write your research paper. Support your claims with facts and opinions.

Go to MyEnglishLab to join in a collaborative activity.

For more about **SOCIOLOGY**, see 1 2 . See also R and OC **SOCIOLOGY** 1 2 3 .

Individual choices impact the global economy.

Writing as an Economist

UNIT PROFILE

In this unit, you will watch a video interview with Professor Marcelo Clerici-Arias who will describe in detail his process for writing a research paper. Have you ever wondered how your professor, or an expert in the field of economics, develops a paper from draft to final product? This is your opportunity to find out more about the process.

EXTENDED WRITING

BEFORE YOU WRITE

Think about these questions before watching the interview with Professor Clerici-Arias. Discuss them with another student.

1. How do you think economists get their ideas for research or writing? How do you get your own ideas?
2. What do you think might be the most difficult part of writing an economics paper?
3. How do you think an economist organizes ideas and research in writing a paper?
4. What role does early feedback play in arriving at a good final paper? Give an example.

THE INTERVIEW

▶ Go to MyEnglishLab to watch the interview with Professor Marcelo Clerici-Arias. Then answer the questions in Check What You've Learned.

CHECK WHAT YOU'VE LEARNED

Answer the questions based on the interview with Professor Clerici-Arias.

1. What is the source of many of Professor Marcelo Clerici-Arias's ideas?

   a. restaurants and theaters
   b. his colleagues and students
   c. suggestions from family and friends
   d. everyday events and observing people

2. Why does he suggest reading a lot to get ideas?

   a. to get the bigger picture
   b. to understand recessions
   c. to get 90% of his ideas
   d. to learn more about microeconomics

3. What does he do with his ideas?

   a. He shares them with other economists to see if they are sound.
   b. He invests his time doing research on his ideas.
   c. He records them so he can remember and later organize them.
   d. He asks a student to do further research.

4. What is the first thing Professor Clerici-Arias does to write an economics paper?

   a. He uses software to combine ideas in different ways.
   b. He writes different pieces of research on index cards.
   c. He reads and creates a literature review.
   d. He gathers all of his references.

5. Why is his software virtual corkboard an important tool in his writing process?

   a. He can use index cards to write down his ideas.
   b. He can give the corkboard to his students to help them understand his classes.
   c. He can write his introduction, literature review, and references using the software.
   d. He can draft and combine the pieces he wants to share.

6. What is Professor Clerici-Arias editing process?

   a. He gets TAs and colleagues to read his papers.
   b. He doesn't get feedback from others.
   c. He only gets feedback from people at his university.
   d. He only gets feedback from other economists.

7. What example does he use to explain his editing process?

   a. a research paper
   b. a journal article
   c. an essay exam
   d. a real-life situation

8. Why does he think getting feedback from others is important?

   a. His audience won't understand him.
   b. His wording may be wrong.
   c. Fresh perspectives help.
   d. He is a perfectionist.

9. What has Professor Clerici-Arias learned from his own experience?

    a. Early feedback is important.
    b. Generating ideas is hard.
    c. Being a perfectionist is helpful.
    d. Intermediate milestones aren't necessary.

10. What is his belief about peer feedback?

    a. Giving feedback to others helps students learn to write.
    b. Getting feedback from someone who isn't an expert gives you a different perspective.
    c. It's best to get feedback early in the process.
    d. All of the above.

THINKING CRITICALLY

Consider these situations in light of what you have heard in the interview. By yourself or with a partner, apply what you know about the writing process to answer the questions about each situation.

Situation 1 Your assignment in your economics class is to use your own observations and experience to analyze the economic factors involved in seeking a post-college job and to develop a research question for further exploration. How will you get your ideas, and what steps will you follow to arrive at a good research question on this topic?

Situation 2 Having a government-mandated minimum wage seems like a good idea, yet some economists say it will result in greater unemployment among the least-skilled workers. How would you research this topic and decide for yourself if you agree?

Go to MyEnglishLab to complete a critical thinking activity.

THINKING ABOUT LANGUAGE

USING REPORTED SPEECH EFFECTIVELY

Rewrite each direct quotation in reported speech by choosing a reporting verb from the box that best expresses the rhetorical purpose. Use each rhetorical purpose at least once. Paraphrase the quotation in your own words and make any other necessary changes to the sentence. Begin each sentence with *He* + reporting verb.

Expressing agreement: agree, endorse, support, acknowledge
Making a claim: argue, claim, assert, believe, conclude, emphasize, insist, maintain, observe, report, reveal, think
Making a suggestion: suggest
Questioning or disagreeing: refute, request, question, dispute, deny, contradict
Making a recommendation: call for, caution, demand, urge, warn, recommend
Making a neutral observation: state, present, illustrate, inform, express, examine, discuss, describe, comment

---

1. Firms are willing to pay workers up to their contribution to production and sales.

   ....

   ....

2. On the supply side, workers' willingness to sell their time as labor depends on the other

   opportunities available. ....

   ....

   ....

3. The workers will accept a wage that doesn't compensate them for the alternative activity they have

   to sacrifice. ....

   ....

   ....

4. If the labor market is competitive, with several firms independently hiring many workers, then the

   market will certainly reach equilibrium at the intersection of demand and supply.

   ....

   ....

5. The fact that a competitive labor market reaches equilibrium does not imply that the equilibrium

   wage will be low or high, nor that it will be great for workers or firms.

   ....

   ....

6. The equilibrium wage is the price that allows the number of hours firms are willing to pay for

   to be equal to the number of hours people are willing to work. ....

   ....

   ....

7. The government needs to comply with a request to legally institute a minimum wage.

   ....

   ....

8. What happens in the presence of a minimum wage? ....

   ....

   ....

USING DIRECT QUOTATIONS AND REPORTED SPEECH

Complete the introductions to the quotations from "Minimum Wages" Use phrases from the table to help you. There is more than one way to introduce each quote. Be sure that the phrase you have chosen works grammatically in the sentence. Use appropriate punctuation for direct quotations. Use each expression only once.

According to + the article / Professor Clerici-Arias

Clerici-Arias / The author / He + observes / reports / informs us

_____ argues / asserts / claims

_____ continues / warns / urges / concludes that

In [the author's / Clerici-Arias's] opinion

---

1. .... when establishing minimum wages, governments usually claim that they are improving the standard of living for workers and reducing income inequality.

2. .... until the 1990s, most empirical tests supported the theoretical predictions of a demand-and-supply model.

3. .... the consensus among economists was that the implementation of a binding minimum wage (above market equilibrium) caused unemployment.

4. .... in 1993 economists David Card and Alan Krueger were able to test these predictions in a unique real-world setting with surprising results.

5. .... Card and Krueger did a number of statistical tests on their available data just before and after the minimum wage increase in New Jersey.

6. .... they found no negative effects on employment, contrary to the competitive market model prediction.

7. .... after Card's and Krueger's 1993 paper, many other economists have explored the impact of higher minimum wages on employment.

8. .... some studies have confirmed the same result (no impact on employment) while others have confirmed the traditional theoretical prediction (lower employment).

9. .... what used to be a consensus point for economists is now cause for contention.

READ

Go to MyEnglishLab to read "Minimum Wages" for more practice reading an extended text and using your reading skills. Then do the assignment below.

ASSIGNMENT

Write a research paper analyzing the development of a new product or service and its likelihood of succeeding. This can be an actual product or service or one you invent for this paper. Research economic factors that would affect the production of the product or inception of the service, such as supply and demand, production, location, raw materials, and so on. Address the externalities of your product or service.

Be sure to conduct research, collaborate and share ideas, and evaluate and organize your research.

RESEARCH

A. Narrow the topic appropriately and write a research question. ....

....

....

B. Discuss your product or service with another student. Then write a few ideas about the product or service that you will be able to research. Write a preliminary thesis statement.

....

....

....

....

C. Create a graphic organizer to develop your ideas.

D. Conduct your research, including searching for appropriate primary and secondary sources. Critically evaluate your sources for appropriate evidence.

WRITE

A. Choose an article that you've found in your research and want to use in your paper. Reread the article and take notes in the margin. Summarize the article. Critically evaluate the source for evidence for your paper.

TIP
Be sure to choose appropriate sources and cite them correctly.

B. Using your graphic organizer and your notes, create a detailed outline of your paper.

C. Write your research paper. Evaluate and integrate evidence to support your ideas.

TIP
Accurately representing the ideas in your sources is essential to providing credible evidence to support your claims.

Go to MyEnglishLab to join in a collaborative activity.

For more about **ECONOMICS**, see ❶ ❷. See also ⟨R⟩ and [OC] **ECONOMICS** ❶ ❷ ❸.

Exploring the secret lives of viruses.

BIOLOGY

Writing as a Biologist

UNIT PROFILE

In this unit, you will watch a video interview with Professor Robert Siegel who will describe in detail his process for writing a research paper. Have you ever wondered how your professor, or an expert in the field of biology, develops a paper from draft to final product? This is your opportunity to find out more about the process.

EXTENDED WRITING

BEFORE YOU WRITE

Think about these questions before watching the interview with Professor Siegel. Discuss them with another student.

1. How do you think biologists get their ideas for research or writing? How do you get your own ideas?
2. What do you think might be the most difficult part of explaining a process in a biology paper?
3. What are important considerations in developing a hypothesis and presenting scientific research?
4. How might a biologist revise and edit a research paper?

THE INTERVIEW

▶ Go to **MyEnglishLab** to watch the interview with Professor Robert Siegel. Then answer the questions in Check What You've Learned.

CHECK WHAT YOU'VE LEARNED

Answer the questions based on the interview with Professor Siegel.

1. Once he gets ideas, what motivates Professor Siegel to write?

    a. the rant of the day
    b. things he reads that he's impassioned about
    c. articles people send him
    d. ideas from newspapers and books he's reading

2. What does Professor Siegel say is most important when starting the writing process?

    a. brooding and procrastinating
    b. organizing ideas
    c. writing down ideas as soon as they come to mind
    d. connecting ideas together

3. Which statement most closely reflects what he does to finish a paper?

    a. He gets others to read it, reads it aloud, and edits the paper.
    b. He gets others to read it and edits it for grammatical errors.
    c. He works on it until it is absolutely perfect before considering it done.
    d. He reads other people's papers and then reads his paper again.

4. What is something Professor Siegel *doesn't* do to make complex processes accessible to readers?

    a. He is methodical and defines all terms.
    b. He runs his ideas by other people to see if they understand them.
    c. He tries to think how he would want something explained if he were an outsider.
    d. He challenges his readers to think about complex ideas.

5. Why does Professor Siegel offer to read people's papers?

    a. He will be forced to finish his paper more quickly.
    b. He wants to learn more about other people's fields.
    c. Other people will read his paper.
    d. Other people will learn more about his field.

6. What is one important way to make sure your writing has clarity and cohesion?

    a. Explain basic processes.
    b. Explain jargon and acronyms.
    c. Combine more than one idea in a sentence.
    d. Use parentheses.

7. What is Professor Siegel's main point for students writing in biology for the first time?

    a. Be critical.
    b. Use a lot of sources.
    c. Copy experts to say things in a clear way.
    d. Write in your own words.

8. What is one important "don't" according to Professor Siegel?

    a. Don't give people background they already know.
    b. Don't write a dumb paper.
    c. Don't have a clear idea of facts.
    d. Don't put things in your own words.

9. What is the hard part of developing a hypothesis for Professor Siegel?

   a. generating good ideas for a hypothesis
   b. finding alternative explanations that are true
   c. controlling what the data is telling you
   d. proving a hypothesis is true

10. What is one of the things people do wrong in research writing?

    a. They don't follow up on ideas in a rigorous scientific way.
    b. They don't have appropriate controls.
    c. They don't interpret the results correctly.
    d. They don't generate good ideas.

THINKING CRITICALLY

Consider these situations in light of what you have heard in the interview. By yourself or with a partner, apply what you know about the writing process to answer the questions about each situation.

Situation 1 For your biology course, you have written a literature review of recently developed vaccines. Your professor tells you to revise your paper because in some areas too much background information is given, and in other areas information has not been fully explained. Your professor also indicates that the organization is not always logical. How would you go about revising this paper? What steps would you take?

Situation 2 You will write an article for a magazine that is largely read by the general public. In the article, you will write about how viruses are being used to fight cancer by describing the process of how viruses modify genes. What organizational pattern would you use for this article: General-to-Specific or Specific-to-General? Why? What information would you include in the introduction? How would you describe this process so that it is accessible to your audience?

Go to MyEnglishLab to complete a critical thinking activity.

THINKING ABOUT LANGUAGE

USING LANGUAGE TO ADD COHESION

Read the passage. Underline all of the cohesive devices (repetition, reference, cohesive nouns, topic introducers, and logical connectors). Compare your answers with a partner and discuss each device and what type it is. Then answer the questions.

(1) Ironically, not only are viruses implicated in causing cancer, they have also played a key role in helping us to elucidate the mechanisms that give rise to all types of cancer. (2) Viruses have helped us to discover that there are a large number of regulatory genes that affect the cell's ability to induce cancer. (3) For the most part, these genes have been classified into two groups: (a) genes that facilitate growth and (b) genes that prevent growth.

(4) The genes that facilitate growth are called oncogenes. (5) Given their relationship to cancer, one might reasonably ask why such genes exist. (6) These genes are critically important during early development, to aid in healing after injury, and to replace the normal loss of cells. (7) Unlike oncogenes, tumor suppressor genes, or TSGs, prevent growth. (8) The normal interplay between these genes allows for cell division when we need it and restriction of division when we do not. (9) An analogy has been made between a cell heading down the path toward malignant transformation and a car heading down a hill. (10) If a cell has an increased expression of oncogenes, it is like stepping down on the accelerator pedal. (11) In contrast, if a cell has insufficient expression of tumor suppressor genes, it is like taking your foot off the brakes. (12) In most cases, it is a combination of aberrant oncogenes and tumor suppressor genes that lead to the development of cancer.

1. What does the word *they* in sentence 1 refer back to? ....
2. What synonym for the word *induce* in sentence 2 is used earlier in the paragraph? ....

   ....
3. What does *their* in sentence 5 refer to? ....
4. What does *it* in sentence 8 refer to? ....
5. What does *it* in sentence 10 refer to? ....

FORMING CONDITIONAL CLAUSES

Complete the conditional sentences with the appropriate form of the verb in parentheses. Consider whether the conditions are real (general truth, fact, or prediction) or unreal (present or past). Use an appropriate modal in the result clause. Some sentences may need passive verb forms.

1. If cancer .... (associate) with certain viruses, then these cancers .... (prevent) by the same vaccination strategies that have been used to prevent viral infection.
2. If cells of our body .... (start) to grow out of control to the detriment of the body as a whole, the cells .... (lead) to loss of organ function and death.
3. Ironically, viruses .... (play, not) a key role in helping scientists understand the mechanisms that give rise to cancer if they .... (cause, not) cancer.
4. If medical scientists .... (develop, not) strategies for using the body's immune system to prevent some cancers, they .... (continue) to use the traditional method of treating cancer after it arose.
5. Unless viruses .... (help) scientists discover regulatory genes, they .... (understand, not) the effect they have on a cell's ability to become cancerous.
6. Regulatory genes .... (call) oncogenes when they facilitate growth, and they .... (be) tumor suppressors if they .... (prevent) growth.
7. Viruses .... (cause) cancer if they .... (modify) genes.
8. People .... (get) cancer when environmental factors .... (combine) with certain viruses.
9. In vaccination, if the body .... (present) with antigens, then the immune system .... (stimulate) to fight off the virus.
10. If doctors .... (continue, not) to create vaccinations against cancer-related viruses, cancer deaths .... (increase).
11. Unless the risk of side effects from the vaccine .... (be) extremely low, the overall risk of vaccinating a large population .... (be) greater than the risk of cancer.
12. More women .... (die) from cervical cancer over the last few years, if doctors .... (create, not) the vaccinations against the H1B viruses.

READ

Go to MyEnglishLab to read "Vaccines That Prevent Virally-Induced Cancer" for more practice reading an extended text and using your reading skills. Then do the assignment below.

> ### ASSIGNMENT
>
> Write a research paper on the causes of a cancer known to be associated with a particular virus. Choose a virus for which there is a vaccination either already on the market or being developed. Research the known causes of the cancer, including the virus, and the possible effects that the vaccination will have on the incidence of the cancer now or in the future.
>
> Be sure to integrate appropriate source material and fully and coherently develop your ideas.

RESEARCH

A. Narrow the topic appropriately by choosing a virus and write a research question about the virus's causes and effects. ....

....

....

....

B. Discuss the virus you are researching with another student. Write notes about the virus and its association with cancer that you will be able to research. Write a preliminary thesis statement about the effects of the vaccination on the virus. ....

....

....

....

C. Create a graphic organizer to develop your ideas.

D. Conduct your research, including searching for appropriate sources. Critically evaluate your sources for appropriate evidence.

WRITE

A. Choose an article that you have found in your research and want to use in your paper. Reread the article and take notes in the margin. Organize the ideas in the source to integrate into your paper.

B. Using your graphic organizer and your notes, create a detailed outline of your paper.

C. Write your research paper. Develop your ideas with concrete and specific support from sources. Arrange ideas in a logical order and use cohesive devices for coherence.

Go to MyEnglishLab to join in a collaborative activity.

> **TIP**
> Be sure to revise your paper for coherence.

> **TIP**
> Check that you fully developed your ideas with concrete and specific support from reliable sources.

For more about **BIOLOGY**, see 1 2 . See also R and OC **BIOLOGY** 1 2 3 .

Education teaches you to love the world.

Writing as a Literary Expert

UNIT PROFILE

In this unit, you will watch a video interview with Professor Robert Pogue Harrison who will describe in detail his process for writing a research paper. Have you ever wondered how your professor, or an expert in the field of humanities, develops a paper from draft to final product? This is your opportunity to find out more about the process.

EXTENDED WRITING

BEFORE YOU WRITE

Think about these questions before watching the interview with Professor Harrison. Discuss them with another student.

1. How do you think writers in the humanities get their ideas for research or writing? How do you get your own ideas?

2. What do you think might be the most difficult part of writing a humanities paper?

3. What do you think is the most interesting part of writing about literature?

4. How do you support an argument when writing a research paper about a work of literature?

THE INTERVIEW

Go to **MyEnglishLab** to watch the interview with Professor Robert Pogue Harrison. Then answer the questions in Check What You've Learned.

CHECK WHAT YOU'VE LEARNED

Answer the questions based on the interview with Professor Harrison.

1. Which statement most accurately reflects how Professor Harrison gets ideas for humanities papers?

   a. Works of literature can inspire ideas when writing about nature.
   b. Nature serves as a better inspiration than literature or newspapers.
   c. Literature, current events, and nature inspire ideas for papers.
   d. Dialogues about something he has been reading can inspire ideas.

2. Why does he think that ideas inspired by nature are most exciting?

   a. They are unpredictable.
   b. They are easy to write about.
   c. They are challenging to understand.
   d. They are interesting to most readers.

3. What does Professor Harrison think is the most difficult part of the writing process?

   a. writing the beginning paragraph
   b. unifying ideas throughout a paper
   c. writing a compelling conclusion
   d. getting past the halfway point

4. What does Professor Harrison find to be the most fun about the writing process?

   a. editing for errors
   b. writing the conclusion
   c. conceiving the initial ideas
   d. revising the style

5. According to Professor Harrison, which of the following is true?

   a. Writing for the *New York Review of Books* is more rewarding than writing an essay.
   b. Writing an accessible paper for a diverse audience is difficult.
   c. Writing an essay is more difficult than writing a book review.
   d. Writing a thought piece shouldn't include your own ideas.

6. How does he feel about the role of tone in writing?

   a. Tone is extremely important and should be monotonous throughout.
   b. Tone is influenced by the topic and should be consistent throughout.
   c. Tone is influenced by the audience and should be varied throughout.
   d. Tone is objective and should be the same in similar pieces of writing.

7. Which statement best captures how Professor Harrison feels about revising and editing?

   a. He takes great care to revise and edit his work in order to satisfy editors.
   b. He carefully revises his work and has an editor review it for any errors.
   c. He takes great care to revise and edit his work until he is satisfied.
   d. He lets the editors make the revisions to his work.

8. What advice does he give to students who are writing a humanities paper for the first time?

   a. Incorporate metaphors and analogies into your paper.
   b. Include your impression of the text when interpreting it.
   c. Coherently present your impressions of the text.
   d. Support your argument with evidence from the text.

9. What is Professor Harrison's view on including citations in papers?

    a. Citations should always follow the *Chicago Manual of Style*.
    b. Citing many secondary sources is critical.
    c. Citations are critical because they give the paper credibility.
    d. Citing only primary sources is best.

10. What is the most important aspect of writing in the humanities, according to Professor Harrison?

    a. analyzing your thoughts through writing
    b. finding your own unique voice when writing
    c. citing secondary sources accurately in your writing
    d. finding a clever metaphor and making it work with your natural tone

THINKING CRITICALLY

Consider these situations in light of what you have heard in the interview. By yourself or with a partner, apply what you know about the writing process to answer the questions about each situation.

Situation 1 Imagine that you are writing a review for the *New York Review of Books* on two recent publications about the medieval poet and philosopher Dante. Where will you get your ideas for this review? What kind of research will you do? What style would be appropriate for this diverse audience?

Situation 2 As a photojournalist, you create a blog that documents the stories of the people who live in your city. You want the blog to be read by people within and outside of your community. How will you organize the blog? In what format will you share the stories? What point of view will you use? What tone and voice do you want to convey to your readers?

Go to MyEnglishLab to complete a critical thinking activity.

THINKING ABOUT LANGUAGE

USING APPROPRIATE ADVERBIALS TO FIT RHETORICAL CONTEXT

Underline the 16 adverbials in the passage. Then identify whether each is a linking or stance adverbial. With a partner, determine the genre of the passage.

I am alluding once again to Book VI of Virgil's *Aeneid*, where the Sibyl of Cumae informs Aeneas that to gain entry into Hades he must first find a tree of gold in the vast forest that surrounds her cave. If and when he finds the tree, he must pluck one of its golden boughs so that he may gift it to Proserpina, wife of Pluto, who will then allow him to enter Hades. The Sibyl can show Aeneas where the forest is, but she cannot help him locate the tree. This he must do on his own. In similar fashion, education cannot put a golden bough into every student's hand. At most, it can send students forth into the forests of literature, mythology, history, art, and whatever else reaches us from the past. With any luck, the students there will discover then—each one on his or her own—the tree whose boughs grants access to the source, that is, to the living springs of history.

The kind of world we live in today certainly makes it easy to forget that such a place—such a source—exists, since the noise, commotion and distraction of the age has a way of drowning out the untimely voices that speak to us from beyond the present. Perhaps this has always been the case. Perhaps it has always taken a special and even heroic effort to keep the source alive and active. One thing seems certain: Hades does not disappear just because we forget it exists. Its dead no doubt wait there for the living wayfarer to animate their voices and learn from them how to move forward into the light.

USING GRAMMAR TO VARY DESCRIPTION

Read the excerpts from "The Odour of Chrysanthemums" by D. H. Lawrence and *The Jungle Book* by Rudyard Kipling. Analyze the descriptive language used. Underline the examples of adjective clauses and phrases, appositives, absolutes, parallel structure, participial adjectives, adjectives out of order, and action verbs. Identify the type of grammar for each example.

"At the edge of the ribbed level of sidings squat a low cottage, three steps down from the cinder track. A large bony vine clutched at the house, as if to claw down the tiled roof. Round the bricked yard grew a few wintery primroses. Beyond, the long garden sloped down to a bush-covered brook course. There were some twiggy apple trees, winter-crack trees, and ragged cabbages. Beside the path hung disheveled pink chrysanthemums, like pink cloths hung on bushes."—D. H. Lawrence

"A black shadow dropped down into the circle. It was Bagheera the Black Panther, inky black all over, but with the panther markings showing up in certain lights like the pattern of watered slik. Everybody knew Bagheera, and nobody cared to cross his path, for he was as cunning as Tabaqui, as bold as the wild buffalo, and as reckless as the wounded elephant. But he had a voice as soft as wild honey dripping from a tree, and a skin softer than down."—Rudyard Kipling

READ

Go to MyEnglishLab to read "The Golden Bough" for more practice reading an extended text and using your reading skills. Then do the assignment below.

ASSIGNMENT

Write a literary analysis of the poem, "Do Not Go Gentle into That Good Night," by Dylan Thomas including a summary of the poem and a response to one or more ideas or images in it.

Be sure to include biographical information about the poet, explaining when and why Thomas wrote the poem.

A. Find "Do Not Go Gentle into That Good Night," and analyze its style, voice, tone, and mood. Note the figurative language used and explain its meaning.

....

....

....

....

....

B. As you read, annotate each stanza, noting the meaning. Make note of areas you have questions about, agree or disagree with, or find especially moving. What is your initial reaction to the poem? Did you like it? Why or why not? Did it elicit an emotional response or a memory?

....

....

....

....

C. Predict what you think inspired Thomas to write this poem. Then do research to find out what actually inspired him. Was your prediction correct?

....

....

....

....

D. Although Thomas wrote this poem about a specific experience in his life, think about the poem's relevance to you. What experience in your life makes this poem relevant to you?

....

....

....

....

....

....

....

....

WRITE

A. Paraphrase the idea(s) or image(s) you would like to explore in your analysis.

B. Using a graphic organizer and your notes, create a detailed outline of your analysis.

C. Write your literary analysis. Stay aware of voice, tone, and use of figurative language.

Go to MyEnglishLab to join in a collaborative activity.

> **TIP**
> Be sure to summarize the poem accurately. Have you included a clear thesis that indicates the idea from the poem that you are responding to?

> **TIP**
> Include evidence to support your thesis.

For more about **HUMANITIES**, see ❶ ❷. See also ⌊ R ⌋ and ⌊OC⌋ **HUMANITIES** ❶ ❷ ❸.

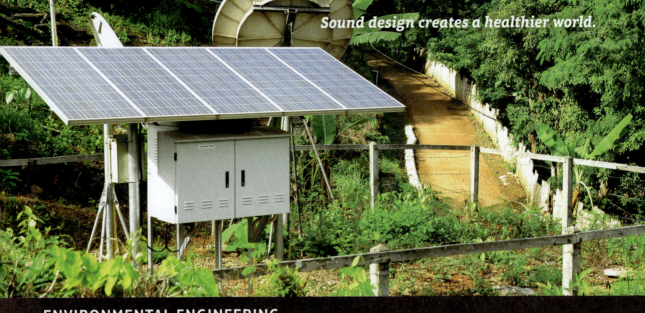

Sound design creates a healthier world.

ENVIRONMENTAL ENGINEERING

Writing as an Environmental Engineer

UNIT PROFILE

In this unit, you will watch a video interview with Professor Lynn Hildemann who will describe in detail her process for writing a research paper. Have you ever wondered how your professor, or an expert in the field of environmental engineering, develops a paper from draft to final product? This is your opportunity to find out more about the process.

EXTENDED WRITING

BEFORE YOU WRITE

Think about these questions before watching the interview with Professor Hildemann. Discuss them with another student.

1. How do you think engineers get their ideas for research or writing? What do you think might be the most difficult part of writing an environmental engineering research paper?

2. When writing a research paper, do you think it's important to begin with the introduction, or can you write another section first? Which section would you start with? Why?

3. How do you determine what visuals to include in a research paper?

4. What do you think is the biggest mistake writers make when presenting their research in a paper? How can writers avoid making this type of mistake?

THE INTERVIEW

▶ Go to MyEnglishLab to watch the interview with Professor Lynn Hildemann. Then answer the questions in Check What You've Learned.

CHECK WHAT YOU'VE LEARNED

Answer the questions based the interview with Professor Hildemann.

1. Lynn Hildemann shared that the topics of her research papers originate from the research she conducts in the field. At what point in her research does she begin writing?

   a. near the end of the fieldwork, after a substantial amount of data has been collected and analyzed
   b. before the fieldwork begins, after the methods used to conduct the study have been identified
   c. after the fieldwork has ended and all of the data has been analyzed
   d. throughout the whole research process

2. Which section of the research paper does Professor Hildemann usually write first?

   a. introduction
   b. methods
   c. results
   d. abstract

3. Which sections of the research paper does she save for last?

   a. abstract and introduction
   b. methods and results
   c. discussion and conclusion
   d. abstract and conclusion

4. What does Professor Hildemann consider when creating visuals for a research paper or conference?

   a. how exciting she can make the data for the audience
   b. which data will be the easiest to produce in visuals
   c. all of the measurements and analyses of the data
   d. the most valuable data for the audience to know

5. What is one piece of advice that she gives to students who are writing a research paper for the first time?

   a. Don't look at other published research papers.
   b. Start with the section that is easiest to write.
   c. Always begin by identifying your visuals.
   d. Check with your classmates to see what they are writing first.

6. According to Professor Hildemann, what is the biggest problem she sees in papers?

   a. Students' papers are usually too short overall.
   b. Students don't include enough information about the methods used in the research.
   c. Students don't include enough information about the key findings.
   d. Students include too much information instead of focusing in on key findings.

7. What aspect of writing a literature review do undergraduates struggle with, according to Professor Hildemann?

   a. They summarize one study at a time instead of analyzing how the studies relate to each other.
   b. They make frequent spelling and grammatical errors and leave out important information.
   c. They do not select related papers in a certain topic area, so it is difficult to compare and contrast.
   d. They do not consult with their professor to determine exactly what should be included.

8. Which statement best captures how Professor Hildemann would define effective writing?

   a. Writing should include a lot of detail and be written in a wordy style.
   b. Writing should be focused and highlight the most important information.
   c. Writing should include a balance of elaborate detail and key information.
   d. Writing should include as many visuals as possible because most people today are visual learners.

9. Why does she think that using correct spelling and grammar is important?

   a. She believes these types of errors are absolutely atrocious.
   b. She thinks using correct spelling and grammar is essential to becoming a better writer.
   c. She believes these errors may cause readers to think the research was carelessly done.
   d. She thinks professors get very upset when they have to spend time correcting these types of errors.

10. Why does Professor Hildemann find it valuable to have students evaluate all of their classmates' summaries?

   a. It motivates them to complete future writing assignments for the course.
   b. It helps them identify what style of writing the instructor prefers.
   c. It helps them notice how organized and structured writing is helpful for the reader.
   d. It keeps them from plagiarizing their classmates' work.

THINKING CRITICALLY

Consider these situations in light of what you have heard in the interview. By yourself or with a partner, apply what you know about the writing process to answer the questions about each situation.

Situation 1 Research shows that using solid fuels, such as coal and wood as an energy source, can increase the risk of respiratory illnesses and contribute to climate change. In some areas of the world, many households still use old cooking stoves that are heated using solid fuels. Improved cooking stoves that have a better technological design have been found to reduce emissions, resulting in lower incidence of respiratory illness. As an environmental engineer, you are conducting a study to measure the health effects of using an improved cooking stove. You will be conducting your experiment in Bangladesh, where many households still use old cooking stoves. You will need at least 300 participants to agree to use the improved cooking stove. What kind of information could you provide to convince people to use the improved cooking stove for the duration of the study? How could visuals be used to communicate this information?

Situation 2 An environmental science journal has asked you to write a paper about the latest solutions for mitigating indoor air quality problems. Considering Hildemann's views on writing a quality paper, how would you edit your paper and visuals to ensure that they are ready for publication? What kind of information would you include in the abstract?

Go to MyEnglishLab to complete a critical thinking activity.

THINKING ABOUT LANGUAGE

EXAMINING SENTENCE STRUCTURE AND SUBJECT–VERB AGREEMENT

Read the passage. Underline the noun that is the subject of the verbs in brackets and circle the verb form that agrees with the subject.

It is estimated that 40% of the total energy consumption in the world [is / are] due to building energy use, and about 30–50% of the energy consumed by buildings [is / are] used for conditioning (that is, heating / cooling) of the indoor air. Because of this, there [has been / have been] a historical trend toward constructing buildings that [is / are] more tightly sealed to slow down the rate at which the indoor air leaks back outdoors. In addition, there [has been / have been] a number of strategies utilized to reduce the amount of ventilation indoors, so that less heating / cooling [is / are] needed. However, a major disadvantage of minimizing indoor ventilation, whether by building design or ventilation use, [is / are] that indoor air pollutant emissions can build up to higher concentrations. What [is / are] the effects of these indoor air pollutants on the occupants?

The effects of low ventilation rates on human health [was / were] seen in the United States, back in the 1970s and 1980s. In 1973, as part of an effort to decrease energy consumption, the US minimum standard for building ventilation [was / were] reduced from 4.7 to 2.4 liters/second of fresh air per person. After many buildings had been constructed that [was / were] designed to meet this lower ventilation standard, it was noticed that the number of complaints about building-related illnesses [was / were] much higher in newer (post-1973) buildings, compared with older buildings. Occupants complained of health- or comfort-related symptoms associated with the time they spent in the building. The term "sick building syndrome" became used to represent the health problems reported, which ranged from rashes, itchy eyes, and allergies to fatigue, headaches, and an increased sensitivity to odors.

RELATING FORM TO FUNCTION

Read the excerpt from "Building Energy Efficiency vs. Maintaining Indoor Air Quality." Highlight or underline key words and phrases. Then create a bulleted list outlining one of the main points. Your bulleted list should follow an independent sentence or an introductory stem. Be sure that your list uses parallel structure.

Even though VAV and DCV systems are less energy intensive, there are some disadvantages. First, it is more expensive to install a VAV system, and even more expensive to install a DCV system—typically, it takes two to five years before the operational energy savings of a VAV system offset the increased capital cost. Second, since VAV and DCV systems are more complex, malfunctions are much more common, so these systems require more frequent maintenance and repairs. Third, for the temperature-controlled VAV systems, if a room or zone is at an appropriate temperature, the ventilation rate will stay minimal, even if indoor pollutant concentrations in that room are building up. Finally, for DCV systems monitoring CO_2, there have been many issues with the CO_2 sensors malfunctioning or "drifting" with time, where they begin reporting concentrations that are systematically either too low or too high. This can cause a room or zone to be chronically under- or over-ventilated.

READ

Go to MyEnglishLab to read "Building Energy Efficiency vs. Maintaining Indoor Air Quality" for more practice reading an extended text and using your reading skills. Then do the assignment below.

ASSIGNMENT

Write a three- to five-page research paper comparing and contrasting the methods, findings, and conclusions of three to five case studies of "sick building syndrome" caused by indoor air quality problems.

Be sure to evaluate how each case study incorporates visuals to support the text.

RESEARCH

A. Look for appropriate sources by starting with an online search. Read the keywords and the hits from your search. Which are most likely to provide reliable and relevant information? Rank the hits from most relevant (1) to least relevant (5) Compare and discuss your rankings with a partner.

....

....

....

B. Choose the case studies you will compare. Write a citation of each source.

....

....

....

....

....

C. As you read, annotate the case studies, noting the methods, key findings, and conclusions in each study. Make note of information you disagree with or have questions about. Highlight information you find surprising.

D. Analyze the visuals used in each study. Determine if the data they contain is relevant, appropriate, and useful as support of the ideas in the study. Are there any visuals you think should be added to the study?

WRITE

A. Create a list of similarities and differences among the case studies.

B. Using a graphic organizer and your notes, create a detailed outline of your paper.

C. Write your research paper. Incorportae visuals as appropriate.

Go to MyEnglishLab to join in a collaborative activity.

> **TIP**
> Report where there is agreement or disagreement across studies.

> **TIP**
> Make sure the organization and structure of your paper are helpful for your audience.

For more about **ENVIRONMENTAL ENGINEERING**, see ①②. See also ⌊R⌋ and ⌊OC⌋ **ENVIRONMENTAL ENGINEERING** ①②③.

Photo Credits

Index

Page numbers in bold refer to visuals (tables and figures).